# REVISITING THE OCEAN

## Living the Blue Economy

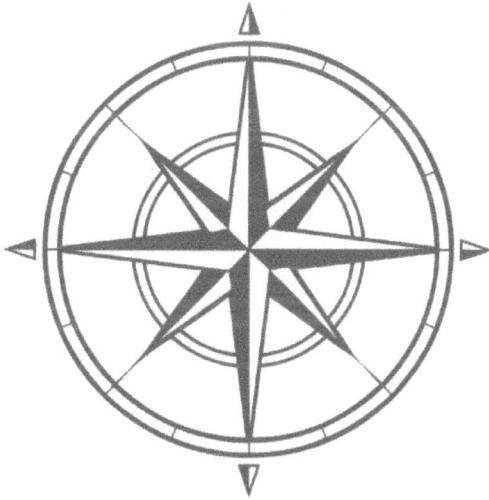

**Also by James Alix Michel**

*A Man of the People: A Collection of Speeches*

*Distant Horizons: My Reflections*

*Island Nation in a Global Sea: Making the New Seychelles*

*Rethinking the Oceans: Towards the Blue Economy*

*Legacy: New Millenium, New Seychelles*

# REVISITING THE OCEAN

## Living the Blue Economy

## JAMES ALIX MICHEL

Enquiries concerning these terms should be addressed to

*Blue Gecko Books*

bluegeckobooks@ymail.com
www.bluegeckobooks.com

Any views, thoughts, and opinions expressed by the author are solely
that of the author and do not necessarily reflect the views, opinions,
policies, or position of the Lloyd's Register Foundation.

Hardback ISBN:978-0-9575685-6-3
Paperback ISBN:978-0-9575685-7-0

Design and formatting by Barbara Velasco (Papel+Papel Creative)

*Front cover:  Seagrass by Inusuke/iStock*
*James Michel by Mervin Marie*
*Back cover:   Photo courtesy of the James Michel Foundation*

*For all at last return to the sea –*
*to Oceanus, the ocean river,*
*like the ever-flowing stream of time,*
*the beginning and the end.*

**Rachel Carson (1950).** *The Sea Around Us*

# Contents

## James Alix Michel
## Former President of the Republic of Seychelles

James James Alix Michel was born on 16 August 1944 on the island of Mahé, Seychelles.

He was the third President of the Republic of Seychelles, succeeding France Albert René upon the retirement of the latter in April 2004, and was elected as president in July 2006, re-elected in May 2011, and again re-elected for a final term in December 2015.

In April 2016, an amendment to the Constitution, proposed by Michel, limiting presidential mandates to two terms of five years in office was approved by the country's National Assembly. Faithful to his commitment not to hold on to power 'for power's sake', James Michel resigned as President barely ten months after taking office, handing over to the Vice-President.

James Michel was responsible for the democratisation of the republic's education system in the early 1980s. Today, all Seychellois children have access to a minimum of fourteen years of non-fee-paying education and equal opportunities to learning. Mr. Michel established the University of Seychelles in 2009, and was its chancellor until he resigned in 2021.

James Michel has promoted Seychelles on the international scene as an ardent advocate of the cause of Small Island Developing States, the preservation of the environment, and the Blue Economy. He has been responsible for the promulgation of legislation transforming half of Seychelles' territory into nature reserves – the highest proportion in the world. He co-chaired the Global Island Partnership and has mobilised political support for the Blue

Economy and marine protected areas within island regions of the world. He is also one of the patrons of the World Sustainable Development Forum.

A recurring theme of Michel's is the need to invest in the youth of the country – the leaders of tomorrow. To that end, he has formulated policy and initiated several programmes aimed at their global holistic development and capacity building. This included the Young Leaders' Programme – an in-service training programme leading to an MBA.

President James Michel is the recipient of several international awards.

## *International awards*

- ✧ Outstanding Civilian Service Medal – Conferred by the United States Army in 1995.
- ✧ Named a Paul Harris Fellow in 1997 by the Rotary Foundation of Rotary International 'in appreciation of tangible and significant assistance given for the furtherance of better understanding and friendly relations among peoples of the world'.
- ✧ Knighthood of Science and Art – Presented by the Presidium of the Russian Academy of Natural Sciences in 2001, in recognition of the 'great personal contribution in the guarantee of the stable development of the Republic of Seychelles and for the prosperity of the Seychelles people'.
- ✧ Grand Cross of the Order Pro Merito Melitensi – Conferred by the Sovereign Military Order of Malta in 2001.
- ✧ UNESCO Gold Medal of the Five Continents in recognition of his work 'to promote the ideals of peace, tolerance and his work to sensitise the international community about the vulnerability of Small Island Developing States' in 2009.
- ✧ Most Innovative People Award (for Natural Innovation) by the Global Leadership Team at the Lebanon 2020 Summit, in 2009.
- ✧ Made Honorary Citizen of Daejeon City (Republic of Korea) in 2009.
- ✧ Special Award for Eco-Safety from the World Eco-Safety Assembly of the International Eco-Safety Cooperative Organization, in 2010, in view of his 'leadership in the field of environment and the long-standing efforts of the Government to foster sustainable development'.

⬦ Grand Cross of the Knightly Order, Special Class, pro Merito Melitensi – Conferred by the Sovereign Military Order of Malta in recognition of the 'exceptional relations that exist between the Order and the Republic of Seychelles' in 2010.

⬦ Doctorate (Phil) Honoris Causa awarded by TERI University in Delhi (The Energy and Resources Institute) for his 'advocacy of the cause of small island states and the preservation of the environment' in 2010.

⬦ Grand Commander of the Star and Key of the Indian Ocean (GCSK) – conferred by Dr Navin Ramgoolam, Prime Minister of Mauritius in 2012 in recognition of his role in 'strengthening the special ties of friendship and cooperation between Seychelles and Mauritius'.

⬦ Sustainable Development Leadership Award in 2013 from the Delhi Sustainable Development Summit, for his 'visionary and strong leadership in the implementation of sustainable environmental programmes, economic and social renaissance'.

⬦ African Development Excellence Award 2013, presented at the 2nd African Investment and Development Award 2013, in recognition of his 'outstanding contribution to Africa's economic growth and development'.

⬦ Recognised as an 'Oceans 8 Champion' by the Intergovernmental Oceanic Commission of UNESCO in June 2017, in appreciation of his efforts to actively promote the Blue Economy concept as a new paradigm of development, as well as his endeavour to develop an innovative debt swap scheme that has enabled Seychelles to finance local ocean science and climate resilience programmes.

⬦ National Geographic Planetary Award, received in June 2019 for his 'commitment to establishing globally protected areas' and having 'worked for years to position the Seychelles at the forefront of ocean leadership'.

# Foreword by Dr. Enric Sala

When you live on an island surrounded by the Indian Ocean, when your dry land is 3,000 times smaller than your marine waters, you know that you and your nation depend on a healthy ocean. But ocean health does not depend any longer on just how your nation and local communities manage their ocean uses – the 'Blue Economy'; it now depends on what the entire world does. This is the frame in which James Michel found himself when he started his term as President of the Republic of Seychelles in 2004, which helped build his enlightened thinking about the present and future of the ocean.

But what is the Blue Economy? As you will read in *Revisiting the Ocean*, President Michel has an optimistic vision of our use of the ocean, where we can keep a balance between production and protection. Yet many see the Blue Economy only as a new opportunity to exploit untapped resources – renewable and non-renewable – for a quick profit. A new gold rush.

Industrial fisheries have vacuumed fish out of the ocean in most seas. We reached peak fish in 1996, and global catches have been declining since. Over three quarters of the populations of commercial fish and invertebrates have collapsed or are overfished. By the shores of the Mediterranean, where I grew up, the sea is all but empty of large animals. But the sustainability of fisheries is paramount to island nations that sell access to their waters as a major source of economic revenue, and to their own food security.

Industrial corporations have promised island nation leaders billions of dollars in revenue for mining their seabed. Studies strongly indicate that such industrial mining could have massive impacts on fragile species and ecosystems living in the deep, on the fisheries these nations rely on, and unknown yet potentially large carbon emissions. A recent survey discovered thousands of new species of deep-sea animals in the Clarion-Clipperton Zone in the Pacific Ocean, contrary to the industry's arguments that 'there is not much down there'.

But these two threats – overfishing and deep-sea mining – can be fixed tomorrow if we so wish, with practical actions by individual countries in their waters. The other major threat – global warming – depends on the behaviour of all nations in the world, especially the Global North. We cannot keep a healthy ocean without solving global warming, and we cannot solve global warming without protecting more of the ocean.

The good news is that, when countries protect areas from fishing, marine life bounces back spectacularly. I have seen it with my own eyes, in many places around the world. I have seen degraded places come back to near pristine within a decade. On average, the biomass of fish inside 'no take' areas increases five times relative to unprotected areas nearby – within five to ten years. And more and larger fish reproduce more and produce more babies, helping to replenish adjacent fishing grounds. I have seen fishers catch more fish around 'no take' areas, and local businesses bring in more economic benefits through diving tourism inside these areas. If we increase ocean protection, we could have our fish and eat them too.

In addition, we know that the more marine life there is in the ocean – from the shores to the deep – the more the ocean can help absorb our carbon pollution. So, protection restores marine life, supports jobs and thriving economies, enhances fisheries, and helps mitigate global warming. It's a multiple win.

Yet currently, only 8 per cent of the ocean is under some kind of protection, and only 3 per cent is fully protected from extractive and damaging activities. But in December 2022, at the COP15 of the UN Convention on Biological Diversity, the world agreed to protect 30 per cent of the global ocean by 2030. There is much to do.

The good news is that a few nations are leading the way. Seychelles, under President Michel's leadership, committed to protect 30 per cent of its waters. And 15 per cent of the Seychelles' waters are already highly protected. This is why I feel so honored to write this foreword to *Revisiting the Ocean*. The world needs Michel's pragmatism – well-earned while leading his country – combined with his optimism and track record. Only hope rooted in realism will save our ocean, and ourselves.

*Dr. Enric Sala*
*National Geographic Explorer in Residence*

# *Foreword by Ruth Boumphrey*

The Apollo 17 astronauts looked back from space and observed a beautiful blue marble planet, an image dominated by the oceans that cover 70 per cent of our planet. Our oceans connect us, protect us, sustain us, and regulate our weather and climate. Wherever we live in the world we are deeply and powerfully connected to the sea, but low levels of awareness and understanding mean that oceans, and the people that work on them, are largely 'out of sight and out of mind'.

Early civilisations were built along coastlines, with trade and fishing facilitated by small boats. Greater ambitions led to increasingly larger ships moving people, food and cargo around the world and providing jobs for millions of workers. Today the interconnected maritime sector is the backbone of international trade, with around 80 per cent of goods transported over the ocean, and growing infrastructure investments in our coastal areas underpin a wider ocean economy. Yet, those who work at sea have some of the most dangerous jobs in the world, often facing risks that are largely hidden to the rest of the world.

While our oceans host vast, biodiverse habitats, provide the largest global carbon sink, and produce over half of the oxygen in the atmosphere, the health of our oceans is already damaged through habitat and biodiversity loss, acidification and climate change, pollution from many sources including plastics and agriculture, and the increased urbanisation of coastal areas.

With the global population estimated to grow to 8.5 billion by 2030 and 9.7 billion by 2050, an increased demand for food, energy, jobs, transportation, and coastal land will bring more pressure on ocean resources and the people that earn their livings there. It's vital that ocean stakeholders collaborate and develop new technologies, approaches, and ways of working to ensure that people around the world are safe and that the natural capital of the oceans is protected and strengthened.

I was inspired after reading James Michel's first book *Rethinking the Oceans: Towards the Blue Economy* which highlighted that solutions to some of the earth's most pressing problems can come from the ocean. Lloyd's Register Foundation has a deep maritime heritage and a mission to engineer a safer world and so I am delighted that we supported this new version of the book and that our *Foresight Review of Ocean Safety*, published in 2021 resonated with the James Michel Foundation and has been included in the text.

This important book highlights many incredible projects already underway to help us on the path to a safer and more sustainable Blue Economy. But we need to act now, with a sense of urgency, increasing capacity and knowledge and supporting people and organisations in geographies most in need, to ensure safety and sustainability is 'baked in' to the growing ocean economy. Lloyd's Register Foundation, is committed to supporting people and communities directly affected who must be seen and heard. A just transition to a low carbon, sustainable ocean economy necessitates investment, education, infrastructure, innovation and decent, safe jobs, all without causing harm elsewhere and without propagating existing inequalities or creating new ones. We really don't have time to waste.

I hope you enjoy reading *Revisiting the Ocean: Living the Blue Economy* and feel motivated to join the journey, in whatever way you can. We all have a role to play, whether it's through sharing our stories and raising awareness, taking action by investing or participating in Blue Economy projects, campaigning for change, or simply becoming better ocean citizens. Together, we can help forge a path to a safe and sustainable Blue Economy that meets the needs of our society for us today, and for the generations that follow.

*Ruth Boumphrey*
*Chief Executive, Lloyd's Register Foundation*

# *James Michel Foundation*

The James Michel Foundation was launched in February 2017. It stems from the experience and legacy of my presidency of the Republic of Seychelles between April 2004 and October 2016, and a continuing commitment to three key areas in particular: the Blue Economy, Climate Change and the Sustainable Development of Small Island States.

Since 2011, I have been lobbying various international agencies, including the UN and the African Union, to give greater importance and visibility to the sustainable development of the ocean as part of the Blue Economy concept. I co-hosted the Blue Economy Summit in Abu Dhabi on two occasions as part of the annual Abu Dhabi Sustainability Week. With Seychelles' leadership and proactive diplomacy, together with several other small island states, the African Union adopted the Blue Economy as part of its economic development policy, and the United Nations included the sustainable use of the ocean as one of its 17 Sustainable Development Goals.

During my presidency, I set up a Blue Economy department in government to promote the concept. In this context, I spearheaded a Blue Bonds initiative to raise capital for the sustainable management of both ocean resources and fisheries, using market mechanisms with the support of development institutions. I was instrumental in securing a unique $21 million 'debt-for-nature' swap agreement with the Paris Club, in exchange for a commitment for investments in domestic environmental conservation and sustainability projects.

The transfer was implemented through the creation of the Seychelles Conservation and Climate Adaptation Trust (SEYCCAT), with aid from The Nature Conservancy (TNC) and generous grants from a group of international conservation foundations, including the Leonardo DiCaprio Foundation. Under my presidency, Seychelles started its journey to become the first country in the world to have a comprehensive marine spatial plan for its entire ocean territory, which continues to be developed through an ongoing full survey of the Seychelles Exclusive Economic Zone. I am also patron of the James Michel Blue Economy Research Institute at the University of Seychelles, where I served as the Founding Chancellor.

*James Alix Michel*
*Founding Chairperson*

# Lloyd's Register Foundation

The Foundation's interest in the ocean is rooted in the heritage of Lloyd's Register, established in 1760 as the world's first classification society. Today Lloyd's Register provides maritime engineering and technology expertise in more than 70 locations, serving clients based in 182 countries.

Lloyd's Register and Lloyd's Register Foundation share a mission to engineer a safer world. The Foundation was established as an independent charity in 2012 to raise awareness of some of the world's most pressing safety challenges, with a focus on engineering and infrastructure.

As a social enterprise organisation, using profits generated by Lloyd's Register's commercial activities, the Foundation grants funds of around £30 million each year to organisations looking to design interventions and deliver research to support our mission. To date, the Foundation has provided more than £160 million via 253 grants to organisations around the world to fund interventions and programmes designed to keep people safe.

The Foundation looks to establish the best evidence and insight on safety-related issues, advocate for high technical standards, and support education programmes and pathways to upskill people around the world with the engineering and safety knowledge they need to help create a safer environment for people, property and the planet.

## The Blue Economy

The Foundation is deeply committed to ensuring a safe and sustainable ocean economy given the vital role the oceans play in supporting society globally.

When it comes to safety, the oceans are still mainly unchartered waters. Yet, more than three billion people rely on the ocean for their livelihoods and more than 600 million people live in coastal areas at direct risk of rising sea levels. Earth's final frontier is dangerous, poorly regulated, under-developed, over exploited and largely unmapped, yet we are dependent on it for our life and our livelihoods.

The ocean economy is booming, with sea-based industries expected to double by 2030. As these industries expand rapidly, we need to embed high standards of safety to ensure the infrastructure that supports these ocean industries, and the people whose livelihoods depend on them, are kept safe, without causing harm elsewhere.

The Foundation's ambition is to raise awareness of the safety challenges in the ocean economy, now and in the future, and form partnerships and coalitions with other organisations to tackle these issues and drive change. While our interest in the ocean is wide ranging, including shipping, ports, alternative fuels, seafarer wellbeing, fishers, ferries, maritime law, blue finance, offshore wind and blue food, our core focus is on the engineering and infrastructure that underpins these industries and ensuring people have the right skills in place to work within these sectors without accidents or fatalities occurring.

## *Requirements for a safer and more sustainable ocean economy*

In 2021, the Foundation published its Foresight Review of Ocean Safety which set out the urgent challenges facing the oceans. These issues require immediate action built on international cooperation to make sure future developments in the ocean economy are safe, sustainable and just.

- ✧ The vital role of the oceans in creating a low-carbon world is under threat unless governments, businesses and wider society **cooperate** to improve ocean safety.
- ✧ The oceans offer immense potential but are poorly governed, over-exploited, and largely unmapped. There's an urgent need to characterise the ocean and seabed and create **open-access data tools** for ocean safety.
- ✧ We need greater **investment** and solutions that address rising sea levels, climate change, pollution, labour and safety challenges.
- ✧ Novel approaches to **ocean engineering** are needed which pursue **nature-positive solutions** that protect the future of our planet.
- ✧ There is a pressing need for new approaches to ocean **education and skills** to ensure we have the skills in place, where they are needed most, for a safe and sustainable ocean economy.
- ✧ We must become better **ocean citizens**, improving our understanding of all aspects of the ocean economy and making better choices in what we buy and build.

✧ The growth in the ocean economy must not be at the expense of **biodiversity** and those whose **livelihoods** are made at sea.

The Foundation is delighted to support this book which highlights many positive examples of work done to date on our collective journey to a safer and more sustainable blue economy. However, it also acknowledges that there is much more that needs to be done.

*Ruth Boumphrey*
*Chief Executive*

# *Acknowledgements*

This book has been written as a contribution to the work of the James Michel Foundation, with the generous support of Lloyd's Register Foundation. I am grateful to members of both bodies for their unstinting encouragement and advice.

For Lloyd's Register Foundation I would like to mention the ever-helpful involvement of Ruth Boumphrey, Beth Elliot, Dagmora Karbowska and Ruth Frankish.

On the home front, I have constantly relied on Debbie Monthy, CEO of my own foundation, to administer the project and liaise with her counterparts at Lloyd's Register Foundation.

Not least of all, I am indebted to Enric Sala and Ruth Boumphrey for each writing a foreword containing kind comments about the book. To enjoy the support of such distinguished individuals is, indeed, a great honour.

Others, too, have helped in various ways and my thanks are due to individuals and organisations from all parts of the world. Let me mention, for a start, a number of ocean advisors, each a specialist in a different aspect of the subject, who have readily shared their knowledge and unique insights. In particular, I would like to acknowledge the expert assistance of Ameer Ebrahim, Vincent Doumeizel, Ginger Garte, and, from NLA International, Jonathan Turner, Andy Hamflett and Bianca Ulan.

Because of the scope and topicality of the book, an independent reviewer of high standing was invited to read the pre-publication text and to offer final comments. My thanks are due to the ocean expert, Belinda Bramley, for so ably undertaking this task and confirming my approach.

I would also like to offer a collective note of appreciation to the many unseen writers and researchers who, on a daily basis it would seem, add to the stock of writings about the ocean. Of course, I acknowledge these in the citations attached to each chapter but I would like them to know that, without their numerous contributions, a scientific understanding of this fast-changing subject would be impossible. Tempting though it is to go on adding new insights, I have had to draw a line in the text at the end of June 2023.

Under the stewardship of Jane Woolfenden, Blue Gecko Books has been responsible for all aspects of production. I have worked with Jane before and, once again, can appreciate the professional standards and care that she and her team devote to every stage of the process. Every author knows how important this is.

Writing a book can be a lonely task and I owe an immeasurable debt to my daughter, Laeticia, for her cheerful company and for reminding me how vital it is that future generations should be able to enjoy all the wonderful qualities of a healthy ocean. To young people everywhere, I dedicate this book.

# Picture Credits

Picture research: Debbie Monthy and Jane Woolfenden

*Page v.* Jane Woolfenden; *Page viii.* From the personal collection of James Michel; *Page 4.* Debbie Monthy; *Page 5.* Stephen Edmonds/Wikimedia Commons (CC BY-SA 2.0); *Page 7.* Jane Woolfenden; *Page 10.* Lisa Carne/Fragments of Hope; *Page 17. (top left)* Ardfern/Wikimedia Commons (CC BY-SA 3.0), *(top right)* Courtesy of Yohan Gallet, *(bottom)* Courtesy of Joanne Muchai; *Page 23.* 人事院/Wikimedia Commons (CC BY 4.0); *Page 25. (top)* From the personal collection of James Michel, *(right)* U.S. Department of State/Wikimedia Commons (PD-US Gov); *Page 33.* From the personal collection of James Michel; *Page 35.* From the personal collection of James Michel; *Page 40. (top)* Warren Talbot/Wikimedia Commons (CC BY 2.0), *(bottom)* Yves Picq/Wikimedia Commons (CC BY-SA 3.0); *Page 46.* © Ameer Ebrahim; *Page 48.* © Ameer Ebrahim; *Page 52.* Courtesy of Lloyd's Register Foundation; *Page 53.* Courtesy of Lloyd's Register Foundation; *Page 57. (top)* Corvair Owner/Wikimedia Commons (CC BY-SA 2.0), *(bottom)* Oceanbird; *Page 63.* Ada Lim/Pixabay; *Page 69. (top)* Gunnery Sgt. Ismael Pena/United States Marine Corps (PD), *(bottom)* Marvin Harris/United States Navy (PD); *Page 71.* Jane Woolfenden; *Page 72.* V.K. Hietanen/Wikimedia Commons (PD); *Page 75.* Jane Woolfenden; *Page 76. (top)* Gordon Brown/Wikimedia Commons (CC BY-SA 2.0), *(bottom)* Jane Woolfenden; *Page 79. (top)* NOAA/Wikimedia Commons (PD), *(bottom)* Claire Fackler/Flickr (PD); *Page 81.* My Lovely Planet/Shutterstock; *Page 89. (top)* Debbie Monthy, *(bottom)* Dimitrina Lavchieva/Shutterstock; *Page 95.* Brataffe/Wikimedia Commons (CC BY-SA 4.0); *Page 98.* Fokke Baarssen/Shutterstock; *Page 100.* Jane Woolfenden; *Page 104.* Chalkie2/Wikimedia Commons (CC BY-SA 4.0); *Page 106. (top)* Georges Seguin/Wikimedia Commons (CC BY-SA 3.0), *(bottom)* Jane Woolfenden; *Page 111.* Berjaya Tioman Resort (PD); *Page 116.* Cindy Ferrer for the Philippine News Agency/Wikimedia Commons (PD); *Page 122. (top)* Derek Keats (CC BY 2.0), *(bottom)* W. Carter/Wikimedia Commons (PD); *Page 124.* Yann Macherez/Wikimedia Commons (CC BY-SA 4.0); *Page 127. (left)* Vegan Feast Catering/Wikimedia Commons (CC BY 2.0), *(right)* Geoffreyrabbit/Wikimedia Commons (CC BY-SA 4.0); *Page 128.* Maoileann/Wikimedia Commons (CC BY-SA 4.0); *Page 133.* Dezeen (PD); *Page 134.* Nazmulhuqrussell/Wikimedia Commons (CC BY 3.0); *Page 141.* Willard84/Wikimedia Commons (CC BY 3.0); *Page 144. (left)* Ørsted (PD), *(right)* Debbie Monthy; *Page 148.* Wonderful Nature/Shutterstock; *Page 151.* Tswgp/Wikimedia Commons (PD); *Page 154.* Dietmar Rabich/Wikimedia Commons (CC BY-SA 4.0); *Page 158.* Ørsted/Wikimedia Commons (CC BY-SA 4.0); *Page 161.* Jane Woolfenden; *Page 163.* NOAA OKEANOS Explorer/NOAA Photo Library (CC BY 2.0); *Page 164.* Pawel Kalisinski/Pexels.com; *Page 168.* V. Gordeev/Shutterstock; *Page 171.* G. Mannaerts/Wikimedia Commons (CC BY-SA 4.0); *Page 176.* IUCN (PD); *Page 178.* Marten Van Dijl/Greenpeace; *Page 186.* Courtesy of Ellen MacArthur Foundation; *Page 189. (top)* Rich Carey/Shutterstock, *(bottom)* Denes Farkas/istock; *Page 195.* W. Kanchanacharoen/Shutterstock; *Page 200.* Courtesy of

# Prologue

In 2016, I concluded my first book on the Blue Economy with the words:

*Let us abandon our entrenched opinions and commit to universal values. Let us believe in our common humanity. Let us, together, move forward. There is still time, but we cannot delay any longer.*[1]

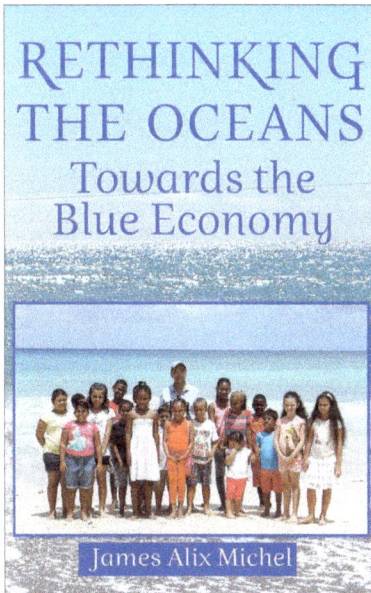

RETHINKING THE OCEANS
Towards the Blue Economy

James Alix Michel

Seven years on, what progress has been made? Much has happened in this short period and the purpose of this new book is to focus on the positives. Of course, opportunities have been missed and old practices persist. There have been unexpected setbacks too. The coronavirus pandemic intervened and, sadly, wars have not been consigned to history. Globalisation has faltered in what was beginning to seem like an unstoppable advance. But, in spite of everything, there are good things to report, not least of all a heightened sense of urgency to realise the true potential of the ocean – a vision that nourishes hope and strengthens the prospect of achievement.

In telling of this new stage in the development of the Blue Economy, sometimes the spotlight will be at a very local level, perhaps on a single beach where a community decides to mount a cleaning operation or restore a degraded coral reef. Or, instead, we might focus on scientists in a laboratory devoting their efforts to discovering new ways to grow crops in seawater. And, at national and international levels, the Blue Economy is emerging as a global priority for the modern age. Along the spectrum, from local to worldwide, we can see an exhilarating range of activities, each a product of novel ideas and energy. No longer can the ocean be dismissed as a residual part of Planet Earth, nor as a threat, but, instead, our very salvation.

To develop my argument, the book is organised in three parts. The first two chapters appear under the heading of 'Recognition', where I show how, even since I wrote my earlier book, there have been important changes. Numerous countries have developed their own policies and there are shared principles which give meaning to the idea of the Blue Economy. A sound platform for further work is now in place.

Then, in subsequent chapters, under the banner of 'Innovation', I gather together accounts of many of the exciting initiatives taking shape in different parts of the world. There is a profusion of activities which are together giving substance to the emergent Blue Economy. A separate book could be written on any one of these themes.

Finally, on the basis of progress to date, I conclude with 'The Reckoning'. In this, I assess the chances of meeting the UN's sustainable development goals for the ocean by 2030. And, in the final chapter, I celebrate the contribution of ocean champions, individuals who care passionately for the ocean and who are really making a difference.

This volume is the work of an optimist but also a realist. I remain optimistic that a healthy ocean will define our future. At the same time, I am realistic in knowing that there is a long way to go. It is hard to deny that humanity has an innate propensity for self-destruction. But, fortunately, there is another side to human nature, too, and, in defiance of negative forces, a new journey has started; a journey that is taking us in an altogether different direction. There are exciting signs of progress. I am not alone in seeing grounds for a better future and I hope you will be convinced too. It is up to us all to make it happen. The ocean, as I have said many times, is our future. It cannot be said too often.

# Part 1

# Recognition

Just a few years ago, whenever I spoke about the Blue Economy I was commonly met with puzzlement. What do you mean by this term, people would ask? Surely, they would say, we have always made use of the ocean. How can you base an economy on water?

This kind of response was perfectly understandable. The fact is that the sea has for millennia been a place for fisherfolk and sailors. And, of course, a vast repository for our waste materials, not least of all sewage and, in modern times, plastics. Landlubbers have ventured to the coast for leisure, to breathe in the fresh, salty air and to tentatively step into the first few metres of a watery expanse. Beyond the horizon and beneath the surface, though, is another world – a world unknown to all but a few.

Our lives have traditionally been grounded on *terra firma*, the sea perceived as merely residual. Little wonder a concept like the Blue Economy meant so little when it was first advocated. It challenged all that we have previously taken for granted; it was like turning the world upside down – or, more accurately, inside out, with the sea offering a new focus for our lives.

What is surprising is that this willingness to look afresh at the world is so recent. Of course, pioneers have been thinking of the ocean's potential for much longer, but it was only at the start of the second decade of the present century that it became a matter of concerted international debate. Fifteen years ago, at most. The Blue Economy is, essentially, a second-millennium concept. In the first two chapters of the book, I will explain how this has come to be.

# Chapter 1
# Matryoshka Dolls
## *Meanings within meanings*

A connection between a set of traditional Russian dolls, nested one inside another, and thoughts of a blue world, might seem overly fanciful. Yet, in seeking a way to illustrate the overlapping meanings and principles embedded in the Blue Economy, the allusion is not as tenuous as it might at first seem.

*A world of embedded meanings and principles*

The fact is that one of the things that has changed most over the past few years is a broadening of the concept. In my previous book, in trying to convey the idea of the Blue Economy, I made two points. One is that the ocean represents an under-utilised resource for the world, and the other was that in seeking to realise its potential all interventions must be sustainable. Nothing should be done, I argued – as it has been over a long history of insensitive development on land – to impair access to the ocean environment for future generations. Sustainability is, for me, a non-negotiable principle, and most people would seem to agree with this. What has changed is that emphasis is also placed on other considerations. And rightly so. Like a set of matryoshka dolls, these additional points are inextricably linked to sustainability and to each other, and each becomes an essential part of the whole.

In an important new book, Helen Czerski makes the same point of interconnectedness in a different way, likening the ocean to a 'blue machine', a single engine powered by sunlight.[2] The health of the planet as a whole depends on its intricate workings and, although the ocean has proved to be remarkably resilient, it is presently under severe pressure from rising temperatures. As any engineer will know, there is a need for constant monitoring and maintenance: no part of a machine can be ignored at the expense of the whole. And failings cannot be left to chance.

From a variety of statements, gleaned from conference presentations and numerous publications, as well as from personal conversations, I suggest that a successful Blue Economy should be widened in scope to include the following dimensions:

- ✧ It must be ethically sound
- ✧ It must be environmentally sustainable
- ✧ It must be regenerative
- ✧ It must be fired by innovation
- ✧ It must yield economic benefits
- ✧ It must contribute to a fairer world
- ✧ It must be supported by adequate funding

Somehow, these different – and to some extent conflicting – ingredients must all be in the Blue Economy mix. It is a demanding set of requirements but expectations are high and any one requirement cannot be ignored.

## The Blue Economy Must Be Ethically Sound

A belief in ethics rests, not on a written code and certainly not in all cases on statutory law, but on a common sense of humanity. It is at this end of the spectrum that one should acknowledge the importance of metaphysical qualities like beauty and tranquility, radiance and reflection, peace and transcendence, truth and love. The ocean is to be cherished not simply for what it can add to a balance sheet but for what it is.

In all respects, the ocean is awe-inspiring. For the whole of the 4.5 billion years since the earth was formed, complex processes have been at work: the cooling of a molten planet, an encircling atmosphere of dust and debris, the gradual formation of a solid crust, and gaseous materials transformed into water. The last of these was the secret of life, with the earth just far enough away from the sun to avoid the wholesale evaporation of liquid yet not so far that it would immediately have frozen. As a result, we have the interconnected ocean and all it can offer, a unique planet with just the right conditions for human development. Have we forgotten, though, how fortunate we are? Do we sufficiently appreciate the treasure of the ocean, and not simply its material properties?

*The value of the sea goes well beyond its material worth*

In a milieu dominated by measurable outcomes and commercial gain, there must always be room for spiritual values alongside, or even above, more conventional criteria. Often these largely abstract attributes are synonymous with religious beliefs but, as well, they can be framed within personal philosophies or those of particular cultural groups. The opening lines of a poem from the North American Wintun tribe (that traditionally inhabited parts of north California) encapsulate in a few well-chosen words the essence of a spiritual view:

> *I am related*
> *in a universe*
> *bigger than*
> *my mind...*[3]

In an article to show the importance of spiritual and cultural values when confronting issues of ecosystem management and conservation strategies, the point is made that the same topic may well be perceived differently by different groups.[4] It follows from this that the Blue Economy must be based on a respect for contrasting viewpoints – an all-embracing ocean that can be seen through a multitude of cultural prisms.

In spite of its apparent roots in abstract qualities, this can also have practical implications. To give a contemporary example within the maritime space of Seychelles, there are extensive reserves of natural gas and oil beneath the continental shelf.[5] Further exploration has been allowed and the pressures are such that this is expected to lead, in turn, to extraction. Economic arguments are offered in justification, and pledges are made that the environmental impact will be minimised. But ethical considerations are given short shrift. The seabed has been left intact for millennia, disturbed only by the natural forces of tectonic movements. What right does a single generation have to upset this balance, not as a short-term inconvenience but for all time? Do we not have a responsibility to respect a diminishing area of pristine waters, to be enjoyed by future generations as well as our own? Is there not hypocrisy in claiming that Seychelles is a paradise when, at the same time, we are prepared to degrade it? And how do we square the circle when, with one breath, we voice our support for renewable energy and with another we might renew our commitment to fossil fuels. The ocean surely deserves better than this.

In contrast, there are other aspects of the Blue Economy where ethical factors can, less contentiously, be addressed. Notable amongst these is the issue of safety at sea. The message could hardly be plainer:

> *Those who work at sea have some of the most dangerous jobs in the world. A just transition to a low carbon, sustainable ocean economy necessitates investment, education, infrastructure, innovation, and decent, safe jobs.*[6]

Traditionally, little thought has been given to the safety of workers at sea. It has been a classic case of 'out of sight, out of mind'. Nearly 150 years have passed since the British politician, Samuel Plimsoll, was responsible for introducing the line (which still bears his name) to show the maximum depth to which a ship could safely be loaded. Great progress in ensuring the safety of crews has been made since then but it is by no means universal. Small trading ships still sail to distant ports, although sometimes the creaking vessels are fit only for the breaker's yard; artisanal fishing boats ply the open seas, with crews often ill-equipped to match the rough seas encountered; while rig workers lead a lonely and dangerous existence, reliant on the robustness of their floating islands.

Nor is it just conditions at sea that need to be monitored and improved.

Ports, too, are hazardous places and require their own health and safety regulations. The problem with these is that they can vary from one jurisdiction to another, making it difficult to achieve the kind of standardisation that is required. It is also a very complex subject, covering all kinds of situations, from the control of dangerous substances, to the prevention of falling objects, from personal injuries resulting from carrying heavy goods to the experience of a lone worker in difficulties.[7]

If the Blue Economy is to succeed as a complex set of modern, scientifically-based industries, the welfare of its workers can no longer be left to chance. Top-quality engineering, investment in modern equipment, greater use of remote operations, and skills education must be integral to all activities at sea. Ethics is a demanding criterion but no part of the ocean's development can escape its reach.

## The Blue Economy Must Be Environmentally Sustainable

Of all the attributes of the Blue Economy, the one that is non-negotiable is surely that everything must be sustainable. The other requirements are, of course, of great importance too; they are all ingredients in the total mix. But unless the way we treat the ocean is sustainable, there can be no guarantee that anything else can be achieved.

The word 'sustain' can be traced back to Latin origins but it was only in the 1980s that 'sustainability' entered the modern lexicon of environmentalists. For that we have to thank the former Norwegian prime minister, Dr Gro Harlem Bruntland, for her seminal report for the UN on environment and development.[8] This now-historic report is well worth revisiting for the clarity of its message:

> *Humanity has the ability to make development sustainable to ensure that it meets the needs of the present without compromising the ability of future generations to meet their own needs... in the final analysis, sustainable development must rest on political will.*[9]

Attention in the report was focused primarily on the use of land but comments on the unsustainable use of the ocean are as apposite now as when they were written: not least of all that 'the underlying unity of the oceans requires effective global management regimes'.[10] Until very recently, with little in the way of concerted action to bring the High Seas into the orbit of international management, there has clearly been a deficit in the kind of political will called for in 1987. But we are where we are and let us not ignore where there has been progress.

The very fact that sustainability is now so widely understood is in itself a step forward. This is no longer an obscure, technical term but one that is as recognisable in communities undertaking environmental projects as it is in international fora. To take just three examples of its centrality in local projects (supported with grants from the UN Environment Programme), we can visit beaches in Belize, Madagascar and Costa Rica.

> *Fragments of Hope, for instance, is a community-based organization in the Placencia Peninsula of southern Belize, which re-seeds devastated Caribbean reefs with diverse and resilient corals. With the grant, Fragments of Hope will expand its work to the northern side of Belize, an area plagued by stony coral tissue loss disease. The condition rapidly kills corals, leaving behind a bright white skeleton. The organization will also support the nationwide mapping of coral reefs that are more resistant to warming seas, considered key as climate change heats the world's oceans.*[11]

*The Fragments of Hope team in Belize*

Elsewhere:

> *...the seagrass in three locally-managed marine areas in the southwest of Madagascar (Velondriake, Manjaboake and Teariake), is threatened by destructive fishing, especially beach seining. Blue Ventures Conservation seeks to train community members to map and monitor the seagrass in the three conservation areas. The organization also plans to help 150 small-scale fishers develop sea cucumber farms, diversifying their income.*[12]

Finally:

> *Misión Tiburon will replant mangroves in the Hammerhead Shark Sanctuary at Costa Rica's Golfo Dulce. The wetlands are a nursery for the critically endangered scalloped hammerhead shark. The project, established in 2009, is focused on conserving other marine life as well by reviving mangrove forests, one of the area's most important and threatened coastal ecosystems.*[13]

In the global scheme of things, these examples might seem as if they barely scratch the surface of what needs to be done. But nothing could be further from the truth. Although the geographical area they cover and the scope of the individual projects is small, they mark a fundamental change in how sustainability must become engrained in the human psyche. The concept, in practice as well as theory, belongs to us all and not simply to a top-down hierarchy. Unless it is embraced by people who confront these issues on a day-to-day basis and whose livelihoods depend on it, sustainability will never be wholly effective. We need the women from coastal villages in Belize, the fisherfolk and others in Madagascar, and young as well as old in Costa Rica, to all embrace the concept and to work towards its realisation.

I favour a pragmatic approach, such as the above, which responds to opportunities where they exist, rather than waiting for a single, grand solution. But I am also respectful of more theoretical explanations of what needs to be done to make the transition to a sustainable ocean. Thus, to demonstrate this, I have taken into account the views of a group of academics who argue that a more sustainable future requires four changes to the way we currently do things.[14] The first is a shift in societal values to embrace the idea of sustainable consumption and production, environmental justice and consciousness of the situation we are in – a shift which I believe is already underway. A second change is to ensure that funding is adequate to support the many ways of making a difference. In fact, there is never enough money to effect social change in its entirety, although I will look (later in this book) to examples of novel ways of raising funds for different projects. Thirdly, this is a global issue and information should be shared across corporate and national boundaries; local ventures are important but news of them and lessons taken must be disseminated widely. Finally, the ethical dimension cannot be left to chance and sustainability must deliberately be sufficiently inclusive to respond to the interests of minority groups as well as mainstream society.

Nor, to add to the views of specialists, should the dissemination of ideas be in one direction only. There are lessons that can be learnt from indigenous groups as well as from highly-qualified scientists. Indeed, it can be argued that indigenous communities bring with them the first-hand experience of generations. In relation to this last point, my own view is that we cannot afford to ignore the wisdom and understanding of the sea that has been accumulated over centuries by people who live by and depend on it for their very existence. For these people, sustainability is not an abstract concept but a way of life.

One lesson to be taken from past experience is that we have to take a long view. In measuring progress over recent years, it is obvious that there is no quick fix. It is like confronting an empty space into which the many pieces of a jigsaw puzzle must be fitted. To date, some pieces are now in place but there is far to go before a picture emerges of a sustainable ocean. But at least a start is being made.

## The Blue Economy Must Be Regenerative

Sustainability remains, for me, the key principle at the very heart of the Blue Economy. I still believe that Bruntland was correct to draw our attention to the importance of conserving finite resources, and that her report remains a landmark in our approach to the environment (at sea as well as on land). A line was drawn between a past where the earth's natural wealth was being consumed indiscriminately, and a future where we might at last learn to live within our means. As she rightly said at the time, consumption of these scarce resources had to be restrained and, for that to happen, political will at an international level was called for. It all made good sense, but the Bruntland Report was published nearly 40 years ago and it is hardly surprising that the global context has changed since then. As a result, the idea of sustainability itself has come under the microscope and there is no longer unqualified enthusiasm for all aspects.

For a start, the necessary requisite of political will – the fuel which powers the motor of sustainability – has not been forthcoming. One has only to observe the performance of nations at the annual COP events, when lip service is paid to the idea of sustainability, and then to see how it is ignored or diluted to a point where it becomes ineffective. Without sufficient political will to make things happen, sustainability will be left (to borrow an image from the ocean) floundering like a beached whale.

Critics also question the theoretical model of 'traditional' sustainability. A basic problem, it is contended, is that it rests on a belief that refraining from development will be enough on its own. The weakness is that it is a linear concept that relies on things being stopped in their tracks rather than taking a wider view of change. Suppose, instead, it were possible to 'energise' the environment, so that it becomes free to regenerate itself (as it would in its natural state). In other words, moving from a linear to an ecological approach, based on the totality of living organisms, no longer confined to human interests and all-encompassing controls.

Regeneration is a powerful concept that is used by some scientists to replace the traditional notion of sustainability. Or, as I would prefer, the two can be used in tandem to supply a sharp, new edge to an existing cutting tool. Leah Gibbons is a leading critic of the old approach and in the title of an incisive article, *Regenerativem – the new sustainable?*, she reveals her hand.[15] She contends that sustainability has passed through successive phases of evolution. First was the idea of its conventional application (which she believes started well before but includes Bruntland's recommendations in the 1980s). For Gibbons, this has now become insufficient, as the focus of the old model 'is anthropocentric and largely on how to enable continued economic development within a context of finite resources'.[16] A second phase is defined as contemporary sustainability, which takes a more inclusive view of systems but which remains fragmented and anthropocentric, 'aiming for human wellbeing now and in the future, within limits'.[17] I am not convinced that this second phase is significantly different from the first but, either way, there are lessons one can take from the two, *en route* to a third stage. This, she calls 'regenerative sustainability', also referred to as 'the next wave of sustainability'. The big difference in this case is that it adopts a holistic worldview in which 'humans and the rest of life' are bound together:

> *Regenerative sustainability's aspirational aim is to manifest thriving and flourishing living systems (i.e., complex adaptive systems) in the fully integrated individual-to-global system. It calls for humans to live in conscious alignment with living systems principles of wholeness, change, and relationship, as nature does.*[18]

The call, to carry forward in a meaningful and socially acceptable way, the Bruntland message of conserving finite resources, has been taken up by successive practitioners as well as theorists. In a study, under the auspices of the Ocean Panel, this is explained clearly when the new ideas – based on regeneration – are applied to the future of the world's seas. The 'new vision', it is boldly asserted, requires an integrated rather than a sectoral approach:

> *It departs from a conservation philosophy of 'minimising destruction' and showcases a balanced model that simultaneously achieves effective ocean protection, sustainable production and equitable prosperity.*[19]

This introductory chapter is not the place to explore in more detail this and other applications (many of which are highlighted later in this book) but I would like to mention briefly the work of one innovator, Juan José Freijo. With an academic background in physics and a passion for sustainability, he is Vice-President of a company specialising in reusable packaging. He explains that he has recently developed a strategy to pioneer a regenerative supply chain:

> *'Historically supply chains have typically consumed natural resources and generated waste; we are now proposing to revert this model and create a supply chain that consumes existing waste and creates natural resources, a truly Copernican shift... We have built an entirely new series of targets under the regenerative banner – shifting from avoiding deforestation to promoting afforestation; making durable circular products from plastic waste; and investing in materials and systems that sequester carbon.'*[20]

Later, I tell about a closely-related concept, the circular economy, and how other innovators are also applying it to their own areas of activity. All of this I prefer to acknowledge as an extension of a totally new concept. Ideas and practices evolve and it is always encouraging to report progress in this critical field.

## The Blue Economy Must Be Fired by Innovation

To bring to life the diverse aims and new frontiers of the Blue Economy, innovation will be the driving force. Without it, the ocean will remain much as it is – poorly used and badly polluted, its vast potential untapped. The fact is that there is so much which is as yet undiscovered that, if handled in the right way, can change all this. Most of the seabed is not even surveyed and the deep ocean remains a mystery. In some ways, we know more about the moon than most of our own planet. If progress is to be made, there are vital questions to be answered. How can we capture the energy of the waves so that, once and for all, we will no longer need to rely on fossil fuels? Is it possible to grow crops in the sea on a scale needed to feed a hungry world? How can we efficiently remove, across the ocean, the accumulation of decades of waste? Science and technology will be constantly in demand to find solutions, to enable us to cross new frontiers, and invention will be followed by much-needed investment and business acumen.

For all of its sometimes-abstract ideals, the Blue Economy will be rooted in a new generation of practical projects. Innovation will be at work in both public and private sectors, although especially the latter. Governments are rarely good innovators and this is best left to entrepreneurs with creative skills, willing to take risks and with a relentless drive to succeed; people who think beyond the limits of a political term of office. Start-ups were pivotal to the emergence of the Information Age, but Silicon Valley was never a government initiative. The same will be said, one day, about the Blue Economy. Indeed, there are already promising signs of this. Great advances have been made in recent years and innovators are poised to take things across further frontiers. There are many examples to draw upon.

BlueInvest, for instance, is a European Union initiative directed to the Blue Economy:

> *[It] aims to boost innovation and investment in sustainable*

*technologies for the blue economy, by supporting readiness and access to finance for early-stage businesses, SMEs and scale-ups. It is enabled by the European Maritime and Fisheries Fund.*[21]

Words are one thing but practical achievements another, and each year a number of the latter are highlighted. In 2022, in what has become an annual event for BlueInvest, one exhibit, in particular, caught my eye, namely, a presentation by a Danish firm called Wavepiston. The significance of this kind of initiative is because it focuses on what could well become the most important source of renewable energy. Unlike wind and solar power, waves and currents are more predictable yet remain largely untapped. Early attempts to convert wave energy required massive, visually intrusive structures close to the shore. In contrast, Wavepiston is developing an entirely different type of technology.

*In the ocean a chain of energy collectors is stretched between two anchored buoys. When waves roll along the energy collectors, plates are moved back and forth. The moving plates pump seawater into a pipe. The pipe leads the pressurised water to a turbine and/or a reverse osmosis system in a dry and easily accessible location for energy conversion and/or desalination. Key benefits of this concept are that: the costs are massively reduced due to the light flexible structure, optimized mooring and modular design. Simplicity and robustness is ensured by the use of standard offshore technologies. The fully submerged system and nonpolluting materials ensure a non-intrusive technology.*[22]

The exciting ideas of Wavepiston are still at a developmental stage and it will be a few years before the business can hope to achieve commercial returns. I hope that this company, and others in the same pioneering field, succeed. It is just the kind of breakthrough that will make the Blue Economy work.

Beyond its European heartland, BlueInvest is making a conscious effort to spread its ideas and support to Africa. To this end, in September 2022, an event was held in Seychelles, the host country selected because of its reputation for advancing the cause of the Blue Economy within the region and beyond.[23] It was an exceptional event, showcasing an exciting array of initiatives that offered a measure of just how much is being done.

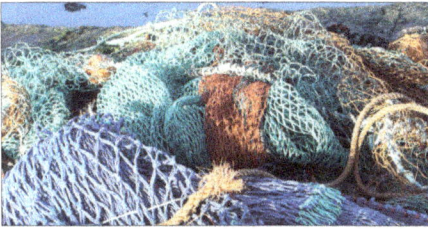

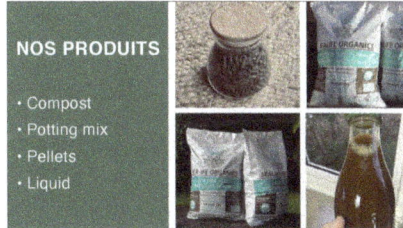

NOS PRODUITS
• Compost
• Potting mix
• Pellets
• Liquid

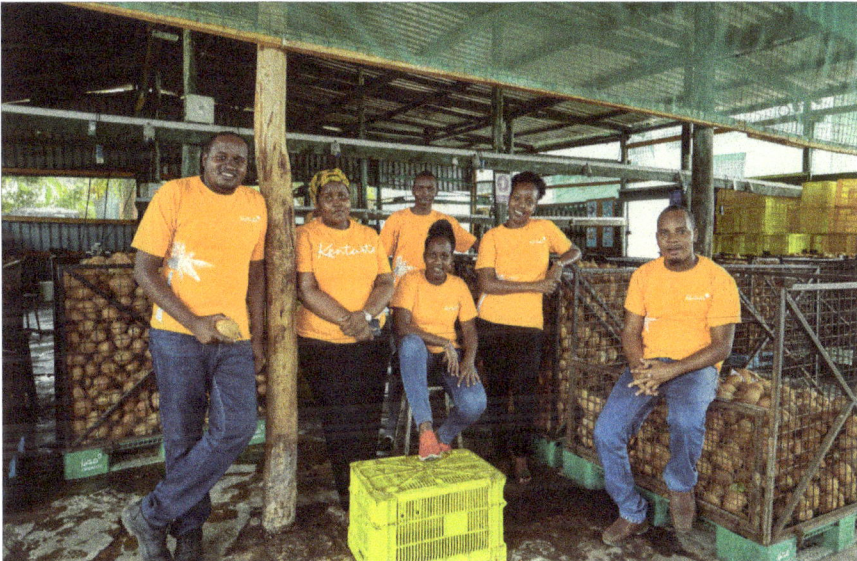

*Variety of innovative ocean-based products*
*(Top left) Brikole is a business startup in Seychelles which recycles the high volume of redundant fishing nets in the surrounding seas*
*(Top right) Fertiliser products from seaweed in Mauritius, pioneered by Sealife Organics*
*(Bottom) Kentaste is a local company reviving the coconut industry along Kenya's beaches*

Different entrepreneurs had their own stories to tell. From Seychelles, M.eco-fabrics could demonstrate high-quality fabrics and designs, using totally plant-based products. Brikole, another local business in the small island state, collects a large assortment of lines, nets, buoys, and other materials discarded in the course of industrial fishing operations and jettisoned or just washed ashore on the many islands. This debris is then sorted and sent to different operators for reprocessing. From elsewhere in Africa, there were examples of shoes made from recycled plastics; fashionable 'leather' goods from transformed fish skin; briquettes generated from plastic waste and then used in construction; several firms using solar power to obtain fresh water from the sea; and harvesting seaweed for a variety of purposes. Powered by the sun, another entrepreneur demonstrated not only how ice can be affordable for small-scale fish farmers but how it can then be transported to market in a container with fresh fish by means of an adapted motor cycle that is also dependent on solar power.

There seems to be no end of innovators with ingenious ideas, with many features in common. They are invariably the brainchild of young entrepreneurs, often engineers and biologists, their firms bearing expressive names like Sealife Organics, Wave Beat, Genius Watter and Island Carbon Consult. Although they share the goal of creating successful companies, they are also sensitive to social needs, and many, if not all, have found ways to help their local communities. A few projects at the Seychelles event have already crossed the threshold from developmental to commercial viability, but even the latter share a need for more investment.

## The Blue Economy Must Yield Economic Benefits

The environmental and ethical arguments for a successful Blue Economy are strong but, however desirable they are, people will always ask if the changes can be afforded and if it will yield ultimate economic benefits. These are wholly justified questions. With a still-burgeoning global population and a commensurate increase in the demand for resources, mistakes cannot be made. Answers have to come from somewhere.

Predictions of what the Blue Economy is worth to the world in economic terms are notoriously difficult to make with any accuracy. Who could have anticipated, for example, the impact on economies of the COVID-19 pandemic from 2019? Or the effects on oil and natural gas supplies of the conflict in eastern Europe that started in in 2022? But, in spite of these interventions, the returns from ocean investment can be expected to increase significantly. In 2016, before either of these global disruptions, the OECD estimated that employment in ocean-related industries would increase to 40 million by 2030. The oceans were, in the year of that report, contributing over $1.5 trillion to the global economy each year and this figure was expected to double by 2030.[24] It would be wrong to rely too much on exact figures but, even with the effects of COVID and then the disruption in oil supplies, positive growth resulting from ocean activities can still be expected.

The fact is that the Blue Economy encompasses a wide range of activities, existing and potential, with growth inherent in each. An indication of this scope is offered in the 2021 Blue Economy Annual Report of the European Union, in which a distinction is made between established and emerging sectors.[25]

## ESTABLISHED AND EMERGING BLUE ECONOMY SECTORS

**Established**
Marine Living Resources
Marine Non-Living Resources
Marine Renewable Energy (Offshore Wind)
Port Activities
Shipbuilding and Repair*
Maritime Transport
Coastal Tourism
*One can assume this includes shipbreaking

**Emerging**
Ocean Energy
Blue Bioeconomy and Biotechnology
Desalination
Marine Minerals
Maritime Defence, Security and Surveillance
Research and Education
Infrastructure

In the associated text within the EU report, a preliminary measure indicates what the different sectors are worth:

*Blue Economy traditional sectors contribute to about 1.5% of the*

*EU-27 GDP and provide about 4.5 million direct jobs, i.e. 2.3%
of EU-27 total employment. Emerging innovative Blue Economy
sectors, such as ocean renewable energy, blue biotechnology, and
algae production are adding new markets and creating jobs. This
is without counting indirect and induced income and employment
effects.*[26]

Even without precise figures there is a simple logic which is hard to deny.
The world presently provides for itself primarily from the use of 28 per cent
of the earth's surface, supplemented by the remaining 72 per cent. If the
latter is in future to be used more intensively (though also sustainably), it
follows that one should expect a commensurate increase in output. This is a
reasonable global expectation but it is fair to assume the impact will be uneven
and that in particular parts of the world benefits will be disproportionate. I
am thinking here of small island states, each surrounded by great stretches
of ocean but disadvantaged by a narrow economic base. Beyond indigenous
lifestyles, they were at first reliant on plantation crops, dependent on the
vagaries of world markets. Then, in the twentieth century, with the advent
of air travel and the global expansion of tourism, and through modern
refrigeration, fishing and tropical-fruit exports became important as well.
When conditions are favourable, these micro-economies can balance
their books but they are especially vulnerable to natural catastrophes like
hurricanes and flooding, as well as downturns in the economies of richer
nations. That is why diversification of their respective economies is essential
if they are to advance.

Fortunately, this is now very much a live issue. I can see the difference in
approach in the few short years since I wrote my first book on the Blue
Economy. Small island states are active in seeking new activities that the
ocean can offer. They acknowledge the importance of training and skills
development, the adoption of ethical business principles, and they speak
of new market opportunities. To make things happen there is a keen
understanding of the importance of attracting sufficient investment and
transitioning to a knowledge-based economy. Fresh ideas are discussed and
shared, a new vision is evolving. Leaders in small island states are no longer
content to limit their economies to how they were in the past:

*To be clear, the examples set by SIDS are not about business as
usual. What island nations are demonstrating is that benefitting
from ocean resources is not a zero-sum game. Conserving the ocean*

*protects marine life and generates economic growth for island and
business communities alike.*[27]

## The Blue Economy Must Contribute to a Fairer World

Although the Blue Economy is about finding new and better ways to use the
ocean's resources, this cannot be pursued in isolation. Notably, any changes
must be designed to improve lives not only for those people directly involved
but also to the furthest extremes of the global community. The ocean belongs
to us all. Divisions between developed and developing nations, between
North and South, 'haves' and 'have nots', should be consigned to the past.
The ocean can help us reshape our thinking about present disparities. If its
immense potential can be realised, the resultant rewards cannot be allowed
to stop at artificial boundaries. The Blue Economy must be inclusive; it
must contribute to a safer and fairer world.

When I wrote my earlier book on the subject, the emphasis was on
sustainable change and what that would mean. At that stage, less attention
was given to social ramifications and concepts like inclusiveness. I am
pleased to see how quickly that has changed and how any discussion of
the Blue Economy would be incomplete without this dimension. If there
can be any doubt about this intention, one only has to look at the UN's 17
sustainable development goals. Only one is devoted specifically to our use
of the ocean but at least five others feature cross-cutting social objectives.[28]
To go ahead with one without embracing the others will miss the point. Just
remember the matryoshka dolls.

Geographically, no part of the world should be left out. Not only coastal
communities but also inland in the various continents. It is an interesting
fact that 80 per cent of the ocean is located in the southern hemisphere
but the Blue Economy is a global concept and everyone should have a fair
share of the benefits. Presently, in many if not most societies, various groups
are disadvantaged. In relation to ocean activities, women, for instance, are
largely under-represented and underpaid. Dona Bertarelli, in her role as a
special UN adviser for the Blue Economy, makes the unambiguous point:

*There is a disparity of work and pay by gender, with women having
a significant presence in processing but not in fisheries management,*

*or ocean decision-making bodies. Many don't have equal access to opportunities, resources, financing, market information, technology, training, mobility and bargaining power. And that has a negative impact on food security.*[29]

Bertarelli argues that improvements need to be made, not only in present activities but, significantly, in 'new areas like sustainable aquaculture, renewable energy, blue carbon, and marine bio-prospection'.

Another group which fares poorly is young people, where in many countries there are high levels of unemployment and limited opportunities to be part of the anticipated changes in this sector. Youth unemployment is a major issue, not least of all in Africa (across the Maghreb as well as in sub-Saharan countries) and, when they do find jobs, these are often unskilled and low paid. New forms of training and education should be directed to turning things round. I have personally always put a high priority on giving every opportunity to the young, as they represent our future. This is one reason why I am pleased to see that in Seychelles, there are new schemes to take advantage of job prospects in the Blue Economy. These include training to increase the capacity of newcomers to work in key activities like water sports, tourism, fishing, port operations and marine transport.[30] A related but different set of initiatives stems from the work of a trust established to deploy funds resulting from a unique 'debt swap' deal that dates from my own time as President. When I reflect on the contribution I was able to make in that period, this is certainly one of which I am especially proud. By the end of 2020 it could be reported that:

*Nearly three dozen 'blue' projects worth a combined $1.4 million have been financed under Seychelles Conservation and Climate Adaptation Trust Blue Grants over the last five years. The 34 projects which emphasised investment in women and youth in the Blue Economy are women and youth-led, have young people and women as beneficiaries and are supporting small-scale fishers.*[31]

The message of inclusiveness has been well taken in general in Blue Economy advocacy, and one can point to a growing number of interesting examples of socially-minded initiatives. I am impressed, for instance, by the recognition of these in the progressive work of NLA International, an action-oriented group of researchers and consultants. In a recent report on this theme, one of the co-authors, Belinda Bramley, points to essential principles for the Blue Economy as well as various projects around the world:

> *Our analysis suggests that the best Blue Economies will be built on approaches that are **regenerative** of the ocean environment; **adaptive** to a changing climate and new knowledge; **inclusive** of all stakeholders, particularly those who depend most on ocean resources; **sustainable** environmentally, socially and economically; and **evidence-led**. Blue economies that follow these principles are most likely to **raise** the quality of lives and livelihoods.*[32]

Amongst the practical initiatives being taken, the report includes the example of the small island state of Antigua and Barbuda, which is benefiting from measures introduced to reduce plastic waste on its beaches and in the surrounding sea. A different kind of operation can be found in the Malacca Strait, where cooperation between the UK (with its own tracking system) and the Malaysian maritime authorities has led to a reduction in illegal oil dumping from passing ships. Elsewhere, another small island state, Palau, has been pro-active in countering illegal fishing and improving measures to reduce pollution (including early detection of oil spills). Or, in the Philippines, the Bantay Dagat or 'sea guardian' programme engages fisherfolk in coastal villages (or barangays) on a volunteer basis to support the detection and enforcement of illegal fishing in coastal waters.[33]

*Japanese fisheries patrol boat and Chinese illegal fishing boat*

I have chosen these few examples because they all illustrate actions taken locally by communities on the frontline of the Blue Economy. And, significantly, they all mean more than mere words. Policies are fine but, in the end, it is people who have the courage to turn back illegal fishing boats, who organise clean-up operations, and who inspire children to value their ocean inheritance, who really count. It is this translation of a broad idea into a myriad of practical schemes that encourages me most. We have come a long way in a short time. There is much further to go – this is only the start – but we are at least travelling in the right direction. And we are already much further ahead than we were when I made my earlier assessment, in 2016.

## The Blue Economy Must Be Supported by Adequate Funding

It is self-evident that for a transition to a Blue Economy, there needs to be a massive injection of new capital:

> *There are enormous needs at the moment, and if we really want to reach the goal of sustainably managed and really healthy oceans, we need to have much larger sources of funding.*[34]

Innovation on a global scale does not come cheap and every possible source will have to be tapped. In effect, there are three financial sectors where sufficient capital can be found, and the skill will be to make use of them all. One is through the contribution of philanthropists and benevolent foundations, a second is through direct government and publicly-based international funding, and a third will come as a result of commercial investment.

Philanthropy is not to be underestimated although it will never be more than a marginal source. There is a limited number of individuals and trust funds with enormous sums at their disposal and enthusiasm to devote their resources to ocean sustainability. Mention has already been made of the personal commitment of Dona Bertarelli; her contribution in so many ways to the cause of the ocean remains immense. As co-chair with her brother, Ernesto, of the Bertarelli Foundation, she dedicates much of her time and prodigious family funds to ocean conservation. To date, the Foundation has contributed to the protection of more than 2.7 million square kilometres in the Pacific and Indian Oceans and in the Caribbean Sea.[35] Amongst its many initiatives is the appointment of five Pew Bertarelli Ocean Ambassadors (of which I am one) to bring their combined global experience to bear on what needs to be done.[36]

*Philanthropy plays an important part in ocean conservation*

*(Top) James Michel, a Pew Bertarelli Ocean Ambassador, alongside Heraldo Munoz, Dona Bertarelli, Carlotta Guerrero and John Kerry*
*(Right) Leonardo DiCaprio at an ocean conference chaired by John Kerry, where DiCaprio announced on behalf of his foundation a new donation for ocean conservation*

Elsewhere, there are examples of ocean philanthropy which lead in different ways to invaluable work to protect and revive the ocean. Sometimes these individuals deliberately keep a low profile, with names little known to the public, such as Ray Dalio, an American billionaire whose wealth comes from a lifetime as an adroit hedge-fund manager and owner of his own company. Dalio has a deep love of the ocean and gives support for exploration to find out more. Amongst his many contributions is a state-of-the art vessel named OceanXplorer.[37] Yet, beyond his own circle, not so many people will have heard of Dalio. In contrast, Leonardo DiCaprio is a household name on the basis of his movie stardom, although not everyone will know that he is a committed conservationist who contributed (through his former foundation) large sums to support the cause.[38]

In turn, whether directly from governments or through international bodies like the World Bank, public monies are used to fund a variety of schemes. Apart from the richest nations, governments will generally find it difficult to fund all but essential projects from their mainstream budgets. Mitigation measures, for instance, to counter the effects of rising sea levels, would be regarded as essential. Beyond these, public funds might be used for demonstration projects or to seek public-private partnerships. In all cases, ingenuity is the order of the day, and during my own presidency I was able to initiate two schemes in Seychelles to augment our own limited funds. As I have already mentioned, one was to negotiate a debt swap arrangement so that monies that would otherwise have gone into debt repayment were redirected to support an ambitious ocean planning project within our waters. The other funding mechanism I was able to start was the idea of blue bonds, designed to attract new funds from the general public and private investors. In both cases, it is rewarding to see that these initiatives are not only well entrenched now within Seychelles but that they are also being replicated in other countries, especially small island states. With the help of bodies like the Nature Conservancy and the Commonwealth, supported with guarantees from the World Bank and the IMF, these ideas are being refined and lessons taken.[39]

After Seychelles (which has already made good use of the new funding), the Nature Conservancy in 2021 enabled Belize to negotiate its own debt swap arrangement. Some 10 per cent of the country's debt was released in exchange for funds (amounting to $4 million a year, through to 2041) to be used for marine conservation. New conservation measures on this scale in Belize, to revive the ailing but potentially rich ocean environment, will have a striking impact for the good:

> *It will double its marine-protection parks – spanning coral reefs,*

*mangroves, and the sea grasses where fish spawn – from 15.9 per cent of its oceans to 30 per cent by 2026. An endowment fund of $23.5 million will finance conservation after 2040.*[40]

Finally, and a vitally important source for the future, the Blue Economy will depend on corporate investment. Public intervention will always be important but change on this scale has never been funded without private entrepreneurs and corporations being prepared to risk their own money and that of investors. The Industrial Revolution in Britain towards the end of the eighteenth century had its origins in inventive minds in small workshops, and in coal mines and canals funded by investors who decided that this was where the future lay. Likewise, the modern Information Age, much of which was moulded by young innovators in garages and studios in Silicon Valley, was at the heart of changes that we now take for granted. And so it will be with the Blue Economy, requiring vision and a belief in all that the ocean has to offer. It calls for a massive step change from a particular way of thinking, one that still sees the ocean as it has always been, compared with the sketchy outlines of how it can be. But once the many opportunities are more widely recognised, money will surely follow. Investing in the Blue Economy will set the pace for new-generation businesses which will undoubtedly make their own mark. Ocean-based businesses for the present century and beyond.

There is, though, an important caveat. Commercial interests are not necessarily at one with the best interests of the Blue Economy. Sustainable tourism is one thing, where development and activities are blended with the surrounding environment and needs of communities. In contrast, interventions which seek only to maximise profits will most likely be harmful. There are all too many examples of the latter. So, too, I view the prospect of seabed mining for minerals with great concern, a subject I explore later in the book. International bodies, responsible governments and NGOs have an important role in moderating the plans of commerce while, at the same time, encouraging investment in projects that are consistent with the principles of the Blue Economy. There is room for all but not if the situation is left wholly to one side or the other.

In a recent article, Belinda Bramley points to the critical role of banks in encouraging and then enabling investors to finance Blue Economy initiatives.[41] As an example, she points to Asian Development Bank's new incubator, which supports sovereign and corporate borrowers who have plans to offer blue bonds. In a keynote address at an event in 2021, organised by the same bank, I was able to add insights based on my own experience. Another example – still at a formative stage – is the World Bank's Blue Economy toolkit to establish a development framework that is clear and can be universally applied. Although the Blue Economy is still a relatively new concept, and potential investors remain wary of committing the very large sums that are called for, there are different ways in which banks can help to build confidence. At different levels – international, regional, national and local – and from different sources of capital, Bramley believes that banks can help to release much-needed investment. If the Blue Economy is to achieve its undoubted promise, much will depend on the ability of banks to achieve this.

Finally, over and above the actions of different financial agencies, there is the underlying issue of a disparity between rich and poor nations. This is a theme which recurs throughout this book, reflecting the fact that the fulfilment of Blue Economy aspirations will fall well short if there is not a correcting mechanism to enable all parts of the world to invest. Different nations have fallen behind in economic development, often through no fault of their own, and it is in the interests of all to provide a more level playing field. The Blue Economy will not be achieved without this kind of recognition.

# Chapter 2

# Eureka!
## *Belated recognition that the ocean is our future*

Archimedes allegedly leapt from his bath to run naked through the streets of Syracuse, shouting *Eureka!* to tell all and sundry that he had made a groundbreaking discovery. Although we need not follow to the letter the example of the ancient Greek scientist, there is a case for celebrating the fact that, at last, the potential of the sea is being recognised for what it is: a golden opportunity for humanity to meet many of its present challenges.

The fact is that the interlinked ocean, which comprises more than 70 per cent of the surface of the planet, has always taken second place to the land in our thinking. Perhaps it should not be surprising that humans hold a land-centric view of the world. Having evolved from the sea as primitive organisms in the first place, there has been no desire to return. Sometimes, resistance is enhanced by an innate fear of the sheer power of the ocean, where lives have habitually been lost and which is still largely unknown. Only sailors experience, day to day, what it is like to go beyond a distant horizon and navigate across a boundless expanse of restless water. Uncertainties might be compounded by superstition and religious belief, like the traditional Hindu depiction of the black sea, *kala pani*, which deters followers to voyage afield for fear of losing their social and cultural hold on life. Crossing the sea, in this sense, has a spiritual meaning.

At a more prosaic level, the ocean has for long been dismissed as a residual part of the world – a vast area over which to cross from one country to another, a place to dump waste and treat with impunity. While it has for millennia provided a valuable source of food, there has, until recently, been little realisation that the supply of fish is exhaustible. As Enric Sala notes in his foreword to this book, 'we reached peak fish in 1996, and global catches have been declining since'. Not that the land has been treated much better, exploited in much the same way, with little thought for the future. Sustainability as a concept – where one takes account of future generations – has only quite recently become entrenched in our everyday thinking.

Even when I wrote my earlier book on the subject, within the past decade, traditional views prevailed. Time and again I encountered, if not resistance, then certainly doubts that the ocean could offer salvation. I argued the case under the banner of the Blue Economy, the term carefully chosen to match the understanding and progress achieved in the parallel, land-based Green Economy. The latter has its roots in the last quarter of the previous century, whereas  the Blue Economy is more recent. Far from being in competition, the two are complementary and both call for economies based on the sustainable use of natural resources. I have, on various occasions, emphasised the complementarity of land and sea, coined in the aphorism that blue is the new green.

As 'the new kid on the block', the Blue Economy has attracted a series of reports and studies which clarify what it is and what it has to offer. As an indicative example of the many explanations and prospectuses, one can look back to the significant publication, *The Ocean Economy in 2030*, produced in 2016 by the OECD and providing a contemporaneous baseline alongside my own book of that year.

> *The new 'ocean economy' is driven by a combination of population growth, rising incomes, dwindling natural resources, responses to climate change, and pioneering technologies. While traditional maritime industries continue to innovate at a brisk rate, it is the emerging ocean industries that are attracting most of the attention. These industries include offshore wind, tidal and wave energy; oil and gas production in ultra-deep water and exceptionally harsh environments; offshore aquaculture; seabed mining; maritime surveillance; and marine biotechnology. The long-term potential for innovation, employment creation and economic growth offered by these sectors is impressive.*[42]

There is little point in replicating this kind of definition as the purpose of my book is to go beyond that and see what, in practical terms, is being done to make the concept a reality. For those, however, who choose to explore comparable statements, I draw attention to a few references (in addition to the above OECD publication) in an endnote.[43]

Perhaps it is an exaggeration to claim that the Blue Economy has come of age. But it would not be overstating the case to point out that at all levels – from international through to local communities – it is attracting growing interest. Policies are not in themselves necessarily worth more than the paper they are written on, but their range in this instance is illustrative of increasing interest and commitment across the world. And one sees that the most effective policies are matched by practical projects to use the sea sustainably and to support its own regenerative properties. The tide is turning; the novel idea of giving priority to the ocean is beginning to realise its promise.

## Global Voices

At the apex of international bodies is the United Nations. It can only work as fast or deep as its member states allow, and for me this is never enough. But the UN has at least placed the sustainable use of the ocean on its global agenda. Reflecting the importance attached to the Blue Economy, it produced in 2015 a set of sustainable development priorities to be met by 2030. Of the 17 goals, one is specifically dedicated to what is termed 'Life below Water'. This 'concerns conservation and sustainable use of the oceans, seas and marine resources for sustainable development, and demands international cooperation for the oceans to get back in balance'.[44]

Half way towards the 2030 marker, progress was reviewed at the 2022 Ocean Conference held in Lisbon. Amongst the outcomes was a reaffirmation of the need for 'an ambitious, future-proof, international legally binding instrument on the conservation and sustainable use of marine biodiversity in areas beyond national jurisdiction, under the United Nations Convention on the Law of the Sea (UNCLOS)'.[45] I have for long worried about the 'free for all' that takes place in the unregulated seas beyond national jurisdictions. The Law of the Sea has made important progress insofar as its reach extends well beyond the shoreline, but it remains far from comprehensive. Apart from breaches within areas of the ocean that are nominally protected, it leaves the greater part of the ocean open to abuse. Bringing the 'high seas' within international control remains absolutely essential if progress is to be maintained.[46] This is why the recent agreement of the UN (in March 2023) to put this into effect is so important and it is why I return to this aspect of biodiversity later in the book.[47]

Hand in hand with the above is the specific objective:

> ...to protect at least 30% of the Ocean by 2030, with a focus on sites of particular importance for biodiversity and ecosystem services in well-connected systems of protected areas and utilising other effective area-based conservation measures, as part of the post-2020 global biodiversity framework.[48]

This is an international goal of the highest importance and one that I was able to advance at a national level during my presidency of Seychelles. As I will explain later, a marine spatial plan for my own small island state is no longer just words but is already partially in force.

The Lisbon Declaration (as the outcomes of the 2022 monitoring event were named) also included a call for 'a moratorium on deep-sea mineral exploitation in marine areas beyond national jurisdiction, and continued vigilance to ensure that human activities do not further contribute to the loss of marine biodiversity or undermine ecological integrity'.[49] Again, this is an issue that I care strongly about and my concern goes further to call for extra protection for areas within national jurisdictions as well as beyond. In a later chapter I explain the situation in more detail but, at this stage, suffice to say that such development runs counter to the common goal of a sustainable ocean.

While the UN is of crucial importance at the international level, it is by no means the only body with a global voice. Foundations, think-tanks and NGOs play their own part too. For example, the Pew Charitable Trusts exemplify how a privately-funded organisation can operate worldwide, in this case seeking to create large marine reserves; end illegal fishing; protect key species such as penguins, sharks, tuna and forage fish; and establish policies that protect, maintain, and restore the health of marine ecosystems.[50] Another example of an independent approach to global issues is the American think-tank, the Stimson Center, which inter alia has been pressing for stronger measures to protect the ocean. Through its annual 'Our Oceans' conference, funds have been raised and publicity given to further the cause. The banner heading for a press release at its fifth annual conference, in 2018, itself speaks volumes: '70 Countries, 100s of NGOs, Pledge New Action to Protect Oceans: Billions in Commitments Show Continued Support of Ocean Conservation.'[51] An influential body like the Nature Conservancy is an especially important source of support for the ocean, as is National Geographic.For the latter, I was honoured to receive an award in Washington DC in June 2019 to mark my contribution to ocean sustainability. It was acknowledged that, as the leader of a small island state, I had played a major part in winning the support of the UN, which proved to be a gamechanger in the campaign. Receiving the award gave me great satisfaction, not simply for myself but for the wider cause of the ocean.

*I received the National Geographic award in Washington, and had the honour of sharing the platform with the ocean advocate par excellence, Sylvia Earle*

In my acceptance speech in Washington, I proclaimed that:

> *We live in the age of the ocean. We have finally awoken to the*
> *sound of the sea around us. It is a late awakening – but, thanks to*
> *organisations like National Geographic, and to pioneering members*
> *like Sylvia Earle and other brave explorers of the sea – it is not too*
> *late.*[52]

I recalled that the great ocean pioneer, Rachel Carson, reminded us many years ago that human evolution started in the sea. Yet that is where survival is now most threatened. Not only for humans but other living creatures too. We cannot allow the loss of a single species. I went on to say that National Geographic does wonderful work and that, through my foundation, I would continue to do everything I can to support its mission, the ultimate vision of which is 'a planet in balance'. In a closing clarion call I urged that:

> *Now is the time for our reconciliation with the ocean! Now is the*
> *time to strike a balance between our needs and the conservation and*
> *rehabilitation of our ocean! With a new compass, we could chart the*
> *journey for the future. There is only one message: Healing, Conservation*
> *and Sustainability. Our shared future is Blue.*[53]

There are other international advocates for the ocean, too, that I can commend, such as two influential NGOs, Greenpeace and the Worldwide Fund for Nature. Additionally, some organisations are dedicated to particular aspects of ocean conservation, such as coral restoration, species protection and clean-up operations, and many of these have an exceptional record of practical achievement. There is no shortage of worldwide ocean advocates and this can only offer hope in reversing the adverse trend of centuries.

A different kind of initiative will sometimes emerge, not through an established institution so much as a response to a particular situation. In the aftermath of the economic impact of the coronavirus pandemic, 17 world leaders came together to establish what is called the Ocean Panel. This has the aim of charting a course of economic recovery by means of sustainable ocean projects. Tellingly, the joint chairs came from Norway and Palau, countries at different stages of economic development but with a shared dependence on the sea; other member states were drawn from different continents. To achieve its aim, the targets are simple but transformative, being nothing less than to secure '100 per cent sustainable ocean management of areas within national jurisdiction by 2025, guided by Sustainable Ocean Plans, and to support a global target to protect 30 per cent of the ocean by 2030'.[54]

## Common Interests

Somewhere between international and national levels of activity, there is an intermediate category of 'regional' initiatives. Their importance lies in the fact that they can reflect a larger cluster of cognate interests than single nations. Not least of these is the voice of small island states. Because of my own background, I am keenly aware of what the Blue Economy means to these, often remote, groups of islands. Surrounded by the sea and with limited land resources, my only surprise is that an ocean-based economy has not been explored more vigorously before. While fishing and tourism have for long been primary sources of income, there is a potential that goes well beyond what is done now.

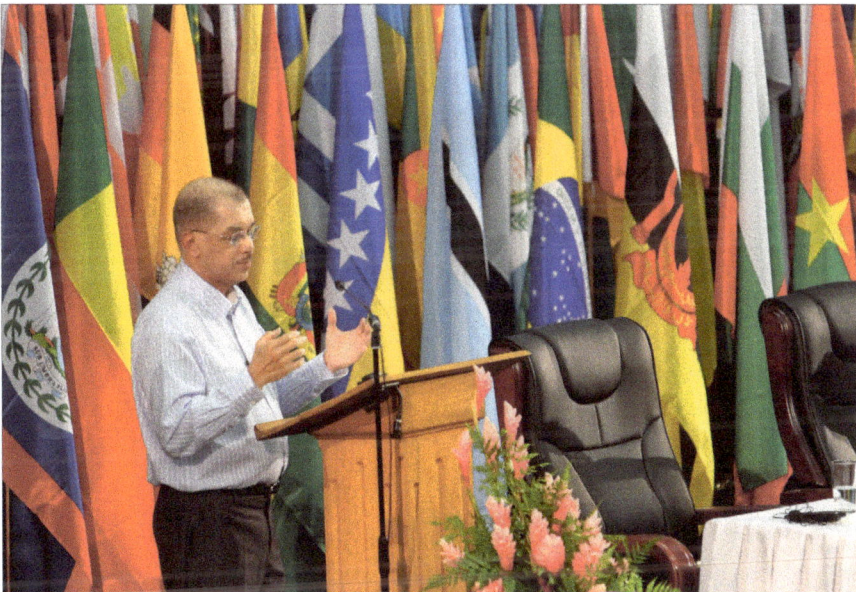

*At the Samoa conference for Small Island Developing States, I did all I could to demonstrate the importance of a healthy ocean*

Looking back, I can see that the UN Rio+20 Conference in 2012 was a turning point in raising awareness. With the backing of the then UN Secretary-General, Ban Ki-moon, a platform was subsequently provided for small island states to make their case. And so it was that, on the Pacific island of Samoa in 2014, leaders of small island states from around the world convened under the auspices of the UN to assert the value of the ocean for all their futures.[55] I made my own speech in Samoa, declarations were announced, and policies were later formulated by the different states. These were given direction by what was called the Samoa Pathway.[56] Best of all, a number of practical initiatives were soon underway in the different islands.

Eight years after Samoa, at a lower-profile UN event in Palau, designed this time to focus on business opportunities offered by the Blue Economy, news of progress was shared. From Seychelles, for instance, it was reported that projects that were started in my own term of office were by then well advanced. I could announce that the world's first sovereign blue bond had been launched, generating $15 million for climate mitigation projects as well as sustainable marine and fisheries support. Two years after that, in March 2020, lengthy negotiations yielded the implementation of the first-ever climate adaptation debt restructuring, in which part of the country's foreign debt was exchanged for the opportunity to designate nearly a third of its ocean territory (the full extent of which extends over an area 3.5 times larger than Germany) as a marine protected area.[57]

At the same UN event, in April 2022, it was reported that the host nation in the Pacific had closed what is one of the world's largest marine protected areas to all forms of extractive activities, including fishing. This followed an earlier decision to use its entire EEZ as a shark sanctuary. As well as protecting the species for ethical reasons, it makes good business sense: the full life of one reef shark, it is estimated, is worth $1.9 million in tourism revenue (compared with just $108 if it is sold on a slab for human consumption).[58]

In a different part of the world, Belize, in the Caribbean, could report on the completion of its own debt conversion along the same lines as the one pioneered in Seychelles. The scale of the exercise is impressive, amounting to a sum of $180 million being secured to invest in the conservation of its marine ecosystems over the next two decades. As in other small island states, tourism is a key source of income and the successful conservation of its reef environment is essential to the wellbeing of its economy.[59]

Arising from a different but related source, Fiji is another small island state intent on rebuilding its economy around its vast ocean reserves. It is a signatory to the aims of the Ocean Panel and is also a Blue Recovery Hub.[60] While subscribing to the general aims of the Ocean Panel it has introduced a welcome moratorium on seabed mining until at least 2030, by which time it is anticipated that more will be known about the potential impact of this activity on the ocean environment.[61]

Small island states represent one kind of regional initiative but there are others which relate more directly to geographical clusters. One which especially captures the imagination is the idea of the Great Blue Wall.[62] This was pioneered by the International Union for the Conservation of Nature, through its regional office in Nairobi, and I was personally very supportive from the outset. Following ratification by its governing body, it was then launched on the margins of the COP26 climate change conference in Glasgow in 2021. The focus of the initiative is on the shared ocean space of countries along the East African seaboard and island nations in the western Indian Ocean. An estimated 70 million people could benefit from the scheme, which is based on a network of proposed coastal and marine protected areas extending over two million hectares. Through concerted and sustainable policies, there is the potential to restore and conserve the sea in this region, with gains that will include the capture of 100 million tonnes of carbon dioxide. Funding could be sourced from the successive issues of blue bonds, a method favoured by Jean-Paul Adam, who heads the climate division for Africa of the UN's Economic Commission (UNEC) and who, coincidentally, was the former head of the Blue Economy department in my own government. At the time of the launch, I offered the following comment:

> The Great Blue Wall initiative is a unique approach for the region, Africa and the world subsequently. It promises to play an instrumental role in helping to achieve a nature-people positive world; a planet in balance. This is a unique opportunity to move forward at an unprecedented speed. I pledge my full support for this visionary initiative.[63]

In a different part of the world, the European Union publishes each year a report to reinforce and update its commitment to the sustainable use of the ocean, highlighting economic as well as environmental aspirations. May 2022 saw the release of its fifth annual report, reiterating the EU's general commitment on behalf of its 27 member states.[64] It is a lengthy report and clarity is clouded by an obvious need to please all parties, although one cannot miss the central message that the adjacent seas – North Atlantic, Baltic, Arctic, Mediterranean and the Black Sea – are all important to the wellbeing of the whole. It is not surprising that separate studies of these specific seas (with fewer members directly involved and with a clearly-defined geographical remit) enable a sharper focus on practical benefits.

A study of the Baltic sub-region, for instance, reveals a wide range of flagship projects.[65] These include ways to prevent chemical pollution from coastal farms; support for cultural diversity and creative industries in the surrounding ports; a concerted approach to increase mussel production; a clean shipping project platform; and cultivating algae sustainably as a potential cash crop.

## Sovereign Rights

International and regional advocacy of the Blue Economy is invaluable but, when it comes to implementing policies, national boundaries define those areas where one would hope to find constructive actions. In principle, the definition of maritime boundaries has a certain order to it. According to the United Nation's International Law of the Sea, a nation's territorial waters – the area over which it has sovereignty – comprise a series of concentric zones. Closest to the shoreline is the territorial sea, extending for a distance of 12 nautical miles (in the rest of that document, referred to simply as 'miles'), in which the sovereign nation has comprehensive rights.[66] This may be extended by a further 12 miles to create a contiguous zone, where restrictions still exist but are less stringent. A further 200 miles is designated as an exclusive economic zone (EEZ), which allows the home nation rights of fishing and other forms of economic activity. In this zone, it may also exploit the resources to be found on the seabed for as far as the continental shelf extends (so long as it is not more than 200 miles). It is in this wider zone that, through illegal actions by external parties, one sees the greatest challenges to sovereignty. Additionally, in both the territorial waters and the EEZ, rights are given to shipping to pass through unimpeded. Beyond these designated areas, as indicated in an earlier section, are the High Seas (comprising most of the world's interlinked ocean) where, at last, there is hope of regulating activities.

Certainly, over the past seven years, national initiatives have made the headlines, with some countries, in particular, showing a deep commitment to the sustainable use of the ocean. When looked at together, the sum total of progressive changes is encouraging, with more stretches of the sea now the subject of protective measures. There is evidence of this in all parts of the world.

To take just a few examples, let me turn first to the South American seaboard of the Pacific, where Chile, with its long coastline, is rightly attracting attention for its commitment to the ocean. On the occasion of World Ocean Day in 2021, Felipe Paredes Vargas, a marine biologist, could report:

> *Protecting and conserving marine resources is imperative and a key feature of a sustainable future. A breakthrough solution in recent years has been the creation of marine-protected areas, in ecosystems of high biodiversity in Patagonia, but mainly in oceanic islands such as Rapa Nui, the Juan Fernández archipelago, and the Desventuradas Islands. In total, Chile today actively conserves 42% of its exclusive economic zone, in more than 30 marine protected areas.*[67]

Within the Pacific, mention has already been made of Fiji and Palau, and there are other archipelagoes with very extensive EEZs where small island states are introducing protective measures. For years their fisheries have been plundered at will by foreign fishing fleets but at last there are signs of these places gaining control of what is rightly theirs.

Australia is a different case, not only because it is a large nation but also because it borders not just one but three of the great seas: the Indian, Pacific and Southern oceans. The oceanic area within its jurisdiction is the third largest of any nation. With much of its interior a desert environment, it is not surprising that the major cities are located around the coast and that the sea offers enormous potential for the whole economy. One feature of Australia's protection of the ocean is the designation of marine parks, amounting to more than 40 per cent of the total oceanic area within its jurisdiction.[68] There are 62 marine parks, the largest of which is the Coral Sea, a broad swathe of protected space off the north-east coast of the country. Second in size, and probably first in recognition, is the Great Barrier Reef. The most recent additions were declared in March 2022, off the shoreline of Christmas Island and in the area of the Coco Islands. The extent of seas covered is impressive although critics will point out that the level of protection afforded is by no means sufficient to maximise conservation.

*With its long Pacific coastline embracing divergent environments, Chile has pioneered a variety of marine protected areas*

The story of nations taking more effective control of their designated waters is replicated in other parts of the world too. Far to the north is Norway, bordering the Atlantic but also extending into the Arctic Circle and the traditionally ice-bound sea that might (in the face of climate change and the warming of the waters) change more than most. Norway is an unusually wealthy country, with a small population and high *per capita* incomes derived from valuable reserves of natural gas and oil, along with rich fisheries and shipping. It is in the enviable position of approaching ocean conservation from a position of strength, going well beyond the mere designation of protected areas, important though those are in themselves.

For Norway, the Blue Economy is deep-rooted and reaches into all parts of its society and economy. Thus, its updated strategy, entitled 'Blue Opportunities', builds on a long tradition of managing ocean resources.[69] Above all, sustainability is projected as second nature in this field and the nation has for some years been investing heavily in science and technology to ensure that all of its maritime activities are state-of-the-art. It has good relations with the EU but is not a member state, choosing, instead, to pursue its own path. On the surface at least, the strategy makes good reading. It goes well beyond the core topics to show how appropriate skills must be developed to support well-paid, interesting jobs; how coastal communities must be an integral part of joint development; and how businesses will be encouraged by numerous investment opportunities. But even Norway, with its many advantages and examples of good practice, is hardly a paragon of Blue Economy virtue. Once a major whaling nation, it has yet to shake off the practice that is reviled by most of the world; and less than 1 per cent of its EEZ is protected from fishing. What is more – against the flow of good environmental practice – the government is showing more than a keen interest in seabed mining for minerals beneath the country's extended continental shelf.[70]

In contrast with this rich, sparsely-populated Scandinavian nation, India and China are shaping their own approaches to the Blue Economy. With their large populations and a resultant need to make full use of their respective resources, the ocean presents an obvious source of interest. India, for instance, with some 7500 kilometres of coastline around the mainland, together with nearly 1400 islands and a sizeable continental shelf, is well placed to integrate potential growth from the ocean.

Prime Minister Narendra Modi has emphasised its importance in graphic terms:

> *To me, the Blue Chakra or wheel in India's national flag represents the potential of Blue Revolution or Ocean Economy. That is how central it is to us.*[71]

China, too, pins the concept very closely to its economic and geopolitical priorities. In fact, in a nation where everything is interconnected and planned to achieve the ultimate goal of overtaking the United States as the world's major power, the Blue Economy has a defined role to play. In the words of Premier Li Keqiang in 2019, the immediate aim is to 'vigorously develop the blue economy, protect the ocean environment, and construct a maritime power'.[72]

It is, in turn, part of President Xi Jinping's 'Chinese Dream', in which, continuing in the spirit of the post-Mao era of 'reform and opening up', modernisation is the key to further progress. The Chinese example shows that the Blue Economy is open to different interpretations and emphases. Reviewing the list of China's ocean economy priorities is indicative: 'Seawater utilization, electricity, mining, salt, chemical engineering, pharmaceuticals, shipbuilding, hydrocarbon, engineering, marine fisheries, travel and tourism.'[73] Elsewhere in policy documents and speeches, there is reference to clean waters and biodiversity but, in the order of priorities, modernisation will always come first.

Globally, the number of nations with Blue Economy policies is increasing, although one has to look at the balance between conservation and development in individual cases. Notable for its limited progress is the United States, which fell behind when the then President, Donald Trump, from 2015 to 2020, led a withdrawal from international initiatives of this sort. As a result:

> *The lack of regulatory support, investor appetite, and ocean-related data means the future of the blue economy is largely led by a fragmented legion of nonprofits and evangelists committed to seeing their vision come to life despite myriad obstacles.*[74]

America has the capacity to recover lost ground – and leading advocates for the cause – but much depends on political will. Belinda Bramley believes that the introduction of the 2021 Bipartisan Infrastructure Law ('Infrastructure Investment and Jobs Act') will help the situation. She observes that one can already see greater investment in coastal community resilience through a mix of competitive and non-competitive funding, and also required use of nature-based solutions in agency facilities, operations, and programmes.[75]

It would be easy to be overly sceptical of the efforts of some nations which could be doing more, but I remind myself of just how recent it is that there were no Blue Economy policies at all. We have already come a long way since then.

## Grassroots Ingenuity

In some ways, it is at the community level where progress can most usefully be measured, as this is where tangible change really takes place. It is one thing to talk at a national level about cleaning beaches and managing dwindling fish stocks, and quite another to take direct action. We can look for evidence at what is being done by people in the coastal communities themselves and also to an international network of NGOs which work locally.

Coastal communities are, literally, on the frontline of the Blue Economy. It is here that one finds experience accumulated over centuries: where knowledge of the tides is measured with precision, where harvests from the sea are a matter of local livelihoods, and where a sixth sense tells of the importance of finely-balanced ecosystems. Around the world, men and women alike take unreported initiatives to maintain a balance with the sea. Recognising the critical role of local communities, the international NGO, WWF, encourages local autonomy but also provides support where this is needed. Under the project banner, Ocean Witness, cases of local interventions are reported from around the world. There are many heartwarming stories to tell.[76]

Patricio Merino, for instance, was for many years a fisherman living on an island off the coast of Chile. After years of working in industrial fishing he realised that a more balanced approach was necessary if the resources of the seas he had come to know so well were to be sustained. His answer was to pioneer a marine protected area, not as a mere line on a map but with community involvement. The result is the Pitapaena-Añihué, a reserve of great diversity, managed by the community and recognised by the national government. It is a model of good governance that Merino hopes others will follow.

Another example is that of Roziah Jalalid, who grew up on the Malaysian island of Omadal and saw an urgent need to reverse adverse trends that were destroying her ocean environment. As others have done elsewhere, she recognised the potential of women to make a difference and is presently chairperson of the Women's Association of Omadal. She explains that a key objective is to secure the designation of a marine protected area but, in the meantime, their members organise patrols for turtle egg collection and to teach young people to care for the marine environment. The women also engage in handicrafts to supplement their income, donating 10 per cent from this to a conservation fund.

There is a great deal more that can be done to benefit from the active participation of coastal communities in marine conservation; these are vitalbuilding blocks in the creation of an all-embracing Blue Economy. But work along the coasts is not confined to locally-born activists, with international participants, too, joining through a network of NGOs. It is here one finds true enthusiasts who commit themselves to making a lasting difference. Ahead of national and international declarations, during my presidency in Seychelles I was always impressed with the range of projects managed by NGOs and the good that resulted from their efforts. Staffed largely (but by no means exclusively) by young people who care deeply about the ocean environment and want, above all else, to make a tangible difference, the range of their work is impressive. To illustrate this sector, I can draw on the example of what continues to be the case in Seychelles, where, because of the unique ocean environment, there is no difficulty in attracting participants. Many of these volunteers come from overseas but there is also a sizeable contingent from young Seychellois who are equally committed to conservation.

Nature Seychelles, led by Nirmal Shah, is the longest-established NGO in the archipelago, with a deserved reputation for research as well as practical operations. One of its many projects, which has been actively undertaken since 1998, is the management of Cousin Island and its surrounding sea. As well as protecting the natural environment, the team also attracts visitors to the island through a successful programme of eco-tourism. Account is taken of the carbon emissions generated by international visitors and actions are taken to ensure that the island achieves carbon neutrality.[77] It is, in all respects, a rounded approach to conservation.

For Seychelles as a whole, along with other countries with coral reefs, degradation of this vital source of marine diversity is a subject that NGOs are called on to address.[78] Restoration is not a quick fix but, as experience is gained, there is a growing understanding of what can be done to recover the reefs. As part of a wider project called Reef-fish, two local NGOs, Marine Conservation Society Seychelles and the Island Conservation Society, have each been allocated different reefs where the aim is recovery. At the same time, they will both continue with related marine conservation projects.

Other NGOs will often focus on the conservation of specific species, like the iconic giant tortoise on the outer islands, as well as turtles and sharks, all of which benefit from the kind of support that dedicated scientists and volunteers can offer. The Green Islands Foundation (GIF) concentrates its work on North Island and Denis Island (on both of which are high-end resorts where guests are encouraged to take an interest in the projects), where the aim is to protect endemic species. GIF is also starting a new fisheries project to reduce the Seychelles artisanal fisheries' impact on globally threatened species.[79] In turn, GVI is an American-based organisation which offers internships to young people interested in being part of a project to study and improve the reproduction rate of the lemon shark.[80]

Of all the islands of Seychelles, though, Aldabra is the jewel in the ocean-conservation crown. More than 1100 kilometres from the country's main island, Mahé, its remoteness undoubtedly helps in the maintenance of a pristine environment and it is, deservedly, a UNESCO World Heritage Site.[81] One of the world's largest atolls, it consists of four closely-located islands which together surround an expansive, inner lagoon. For all its remoteness, it was only by good fortune and public pressure that it escaped an ill-conceived plan in the 1960s for the British government to use it as a Royal Air Force Base and telecommunications centre. Since then, it has become the home of numerous conservation projects and a showcase for marine diversity.

To recognise its importance, Aldabra is protected by government legislation and managed by a public trust, Seychelles Islands Foundation, rather than an NGO. Amongst its many successes is the revival of species that were once close to extinction, the green turtle being a case in point. It is also one of only two breeding sites in the world for the Greater Flamingo. The giant tortoise is probably the most iconic beneficiary of sustained conservation, with a number in excess of 100,000.[82] Access to Aldabra is tightly controlled but for an insight into the richness of marine life in the western Indian Ocean, there is nowhere more stimulating. For volunteers, this offers the experience of a lifetime.

*Aldabra, so nearly lost to military development in the 1960s, is now an ocean treasure of international importance*

# Part 2

# Transition

A great deal is changing in the transition to a more ocean-centred world. It is a mixed story and not all of it is what one would necessarily hope for. But there is also no shortage of good news to tell. The fact is that progress is dependent on a wide range of activities and each moves ahead at its own pace – some exceeding expectations, others lagging behind.

In this section of the book, I start with the two traditional pillars of the ocean economy, shipping and fishing, with the former showing more concerted efforts to become sustainable than the latter. I then move on to tourism, which has an enormous impact on the maritime environment and certainly raises many questions. In contrast, when it comes to finding ways to harvest new sources of food from the ocean, there are more obvious signs of progress; this is, in fact, one of the most uplifting topics I address.

Ocean energy is the subject of the next chapter and this, too, shows plenty of positive change but by no means fast enough to counter the relentless effects of climate change. If that is a mixed story, in contrast, when it comes to seabed mining, I can find nothing to report that supports the idea of sustainability. We are told that the world needs what is embedded on the sea floor but certainly not everyone is convinced. Moving on, using the ocean as a dumping ground for waste generated on land continues to be a cause for serious concern, although even here one can take heart from new ideas and worthwhile projects.

A pristine sea exhibiting biodiversity is at the heart of a sustainable transition and, in the penultimate chapter, there are certainly some promising developments but, as with other activities, there is still a great deal more to be done. Finally, I turn my attention to the seashore, which is not always seen as part of the Blue Economy but should be, as coastal development plays its own part in contributing to the ocean as a whole.

Over such a broad range of activities, I suppose it is inevitable that some of these demonstrate more progress than others. But time is not on our side and the achievement of a sustainable transition depends on all moving faster than they are. In pursuit of measurable improvements, one cannot be other than critical of what has been done so far. Some of it is very good but it is not enough. The ocean deserves better. There is more to be done – on all fronts.

© Roger Ebrahim

# Chapter 3

# Godspeed and Safe Passage
## *Safe and clean shipping at the heart of globalisation*

Shipping has always been the great conveyor of goods between nations. And it still maintains that dominant role, by far. Estimates vary but a generally accepted figure is that at least 80 per cent of total international trade by volume, worth 70 per cent in terms of value, is seaborne.[83] The present, complex web of globalisation is dependent on the safe and timely means of transport that shipping offers. No discussion of a sustainable transition to the Blue Economy would be complete without an understanding of this most crucial of activities. What is more, the situation is far from static and not long ago it was predicted that trade across the seas might increase as much as threefold by the middle of this century. While still anticipating an upward trend, more recent forecasts are looking towards a lower rate of growth.[84]

Regardless of precise numbers, shipping is, indeed, indispensable. But there is a downside to what is, in terms of meeting the world's needs, a success story. The fact is that, essential though it is, shipping is not presently sustainable. So what needs to be done to change this in the years ahead? The energy to propel ships over long distances has evolved across the centuries, most notably from the days of wind and sail – the ultimate renewable combination – to coal-fired and diesel-driven engines. In 2018, shipping accounted for more than 2.9 per cent of the world's carbon emissions and, if allowed to continue at the present rate, the figure will continue to rise, year on year.[85] With fossil fuels the main source of power, and the cause of increasing carbon emissions, the challenge is to find new, more sustainable methods of propulsion. The first step, therefore, on the journey to sustainability, is to look at the various fuelling options that are now available, the agreed goal being to reduce carbon emissions and to do so urgently. Creating a decarbonised industry is about much more than changes to the operation of ships themselves; the multiple activities of ports and, in turn, the land transport generated to serve them, add to the complexity of the challenge. Little short of an ocean revolution is required if sustainability is to be achieved.

Decarbonisation heads the agenda, although it is by no means the only aspect of shipping in need of radical review. Thus, other practices, too, which have long been tolerated, do not necessarily pass muster in what is rightly a more critical age. A second step, therefore, is to improve the safety of all aspects of carriage by sea. This will include a review of the legal and regulatory framework for safe and efficient movement on the open seas. Are the rules up-to-date and, significantly, are they effective? A review of safety should also include a fresh look at the training and welfare of seafarers, who too often still endure conditions that are unacceptable for a modern industry. Their various hardships and courageous deeds in the past have coloured numerous works of fiction but that is hardly a reason to continue without reform. And a final aspect of this review of safety will be the specific case of ferries, where the incidence of accidents and fatalities in this often-neglected sector calls for its own scrutiny.[86]

## Ocean Revolution

The bottom line is that, if shipping is to become more sustainable, the present reliance on fossil fuels must be drastically reduced, if not totally removed. Certainly, the case to do so is clear enough. The UN's agency for shipping, the International Maritime Organization (IMO), has called for a 50 per cent reduction in greenhouse gas emissions by 2050, and their total elimination 'as soon as possible' in this century.[87] Critics have since countered that this level of reduction is not enough and that a vague aspiration to achieve further change 'as soon as possible' is not sufficient to convey the sense of urgency that underlines the issue.[88] In fact, the challenge is even greater than these figures suggest, the reality being that 'ships will have to reduce their output of carbon dioxide by 85 per cent per nautical mile, to take account of an increasing number of ships, and possibly more activity over coming years'.[89]

Rapid progress needs to be made in the present decade if there is any chance of keeping pace with existing traffic in the years beyond. In the words of one specialist:

> *The 2020s will be a vital time for piloting and prototyping new fuels and hybrid propulsion arrangements. Vessels will need to transition from fossil-based fuels to zero carbon energy sources and technologies, while simultaneously increasing efficiency.*[90]

Gradual evolution is no longer an option; drastic change is needed, and there is little time for this to happen.

As good a starting point as any is to go to the heart of the problem and question why there is so much traffic in the first place. What is in the numerous containers that are piled high and transported to distant destinations? And, likewise, why are there so many bulk carriers? Do we really need them all? Can we cut back on the volume of traffic and, by that means, reduce the polluting effects of shipping?

The answer to the basic question of why there is so much traffic is simple enough. Firstly, each year there are more people in the world and, consequently, a greater demand for goods and services. It is commonly thought that the total population level will tail off later in the century but, apart from the fact that predictions of this sort are notoriously unreliable, it will still represent many more people than there are now. Secondly, even if the population were static, demand would still increase because of the numbers coming out of poverty and finding themselves, for the first time, with even a modicum of disposable income. For ethical and political reasons, neither of these two trends can reasonably be reversed.

There is, however, a third reason which, on the face of it, might be more amenable to change and that is to be found in the dynamics of consumption. Globalisation has made possible the creation of a worldwide consumer society. Hidden within the anonymous casing of containers are vast numbers of cheap clothes and trainers, plastic toys and bicycles, laptops and mobile phones, furniture and fabrics; while in the bulk carriers are materials for construction and food processing, chemicals and cars, destined for factories and farms, for refineries and showrooms. And this is not to mention the specially-designed tankers used to transport crude oil, which is a smaller proportion of seaborne trade than it used to be but still a major source of carriage. Distance is no obstacle in what amounts to the delivery of consumer choice, meeting demands that become ever more voracious and discriminate. Logic would tell us that consumption has moved well beyond what people actually need, and that it has a dynamic of its own.

Yesterday's luxuries become today's necessities. Yet logic will also tell us that, without draconian measures, these trends cannot, in practical terms, easily be reversed. Perhaps the sheer urgency of such measures will one day force extreme change but consumers will not readily accept such actions now. Politically, one may be able to chip away at particular items but overall, for better or worse, it is hard to see how the general flow can be stemmed. Once toothpaste is squeezed from the tube there is no obvious way to get it back.

*Container ships are the engine room of globalisation*

A change of mindset is called for but this will need to be accompanied by innovative options that might offer different ways to solve the problem. Once again in this book, I can visualise how bright scientists and young entrepreneurs will work together to power fundamental change. In relation to different aspects of the transition to a Blue Economy, I take every opportunity to commend the contribution of business start-ups to provide fresh ideas and the impetus to make them work. What is especially encouraging in the case of shipping is that there is also scope to align these initiatives with the muscle of large corporations committed to a 'net positive' approach. Leading companies are not always quick to change timeworn ways – generations of executives attending business schools are indoctrinated with traditional practice – but when they do make a move they can be surprisingly fast. One comparative change in a different sector is to note the rapid introduction of battery-fuelled cars when, up to now, petrol and diesel have been the dominant sources. Changes in consumer preference led to a remarkable U-turn. Even ten years ago, the speed of change that has since taken place in that industry would have been hard to imagine. It is striking what can be done when the need is recognised.

## A Decade of Decarbonisation

There are, indeed grounds for hope. But no one who understands the problem is sanguine about how much needs to be done. Charles Haskell, for instance, the programme manager of Lloyd's Register's initiative, 'Maritime Decarbonisation Hub', expresses it this way:

> *The challenge is to advance from fossil-based fuels, to net-zero energy sources and technologies in a safe, fair, equitable and just way. Stimulation of investment is critical, which in turn requires an understanding of both supply and demand of zero carbon shipping fuels.*[91]

It is not only a technical challenge: in the end, being able to make a strong business case is essential. Although there is undoubtedly a steep slope to climb, there is already a menu (as illustrated in the table opposite) of ways to replace fossil fuels in shipping.[92]

## POTENTIAL ALTERNATIVES TO FOSSIL FUELS IN SHIPPING

| | |
|---|---|
| ✧ **Liquefied Natural Gas (LNG)** Derived from natural gas that is liquefied at very low temperatures. Transported to port terminals by tankers. Zero sulphur content and low carbon dioxide emissions. Already widely used. | The main disadvantage is that LNG is highly flammable. Seen as a bridging solution while working towards safer and longer-term, renewable sources. |
| ✧ **Hydrogen and Fuel Cells** Compressed or liquefied hydrogen has a number of advantages: it produces zero carbon emissions, is non-toxic and odourless. Especially attractive for smaller ships but can be scaled up. | But its production is dependent on large amounts of energy. It is also quite highly flammable. It has low ignition energy. And is not efficient in deep-water conditions. |
| ✧ **Biofuels and Biodiesel** Produced from biomass, whether specially grown or organic waste. Renewable and low in carbon emissions. Suitable for blending with other fuels. | Must be sourced from sustainable materials. Can be environmental problems if large scale. Still technical issues at the production stage. |
| ✧ **Ammonia** 'Green ammonia' produced from renewable sources. Applicable to fuel cells or internal combustion engine. Does not contain carbon: effective source of zero emissions. Low-cost way of using hydrogen as a marine fuel. | Problems to be ironed out before promising potential can be realised. Ecological threats in cases of spillage. As a toxic fuel, has to meet strict regulations. |
| ✧ **Battery/Electric** Another zero-emission option. Can make use of solar sources. Fully electric applications still developmental. But potential to design generators for on-board charging of batteries. | Currently only practicable for short distances such as ferries. Much depends on emerging battery technology. |

| POTENTIAL ALTERNATIVES TO FOSSIL FUELS IN SHIPPING | |
| --- | --- |
| ✧ **Nuclear**<br>Proven effective in military vessels.<br>New developments will reduce lifecycle costs and improve safety. | Public opinion will question safety aspects.<br>Also a need to adhere to international non-proliferation agreements. |
| ✧ **Rediscovering Wind, Tapping into the Sun**<br>Can be used to supplement other forms of power.<br>Already in limited use.<br>The ultimate in renewable energy.<br>Solar power as well as wind a valuable supplement. | Needs new designs to capture wind and solar power.<br>Challenges of grid connections and storage. |

It would be misleading to suggest that any one of these various options is, as yet, either technically or commercially ready for wholesale application, although some are more advanced than others. The reality, in any case, is that any one option, even when further developed, will be unlikely to answer all the questions. Probably, solutions will be found which use different applications in combination, or which respond to particular circumstances. Why not, for instance, the use of, say, green ammonia as a ship's main fuel, supplemented by wind power when conditions are favourable?

In deciding which of these different fuels are most appropriate, account must be taken of a number of variables. For instance, the configuration of different shipping routes is an important factor, on the basis that it is easier to plan (at refuelling stations as well as at sea) for regular traffic between two ports than for an unpredictable number and distribution. One also needs to know whether demand will be generated by large vessels or small, and for long-distance traffic or more localised routes. Will speed be the main consideration or should costs be reduced by taking slightly longer? Geography is also a factor, on the basis that some countries will be in a stronger position to produce certain of the new fuels than others. In the case of Morocco, for instance, solar energy will be more important than in countries with a high level of cloud cover. Chile is also well endowed with renewable sources of power (including water) and will naturally favour applications which use these effectively.

*Wind power – the traditional source of power for shipping – may yet return to supplement other renewable options*
*(Top) A modern version of the original Royal Clipper, equipped for passengers*
*(Bottom) Oceanbird – a planned new venture into the world of modern sail*

If carbon emissions are to be drastically reduced, time is short to make the required transition; there is painstaking research and development still to be done in order to provide genuine alternatives to fossil fuels. Different solutions remain just beyond reach, the main barrier to their adoption at present being the difficulty of making an effective business case to attract investors. Rather than wait for individual solutions to be perfected, the best approach, instead, is to advance on all fronts, to continue with R & D while at the same time anticipating how best to make a progressive transition of the industry as a whole. There is nothing so effective as monitoring particular applications in practice. Central planning is not the answer; local innovation offers better prospects for change.

One thing is certain, the transition from one form of energy source to another will not be a seamless process in which the world's operators all fall into a single line. Instead, it will occur piecemeal, 'starting from niche markets until their expansion merges and substitute with the current regime'.[93] It will be a complex set of actions, in which different zero-emission fuels are refined and evaluated, in which required changes to port facilities are assessed, and where the relative costs of retrofitting new systems are compared with newly-built vessels. Some countries will emerge ahead of others, just as commercial operators and investors will see different opportunities to overtake their competitors.

Even now, the route to 2030 and beyond is hard to determine with any certainty. The landscape is muddled, with a web of innovative organisations and scientific projects intersecting and overlapping. Look more closely, however and common themes will start to emerge. Above all, in spite of some scepticism as to whether the transition can be achieved in such a short time, there is a powerful desire amongst most parties to cut the volume of carbon emissions. This means that, although there are numerous starting points and different approaches are taken, there is also the unifying factor of generally shared goals. Although an attempt in June 2023 failed to secure international agreement for a global tax on offenders, it is believed that change will soon follow.[94]

There is certainly no shortage of effort in the search to cut levels of carbonisation and from this we can take hope.

## First Movers, Fast Forward

Targets have been set. We are already a few years into this critical decade. The 'fast forward' button has been pressed and the race is underway. Working towards the decarbonisation of shipping is the common destination. After nearly two centuries of bunkering with coal and oil, and never mind the consequences, a new generation of ships will have a choice of zero-emission fuels. It is not just the shipping operators who will decide which will suit their needs best but also the customers, in the form of companies wishing to transport their goods from production to dispersed markets. Some major producers have already staked their reputations on the transition to clean energy, and the questions are whether they will stay the course and who will join them? First movers hope to keep their advantage, although always aware that there is a risk in committing to be out in front. The scene is rather like the start of a cross-country race, where runners jostle for position before the starting gun is fired. Amidst the pack of runners, one can see producers and consumers, shippers and regulators, scientists and technologists, lobbyists and politicians. Investors are there too, understandably cautious but attracted by the prospect of huge gains for those who get it right. The money will flow once there is a strong business case for investment.

Without continuing research and development, and then the right level of investment, the runners will remain in a huddle. As already explained, it is unlikely that consumers will be willing to shed their reliance on imported goods (although different patterns will constantly evolve), so the decisive agents of change will be found amongst suppliers. Theirs is a pivotal position. Suppliers are the key: the fact is that, for all the diversity of products that are transported round the world, they originate in workshops and factories, whether from small firms or through multi-national corporations. Goods are taken to the ports and then loaded onto waiting ships. So begins their journey to the various markets. Clearly, it is not in the interests of shipping operators to stop supplying what is in demand. Instead, or as well, it is producers who have a crucial opportunity to make transactions more sustainable – in terms of the design and raw materials for their products, and then their ability to influence how their goods are transported. At least there are signs that this is, increasingly, being recognised and that change will come from within. Traditionally, businesses were interested only in the bottom line, in maximizing profits for themselves and their shareholders. Obviously, they still have to be profitable but there are other considerations too.

## Changing the mindset

Under the banner of 'Net Positive', Paul Polman and Andrew Winston argue that businesses can serve their own interests while at the same time addressing social and environmental issues. They can make a contribution to solving some of the world's problems while also improving their own reputations as progressive businesses. 'We define a net positive company,' say the authors, 'as one that improves wellbeing for everyone it impacts and at all scales – every product, every operation, every region and country, and for every stakeholder, including employees, suppliers, communities, customers, and even future generations and the planet itself.'[95] A net positive company, they continue:

⬧ improves the lives of everyone it touches, from customers and suppliers to employees and communities, greatly increasing long-term shareholder returns in the process;
⬧ takes ownership of all the social and environmental impacts its business model creates. This in turn provides opportunities for innovation, savings, and building a more humane, connected, and purpose-driven culture;
⬧ partners with competitors, civil society, and governments to drive transformative change that no single group or enterprise could deliver alone.[96]

Even before the publication of the book to explain the concept, Polman (formerly CEO of Unilever) was instrumental in getting a number of major companies to join in a commitment to zero-emission shipping by 2040.[97] Amazon, IKEA and Michelin were amongst other multi-nationals which signed up to this goal. The intention was not only to encourage ocean operators to make the change in their fuel systems but also to give confidence to investors in building the necessary port infrastructure to replace obsolete facilities. And, in the course of their actions, it was intended that reputations would be enhanced.

Other global initiatives and studies, too, point in a similar direction. From commercial operators, we can see, for instance, Shell plc's *Decarbonising Shipping: All hands on deck*,[98] and the formation in 2020 of the Mærsk Mc-Kinney Møller Center for Zero Carbon, which will generate updated statistics and promote new findings.[99] Meanwhile, indicative of an international pressure group, the International Renewable Energy Agency (IRENA) in 2022 produced its own report, *A Pathway to Decarbonise the Shipping Sector by 2050*.[100] In fact, searching the literature on this subject is like being in an orchard and picking low-hanging fruit. There is no shortage of enticing possibilities.

To illustrate what is available, I can turn the spotlight on what is being done through the Lloyd's Register's 'Maritime Decarbonisation Hub'. Formed in 2020, its mission is 'to accelerate the sustainable decarbonisation of the maritime industry, by enabling the delivery and operation of safe, technically feasible and commercially viable zero-emission vessels by 2030'.[101] One of the strengths of the hub is in bringing together like-minded partners, each of which contributes its own specialist ideas and experience. It shows, too, that no single organisation is alone on the frontier and support is never far away; they each have something to offer and the whole endeavour is greater than the sum of the various parts. Thus, one of these partners, the Sustainable Shipping Initiative, brings together leading agencies to improve the sustainability of the industry as a whole, in terms of social, environmental and economic impacts. Lloyd's Register was a founding member of this body as long ago as 2011, when the issue was not generally recognised as the priority it is now. A second partner is the Global Compact, which works in the business sector to champion the principles and objectives of the UN's Sustainable Development Goals. And, a third collaborator is the eponymous Getting to Zero Coalition, the purpose of which could not be clearer. The Coalition is itself in partnership with the Global Maritime Forum and the World Economic Forum, and within that framework it is:

> ...*a powerful alliance of more than 200 organizations (including 160 companies) within the maritime, energy infrastructure and finance sectors, supported by key governments and IGOs. The Coalition is committed to getting commercially viable deep sea zero emission vessels powered by zero emission fuels into operation by 2030 towards full decarbonization by 2050 – maritime shipping's moon-shot ambition.*[102]

This joint approach by various partners is exemplified through the initiative of green shipping corridors, most commonly defined as shipping routes where 'the technological, economic, and regulatory feasibility of the operation of zero emissions ships is catalysed through public and private actions'.[103] In this context, the Lloyd's Register initiative affirms a belief that solutions have to be matched to the different needs of ship operators and preferred routes. Working through a fleet-specific case study – that of medium-size container ships, plying the busy route to and from Singapore and Hong Kong – the researchers are able to draw particular conclusions. [104]

✧ One is that, although it is likely that different fuels could be used to reduce carbon emissions, each has a different cost and other implications. As a result, some will suit particular situations more than others.

✧ Another conclusion is that, while one fuel might offer short-term advantages, it is the long-term scenario that has to be assessed. The level of investment in each case – in infrastructure and on-board changes – will be extremely high, and reducing costs over the life cycle of a ship is an essential factor.

✧ One of the longer-term considerations is that an estimated 26 per cent of the fleet will need to be retrofitted to accommodate new fuels, with the rest being redesigned at the time of replacement.

✧ Of all the costs incurred by an operator, the actual voyages account for the highest proportion. If fuel costs can be reduced this will have the largest impact.

✧ Finally, early decisions have to be made on where fuel supplies will be sourced; if natural gas is a key element, along with ammonia and methanol, it may be that the main producers for this particular fleet will be in Saudi Arabia and Australia. Decisions cannot be taken in isolation from the wider context.

## *Singapore's blueprint*

I am not always confident about the contribution that can be made by individual countries, where short-termism better suits the life expectancy of elected governments. But there are notable exceptions, where particular nations are taking commendable steps to make their own maritime industries more sustainable. The example of Singapore can serve to illustrate ways in which this can be achieved.

Singapore is inherently an innovative island state, left in ruins after the Second World War and only achieving sovereign status in 1965. Since then, under inspired leadership, it has become a model of industrial efficiency and social progress. Located at a strategic nexus in the vibrant trade of South-East Asia, it is the world's second busiest port in terms of container throughput and the leading hub for bunkering. Its commitment to contribute to cleaner shipping is, therefore, not to be underestimated. Setting out its intentions, in 2022 the government produced its own blueprint for decarbonisation, comprising 'ambitious and concrete long-term strategies to build a sustainable maritime Singapore'.[105]

*Singapore's blueprint for decarbonisation of its busy harbour is a world leader*

The blueprint makes fascinating reading, bridging the gap between ideas and application. It has a sense of immediacy about it which helps one to understand the many questions which surround the transition to decarbonisation. Just a few extracts will illustrate the wide range of ideas and actions underway.

- ◇ Strategies [for its port terminals] include the greening of port handling equipment, port vehicles, and terminal buildings, as well as improving energy efficiency and adopting cleaner energy alternatives.
- ◇ By 2030, [Singapore] aims to reduce absolute emissions from the domestic harbour craft fleet by 15 per cent from 2021 levels, through the adoption of lower carbon energy solutions such as blended biofuel, LNG, diesel-electric hybrid propulsion, and full electric propulsion. By 2050, the port authority aims

for the harbour craft fleet to halve 2030-level emissions by transitioning to full-electric propulsion and net-zero fuels.

✧ While not favouring any particular fuel type, [Singapore] expects hydrogen and its carriers (including ammonia, e-methanol) as well as bio-LNG to potentially play important roles in the decarbonisation of international shipping in the mid to long term.

✧ Under its ship registrations scheme, Singapore will recognise, incentivise and guide shipowners to meet the targets under the IMO Initial Strategy and achieve their sustainability ambitions.

✧ As a leading global hub port, bunkering hub and shipping registry, Singapore will advance strong, credible and inclusive climate action at the IMO and international fora... [and] supports a global carbon levy on international shipping in the medium to long-term.

✧ Singapore will be a global hub for maritime decarbonisation R&D solutions, enabled by a vibrant ecosystem, with the talent and expertise to develop, trial, deploy and commercialise innovations.

✧ To build Singapore as a green maritime finance hub, MPA will continue to strengthen capabilities in carbon accounting and reporting and promote green financing within the maritime industry.

Clearly, the blueprint of one country will not necessarily suit another, but it hard to see why this could not offer a template of measures that others might consider, if not to use in their entirety. It is comprehensive, relevant and innovative, pointing in different ways to the common goal of decarbonisation.

This brief review, not only of the example of Singapore, but of other initiatives too, affirms for me that there is exciting work underway, in different sectors and across the world. It is a sea of discovery and I cannot be other than hopeful that further pointers to a decarbonised future will be found.

## Safer Shipping

Most of us, who have never had to work at sea, cannot expect active seafarers to continue to put themselves in needless danger on our behalf. As beneficiaries, we have our own part to play in ensuring that conditions are as conducive as possible for a safe and satisfying life on the waves.

The reality is that, for as long as boats have left shore, the sea presents a constant challenge. Sometimes this is a result of our own laxity in failing to adequately prepare, but at other times it is the natural force of the ocean environment itself which is overwhelming. Histories of seafaring abound with accounts of shipwrecks and loss of life, of mountainous waves and icebergs that cannot be overcome, and of brave but untrained boys who were sent to climb tall masts for lookouts and to free entangled sails. The sea will always remain a challenge but in the rest of this chapter I will point to three aspects of shipping where new measures can make a difference: the enforcement of sensible rules and regulations, the need to recognise the safety and welfare of seafarers, and the specific case of accident-prone ferries.[106]

### *Enforcing the rules*

In many respects, the shipping industry is replete with well-intentioned rules. These are not just the result of altruism but also the self-interest of merchants, shipowners and other investors who all want to ensure the security of their business. A perennial problem, however, is that, unlike other forms of transport, for most of the time ships are not closely monitored. That is the nature of the activity. Once a vessel is over the horizon there is latitude given to a captain that goes beyond, say, an airline pilot or a factory manager. This is not to suggest that captains are any less responsible than their counterparts, so much as to recognise an important difference in context. Nor is it just the navigation of legitimate craft which may be at fault, as the present century has revealed new versions of the ancient practice of piracy and the intervention of organised crime.

For all the romance associated with piracy in history, it is and always has been an indefensible flouting of rights and the rule of law. In the popular imagination, it belongs to the past but, as I discovered myself when Seychelles faced a succession of assaults by pirates emanating from the long coastline of Somalia, it has resurfaced as a contemporary problem. With the support of international partners, we were able to rebut that particular outbreak of lawlessness, but only at great expense at the time and the continuing costs of naval containment to prevent fresh instances.[107] Moreover, it has not been confined to this one region, with other attacks on merchant shipping taking place in South-East Asia and off the west coast of Africa. Looking towards a sustainable Blue Economy, what can we learn from these recent examples to create a more peaceful sea?

The fact is that the reasons for piracy are by no means straightforward: does it occur because there is weak governance on land or should one look, instead, to the fact that EEZ fisheries in such countries are ruthlessly plundered by more powerful nations and organised crime?[108] My personal experience of Somalia pointed to the fact that it is still a lawless state and, until fundamental issues can be resolved there, the threat of piracy will remain. In the 15 years or so since the first pirates unlawfully boarded ships passing down the East African coast, the situation in that troubled state has not significantly improved. Further incidents today are only prevented through containment by naval forces. It is a costly process but the international community cannot relax its efforts to bring Somalia and other nations where piracy occurs into the fold. If it is allowed to persist, there is then the added threat of organised crime controlling the activity, along with related illegal acts like people smuggling, wildlife contraventions and trade in narcotics and weapons.[109]

Yet, while maintaining my position, I would be the first to lament the related fact that the loss of valuable fisheries along Somalia's lengthy coastline have forced its population to find alternative sources of income. It is a sad reflection of the state of international cooperation that a binding agreement has yet to be reached in which the whole of the ocean becomes subject to effective controls. The transition to a Blue Economy is dependent on progress in embracing all parts of the ocean, without exception. In pursuit of that goal, controls can be strengthened through the judicious use of new technologies to monitor shipping, even when vessels are far from the eyes of conventional tracking.

But the road ahead is not easy. In an earlier (but still illuminating) article on maritime security, Christian Bueger analyses the complexity of the concept and, because of this, the difficulties in framing solutions.[110] Is maritime security the sole province of respective navies or is there a wider policing role? How can short-term issues of extreme urgency be reconciled with longer-term interests? Are the offenders the result of political interventions or, as is increasingly the case, because of the operations of organised crime? And are there particular parts of the ocean that seem to be especially vulnerable? There are many other questions too raised by Bueger but it is hard to be optimistic about the means of addressing threats to maritime safety and adherence to the rule of law. The fact is that attacks on shipping call for a commensurate response, yet that is the weak link in ocean governance. Pronouncements can continue to be made about rights of free passage but, ultimately, it is what happens at sea and in the ports where illegal transactions are located that really matters. Unfortunately, this reality, which is directly at odds with the aim of a peaceful transition to the Blue Economy, seems no closer to being resolved. Ways must urgently be found for those who believe in the rule of law at sea to gain the upper hand. Of all the issues, this remains a major impediment to progress.

## *Thinking of seafarers*

In response to successive changes in shipping practices in the past, it has been largely left to seafarers to adjust to new circumstances. Since the second half of the twentieth century especially, irresponsible operators have taken advantage of sailing under flags of convenience, enabling them to evade what are seen as onerous maritime regulations in their own countries and to cut costs to an absolute minimum. Seafarers inevitably suffer in the process, potentially working on vessels which are unsafe and in unacceptable conditions. Even in the new millennium, the UN's International Labour Organization could cite instances where crews are paid at very low rates or not paid at all, and sometimes abandoned in distant ports.[111] Poor standards that have prevailed in the past cannot be allowed to continue, not only for the good of seafarers but also to ensure the progressive development of the whole maritime industry. The case is well made in the Lloyd's Register review of ocean safety:

> As we move toward a sustainable ocean economy, we must plan for a just transition of the workforce that leaves no one behind. Efforts to address climate change should create better, safer work rather than job losses or economic disadvantage... [A just transition] therefore necessitates investment, education, infrastructure, innovation, and dignity of work. These must foreground occupational safety and health, actively protect workers and vulnerable groups, offer technology and knowledge transfers between countries, and ensure

*diversity and inclusion across programmes and sectors. From a skills perspective, workers should not be left behind.*[112]

With some 1.6 million seafarers working in the industry, this is hardly a marginal issue. It is, at least, encouraging that the situation is rightly attracting more attention, and some operators are taking their responsibilities seriously. But there are still too many gaps and numerous examples of poor practice. The real challenge is that the industry is rapidly remaking itself, yet the necessary changes to enable the workforce to keep pace are lagging. Gone are the days when the job of a seaman was based heavily on manual tasks – coiling and uncoiling ropes and scrubbing the decks; when the engineer and his team emerged from the engine room streaked with sweat and heavy grease; and when a weather-beaten captain used all his strength to steer his ship through hell and high water. The sea is still the sea, and will always be a place of toil and potential danger, but the way that ships are operated is starting to look very different.

As in other industries, the future will see a greater use of digitalisation, smart technologies, and artificial intelligence, and will require higher levels of scientific understanding. Many of the traditional tasks will be replaced by remote control and the new fuels will demand their own high-level skills if they are to be safely operated. The industry will be more open to a gender balance in the workforce than in the past, with young people seeing it as a career opportunity. In the words of one young woman who has committed herself to a career in shipping, the future will be very different from the past and is in urgent need of rebranding if it is to attract a new generation of seafarers:

> *More and more shipowners and ship managers are migrating their control centers in cloud-based services and platforms, enabling big data analytics, machine learning and artificial intelligence for decision support and operations. Repetitive tasks would be delegated to AI, self-cleaning and self-healing smart materials would mean less maintenance work, automated systems hold the promise of safer ship operations, but cyber security would become an even bigger consideration. Despite having the same job description, the able-bodied seafarer of 2050 would also be able-skilled – digitally native, data-driven and discerning – to handle the changes in technology.*[113]

*For modern seafarers safety and amenable working conditions are a priority*

*Women are playing an increasingly prominent role in operations at sea*

Predictably, some of the richer and socially responsible countries and operators are leading the way in the transformation. The European Union, for instance, issues voluminous guidelines urging consistently higher standards and better training across all of their maritime states.[114] Another indication of this trend could be seen in discussions at the UK Maritime Safety Week in September 2022. Amongst the points at issue were the facts that there is generally a higher rate of accidents at sea than in occupations on land; that fishing boats have the highest *per capita* risk for their crews; that badly-managed seafarers are forced to work long hours, with evidence of stress and resultant mistakes being made when this occurs; and the persistence of specific problems like the inadequacy of rope ladders for harbour pilots boarding ships for the last stage of a voyage (ironically, when safety is the very reason for the operation). Perhaps the most consistent message in such gatherings is the constant emphasis placed on improved training to support mariners to play meaningful roles in the fast-changing industry: 'Our maritime professionals must be given the opportunity to train and learn new skills, so they can be active participants in the future of the maritime industry, an industry they already know, and many will have worked in for their entire lives.'[115]

In a timely report, *A Fair Future for Seafarers*, the authors synthesise the various arguments and highlight the role of innovative business startups as well as major operators to make things happen. As well as the importance of training, the report concludes with three recommendations to improve welfare for seafarers. The first is to establish a global organisation to lobby for better welfare and to support individual seafarers; the second calls for a review of available services for seafarers around the world; and the third points to the greater use of digital services that can be accessed when onboard.[116]

One way and another, serious thought is at last being given to the situation of seafarers, and early initiatives provide hope for changes that will match the rate of transformation of the industry as a whole.

## *Ferryman, ferryman*

Ironically, it is on some of the shortest voyages that a disproportionate number of accidents and fatalities occur, with higher rates in this one sector than those in aviation and on the railways. Belatedly, the subject has attracted the recent interest of researchers concerned with issues of shipping safety.[117] Although a reference to ferries includes those which occur on rivers and lakes (where some of the worst accidents occur), many are also for estuary and short sea crossings, often in countries where there are regular trips between islands.

*Often it is the smaller ferries which are most vulnerable*

In a detailed study of accident statistics over a recent half-century period, 681 fatal ferry accidents were recorded worldwide, resulting in nearly 60,000 deaths.[118] Most of these occurred in tropical regions, in which 80 per cent were in just ten developing countries. What is more:

> *...about 88% of the accidents and 98% of the deaths are directly attributable to human error. This is mainly in the form of unseaworthy vessels, poor lookout, overloading, general negligence*

*and poor seamanship. These factors are exacerbated by evacuation, lifesaving equipment and search and rescue deficiencies. Put simply, the causes are overwhelmingly behavioural and cultural rather than structural or mechanical.*[119]

In spite of these general conclusions, there is also evidence of major ferry accidents at sea where the main causes were technical. Ferry disasters are by no means an exclusive problem for poorer countries. Two legendary cases in Europe were the sinking in 1994 of the MS Estonia in the Baltic (with the loss of 852 lives) and the Express Samina in the Aegean in 2000, in which 81 passengers and crew were drowned. In the first case, alternative findings both pointed to problems surrounding the reliability of the bow door in storm conditions;[120] in the case of the Express Samina, storm conditions were also present, which had a greater effect because of the age of the vessel and an over-reliance on automatic procedures without adequate crew supervision.[121] Invariably, general lessons are taken from such incidents although these are not necessarily adhered to by all ferry operators and, in the absence of compliance, this kind of experience fails to prevent recurring issues elsewhere.

*Fatal ferry accident in the Baltic*

The in-depth study of ferry accidents referred to above concludes with recommended solutions to prevent the historic rate continuing.[122] Basically, there are three things which can be done. One is to reduce the scope for human error through responsible ownership, better management and more rigorous training and safety procedures. The approach makes good sense but in the end it comes down to local implementation, where developed countries are more likely to be in a position to introduce these changes than developing countries. In the latter, investment opportunities are fewer and vessels continue to be used long after they should be. So, too, in the interests of maximizing income for each journey, overcrowding frequently emerges as an issue. A second approach is to replace obsolete designs with new ones where safety is a major consideration. The main weakness in traditional practice is the use of hulls with a single compartment, so that if water enters through the bow doors there is nothing to prevent it filling the whole space and destabilizing the ship. In response to accidents of this kind, the hulls of new vessels are fitted with multiple compartments. Finally, Neil Baird, the author of the study, reserves his strongest criticism for the IMO, the international body which is charged with the duty of spreading good practice and putting pressure on lax operators to mend their ways.

The underlying problem with the IMO, in the view of Baird (a view which is shared by others), is 'a disappointing perception of disengagement and remoteness and an appearance of being much too North Atlantic focused'. It suffers from what he describes as 'a self-serving culture' and seems unable or unwilling to address the inherent failings of ferry operations. Effective actions are few and far between.[123] Other critics, too, believe that the IMO is no longer fit for purpose, although this view is balanced by an understanding that the powers of an international agency are limited by the will of its member states.[124] In other words, the IMO can produce well-intentioned strategies but, in the last resort, if its members are not willing to see them through there is little that can be done. International bodies can speak with a loud voice but they need more than that to enforce their will.

For all of its limitations, Baird suggests (somewhat surprisingly, in view of the general tenor of his conclusions) that a reformed IMO is better than no IMO at all. But he hedges his bets, with the caveat that if it is not receptive to change then it should be replaced by a different kind of body that will not be so restrained by bureaucratic norms and diplomatic protocols. His preference in that case is for a global NGO to promote greater ferry safety.

The new organisation:

> ...*should use 'naming and shaming' techniques similar to those used by Amnesty International, Greenpeace, WWF, Transparency International and Sea Shepherd, for example, to expose the greed and negligence of bad shipowners and corrupt bureaucrats. Market forces should then encourage those shipowners to reform.*[125]

With effective global networks and the universal use of social media, this might well be a way forward for other international agencies too.

# Chapter 4

## Prospects for Pescatarians
### *Ways to ensure that fish stocks remain abundant*

Another central pillar of the ocean economy is to be found in the fisheries that provide the world with an essential supply of food. The connection in our minds between fish and the sea is inseparable, and there is nothing new about this. Traditional coastal communities have always relied on local fishing to supplement or, more often, to serve as a staple part of their diet. People in those locations knew from experience that eating fish was healthy but it was left to modern nutritionists to explain why. It is valued today as a low-fat, high-quality protein, with exceptional properties – including omega-3 fatty acids, and a variety of vitamins (especially D and B2); as well as being rich in calcium, phosphorus, and minerals such as iron, zinc, iodine, magnesium, and potassium.

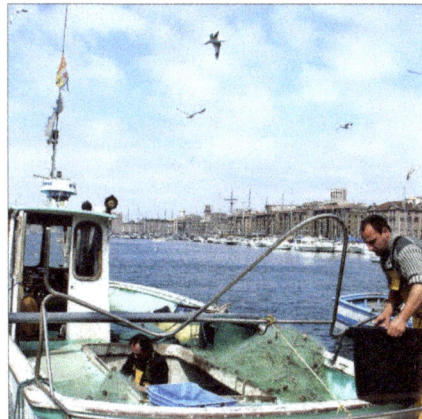

*Artisanal fishing is, by definition, on a human scale*

*Industrial fishing is an altogether different activity'*

*Road-side fish market*

Fish is something of a 'wonder food' but there is one serious drawback: with a growing population worldwide, there is simply not enough in the wild at the present rate of extraction to meet a seemingly inexhaustible demand.[126] This widening gap is at the heart of a key problem for a sustainable Blue Economy, namely, to ensure that natural stocks in the ocean are not further depleted to meet short-term interests. Governments will often take a lax approach to restrictions in order to ensure constant supplies to feed their people, while commercial operators see in high prices in the markets an opportunity to maximise profits. These are practices which cannot be sustained.

A new balance between supply and demand has to be achieved and, for all the political and economic difficulties, the way ahead is, in theory at least, really quite simple. One solution is to manage natural stocks more effectively than is the case now, and a second approach is to increase the output and quality of farmed seawater fish.

## We Can No Longer Be Hunter-Gatherers

We speak of hunter-gatherers as if they belong to a distant past and yet what is fishing now if not a new version of old ways? And far more destructive in the process. It is not, in the original use of the term, a question of individuals seeking their daily sustenance. Instead, modern fleets hunt as a pack, appearing over the horizon like an armada in full sail, the effects of their indiscriminate activities being to extract everything in their wake – not only fish but also vulnerable bycatch, and in the process often destroying the ecology of the seabed. We may still nurse images of brave fisherfolk in sou'westers pitting their wits against mighty waves and strong currents, but industrial fishing is very different. Instead of taking to the sea in isolation, ships in a convoy are in constant radio contact with each other as they close in on unsuspecting shoals. The hunters are guided by sophisticated sonar and other electronic equipment, with skippers monitoring readings on a single control panel. And the statistics show what this kind of activity means for fish stocks: while the world's fishing fleet has more than doubled in size from the middle of the past century, the catch actually fell by 80 per cent in the same period.[127] It lends weight to concerned observers like Ilaria Perissi and Ugo Bardi,[128] who have written about what they call 'the empty sea'. The sad fact, as those two authors assert, is that 'human beings do not know how to manage what makes them live'. [129]

The most voracious consumers of fish come from East and South-East Asia – it is estimated that China's fleet alone accounts for half the world's open-sea operations, its activities extending across all of the major seas including the north and south polar extremes.[130] To add to the global dilemma, the use of subsidies in many countries encourages fishing to continue even where it might be uneconomic. So, too, the situation is worsened by the combined impact of illegal fishing[131] and organised crime,[132]in both cases where no thought is given to longer-term implications. Fish are treated as just another commodity for indiscriminate gain. Even within what one would assume to be the protective boundaries of national EEZs, governance is invariably not as effective as it should be if stocks are to be conserved. It is, in many ways, a bleak situation, exacerbated by the fact that the High Seas, which extend over most of the ocean, still remain largely beyond effective regulation. Repeated attempts to introduce a more stringent legal framework have been rejected by a majority of nations, although a recent breakthrough in relation to biodiversity holds out hope of much-needed change.[133]

As one can see, fishing tells a sorry story of human greed and folly but, as always, I am keen to identify counterpoints of good practice which might offer hope for a more sustainable future. Maintenance of fish stocks is too important a part of the transition to a Blue Economy for this not to happen. We must look for every opportunity to retrieve the situation. The fact is, like so many environmental problems, possible solutions require, above all, political will rather than needlessly complex and ineffective strategies. But nothing is impossible and, in searching for examples of good practice, I explore below five aspects of fishing where negative trends are now being challenged. Thus, I look at marine protected areas and marine spatial planning; at localised conservation projects; at largely administrative attempts to improve EEZ governance; at a growing recognition that subsidies are not in the best interest of fisheries management; and the urgent need to end illegal fishing and banish international criminal involvement.

## *Celebrate the success of creating ocean sanctuaries*

I am a great believer in the value of marine protected areas (MPAs) and, when I was President of my country, seized the opportunity to promote them in our own region and worldwide. As a result, I was greatly heartened to read of some recent findings in the Pacific, in the vicinity of the enormous Hawaiian reserve, Papahānaumokuākea.[134] Almost four times the size of California, it was originally created to protect unique biological and cultural resources. Fishing remains largely banned within the MPA boundaries, enabling it to evolve as a genuine marine sanctuary. What scientists have discovered, however, is that, in addition to its primary purpose of protecting biodiversity in the world's seas, the undisturbed environment has resulted in fish stocks in the surrounding seas returning to previous levels. Thus, in this fringe zone, 'catch rates for yellowfin tuna had increased by 54 per cent, bigeye tuna by 12per cent, and all fish species combined by 8 per cent'.[135] This is good news in itself but I believe it endorses my long-held view that the worldwide recovery of the ocean is dependent on the creation of more marine protected areas.[136]

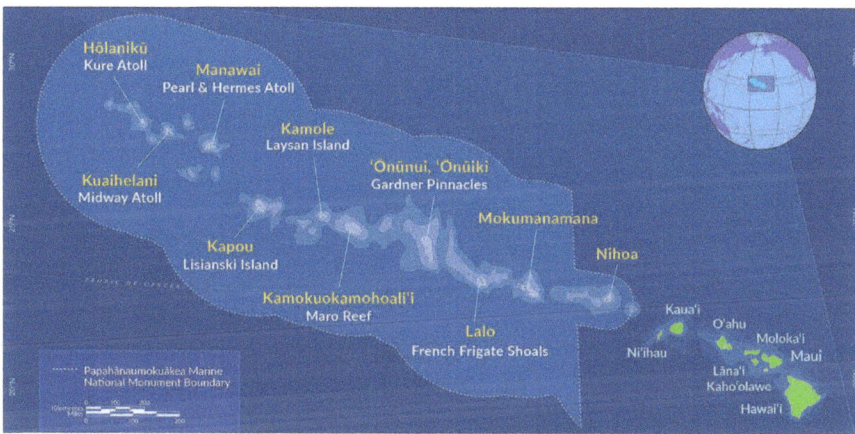

*Ocean sanctuaries put nature first on a scale which provides unparalleled protection*

Papahānaumokuākea is a unique example because of its size but it is encouraging to see how many other reserves are being created in different parts of the world. Indonesia, for example, 'has pledged to secure 10 per cent of the country's territorial waters towards biodiversity protection and sustainable use by the end of this decade, and triple the size by 2045'.[137] Ecuador offers another example, with a protected area to support the unique marine environment surrounding the Galapagos Islands.[138] Fortunately, there are other examples, too, which support the simple strategy of reducing catches for a period if not permanently as a way of allowing stocks to recover. In Seychelles, a local fisheries expert could report on a particular experiment, where:

> ...following a six-month ban on fishing within a particular bay, the size and quantity of fish were recorded to be significantly greater than prior to the closure. This demonstrated clearly how empowering fishermen to take control of their industry could lead to sustainable management of the resource.[139]

Elsewhere, around the North American coastline there is a profusion of protected areas, each with its own priorities. The Florida Keys Marine Sanctuary, for instance, keeps the underlying coral reef healthy and allows fish populations to grow. Another southern reserve is the Reserva de la Biosfera Sian Ka'an, off the Yucatan Peninsula in Mexico, which is designed to preserve mangrove forests along the shoreline, with their rich diversity of fish and bird life. A little further north is the Channel Islands National Park, off the coast of Los Angeles, where the priority is to protect underwater kelp forests, with rare deep-water marine life like cold-water corals. Far to the north-east, off the Canadian coastline, a very different example is the Gully Marine Protected Area with its underwater canyons that offer safe habitats for their own variety of marine life.[140]

Over the past decade, with the guidance of the Nature Conservancy, 34 countries around the world have embraced the idea of sanctuaries, covering a combined area of 7 million square kilometres of previously unprotected ocean.[141] Even though not all of the world's newly protected areas can be matched with sufficient enforcement to wholly achieve their goals, the fact of their designation itself is encouraging. Over time, one can reasonably hope that, where needed, their management will improve. One can hope, too, that their coverage will increase across all EEZs and, with MPAs, achieve the global target of protection for 30 per cent of the ocean by 2030.

Complementing MPAs (with their primary focus on biodiversity), I also have a personal interest in acknowledging the value of marine spatial planning (MSP). This is broadly comparable to land-use planning, offering the opportunity to create designated zones within a country's EEZ. Just ten years ago, Seychelles, for instance, had in place measures to protect 47 per cent of its land area but only 0.04 per cent of its seas. This has since changed dramatically, with 15 per cent of the country's EEZ now planned to be completely free of any form of fishing activity and a further 15 per cent protected to a lesser extent. While it presents the challenge of enforcement, the prospect of making a real difference to fish stocks is a major inducement to its adoption. Implementation of the Marine Spatial Plan for Seychelles is already underway.[142]

*St. Anne Marine Park, Seychelles*

## *Build on the example of good conservation projects*

In addition to designating large stretches of the ocean, there are many projects which focus on specific locations and active conservation objectives. A few examples of these can be found, for instance, in the northern waters of Canada, where the effects of climate change are already evident in melting ice and changing environmental conditions. Traditionally, this has been the home of the indigenous Inuit, where as many as a million people met their essential needs in the inhospitable environs of an Arctic landscape. The challenge for people who live there now is to adapt to what will become quite extreme physical changes.

To assist in the transition, Pew Charity Trusts are making their own contribution, working closely not only with the local population but also Canadian marine scientists and natural resource officials.[143] To take the project forward, three ecologically significant locations have been selected for various actions. Firstly, Lancaster Sound provides the venue for a large national marine conservation area. It is acknowledged as a world-class environment that has an abundant variety of mammals and seabirds, as well as its own cultural and historical legacy. The designation is intended to offer protection in the face of the growing demands of commercial fishing, offshore oil and gas development, and marine shipping. A second initiative is for a fisheries management plan in the Beaufort Sea. A highlight of the plan is to close the waters to commercial fishing until ways are found to regulate it so that the changing Arctic ecosystem is not harmed and also to respect the land rights of indigenous people.

Thirdly, a sustainable fishing plan is being prepared for Baffin Bay. This is designed to 'respect Inuit traditional practices and protect marine mammals, cold-water corals, and sensitive habitats while providing jobs and fishing income over the long term'.[144]

Fortunately, Pew is not alone in supporting ocean conservation with practical projects, another example being the Ocean Foundation. This is a twenty-first-century body which has grown rapidly since its inception. Based in California, it is responsible for projects elsewhere in the US and also in other parts of the world. Indicative of the range of its work in pursuit of a healthy ocean:

> The Ocean Foundation is currently leading a large-scale seagrass and mangrove restoration project at the Jobos Bay National Estuarine Research Reserve in close partnership with the Puerto Rico Department of Natural and Environmental Resources, and Conservación ConCiencia, a Puerto Rico-based nonprofit. In addition, with support from the U.S. State Department, TOF is currently funding a mangrove restoration project in Fiji that focuses on the role mangroves play in mitigating ocean acidification.[145]

The Ocean Foundation is entirely self-funding and for me this itself is a promising sign of public awareness and support for ocean conservation. Even if governments are sometimes slow to act, this kind of populist groundswell provides a strong source of hope.

## *Seek nothing less than good governance*

Overfishing is very largely a result of poor governance and a seeming inability to prevent the flouting of common-sense rules. This is widely acknowledged, as illustrated by the following assertion:

> *Overall, improving governance of the oceans to achieve a more sustainable future – a better future than we can expect under business-as-usual conditions – is both a challenge and a crucial opportunity for the coming decade.*[146]

A challenge and an opportunity. So let us start there: what examples are there of good governance that might offer a more sustainable future? Given the difficulties in bringing change to the High Seas, the obvious starting point is to look, instead, at the extensive areas which come within national jurisdictions. Effectively, this means concentrating for now on the network of EEZs.

There is no shortage of bodies with responsibility for fish stocks in their respective national jurisdictions but the collective record in really making a difference is very patchy. Words alone are never enough on their own to lead to improvements; nor are mere lines on a map, showing where particular rules apply. In response, Pew is working with many organisations to help them improve their management strategies:

> *…by adopting precautionary harvest strategies for the stocks they manage; reforming oversight of longline fishing and trans-shipment practices; implementing robust enforcement and compliance systems to ensure that the rules set for these fisheries are followed; and promoting protection for vulnerable species and critical habitats affected by these fisheries.*[147]

A recurring problem with existing strategies is their tendency to focus on particular fish species rather than taking account of the wider environment. Sometimes this narrow focus can lead to unexpected damage to the latter. Thus, in place of that approach, Pew puts its faith in what is called 'ecosystem-based fisheries management', and there are already promising signs that this new approach is being adopted by different jurisdictions.

> *To date, many decision makers around the world have made political*

*– and, in some cases, legally binding – commitments to adopt EBFM. The United Nations Food and Agriculture Organization and the U.N. Convention on Biological Diversity have strongly encouraged governments and international fisheries management bodies to adopt ecosystem-based management approaches. In the Northeast Atlantic Ocean, the European Union, the United Kingdom and Norway, among others, have included commitments relating to EBFM prominently in their domestic fisheries policies.*[148]

If I look to Seychelles, I can see that this recommended approach of ecosystem-based fisheries management now underpins various initiatives.[149] These include what is known as a harvest strategy policy, focusing on what is taken from the sea and designed to prevent overfishing in particular areas; an internationally-funded project (supported by the Nature Conservancy) to improve stakeholder engagement and to reduce the bycatch of sensitive species in tuna fisheries; and another international project, in this case to increase transparency and participation in fisheries governance for the benefit of a more sustainable management of fisheries resources. A common feature in each of these is that they concentrate on sharing information on fish stocks and seeking stakeholder engagement. These initiatives are certainly laudable in many ways but I do wonder if the basic problem of too many fisherfolk chasing too few fish is being sufficiently addressed. Iceland, for instance, has taken a more direct (some might say, aggressive) approach and, as a result, its fisheries are healthier than they were.

Elsewhere, examples are too often well-intentioned but far from impressive in outcomes, amounting to little more than words (important though these are as part of a concerted response). The South Pacific Regional Fisheries Management Organisation, for example, is an inter-governmental organisation that is committed to the long-term conservation and sustainable use of the fishery resources of the South Pacific Ocean.[150] Its aims are worthy, even more so because it is trying to bring some order into the unregulated space of the High Seas. To extend its influence, it has joined with others in the region such as the Inter-American Tropical Tuna Commission, the Commission for the Conservation of Antarctic Marine Living Resources, and the Permanent Commission of the South Pacific. For all the fine words and formal agreements, however, there is a sense that, until there is an effective legal framework for the High Seas to give support to good intentions, little will be achieved in practical terms to regulate catches in the region.

## *Get rid of wasteful practices like subsidies*

Government subsidies for the fishing industry have an adverse impact on sustainability. Quite simply, they result in more fish being taken from the sea than would otherwise be the case. The figures are stark. According to the United Nations:

> *Fishing subsidies are estimated to be as high as $35 billion worldwide, of which $20 billion directly contributes to overfishing. These subsidies effectively mean that taxpayers are paying industrial boats to degrade the environment and to destroy the food security and livelihoods of vulnerable coastal communities. By fueling unfair competition between large fleets and individual artisanal fishermen, they are also fostering inequality.*[151]

Such is the importance attached to this issue that one of the UN's SDG targets calls for the elimination of subsidies, not by the general date of 2030 but ten years earlier. Unfortunately, the 2020 date was missed; rather like the earlier failure of negotiations to bring the High Seas under the effective rule of law, the target of ending subsidies met with resistance from nations that put their short-term interests before the common good of the ocean. However, negotiations persisted and in June 2022, an historic agreement was reached that offers the prospect of ending the harmful practice. Like any international agreement, the outcome was not to everyone's liking and further discussions will undoubtedly be held to try to seal any gaps. The present agreement, for instance, does not apply to mariculture or inland waters. Overall, though, it was announced by the World Trade Organization as 'a first but significant step forward to curb subsidies for overcapacity and overfishing by ending subsidies for fishing on the unregulated high seas'. [152]

If it can be sustained, removing subsidies is an important step forward, even more so if it can be matched by what is, effectively, the other side of the coin, namely, for nations to apply fishing quotas. The case of Iceland is exemplary.[153] Although dependent for generations on its rich fisheries in the cold waters around its shores, evidence in the 1980s showed that present catch levels could not continue; if they were allowed to do so, scientists predicted a catastrophic decline of remaining fish stocks. As a result, the Icelandic government moved quickly to introduce a system of quotas and, at the same time, to remove existing subsidies. The industry acquiesced as it was already evident that catches were becoming uneconomic.

A feature of the quotas was to allow them to be traded so that holders were guaranteed a secure income. Catching particular species like cod were targeted, and wasteful practices such as throwing smaller fish back into the sea were forbidden. Another conservation measure that captured worldwide attention was the '100% Fish Project', which showed how it is possible to use most if not all of a fish for productive purposes. The outcome of these various measures was dramatic, restoring the health of stocks and achieving sustainability into the future.

Restricting the size of fishing fleets is a related issue. In contrast with fishing fleets in Asia, those in the EU have, in recent years, steadily been decreasing in size. Over a ten-year period from 2008, 'the number of vessels was down by 4 per cent, the overall gross tonnage was down by 17 per cent and engine power was down by 10 per cent'.[154] Regulations are strictly enforced although part of the downsizing is due to the greater efficiency of fishing boats, rather than solely recognition of a need to reduce catches. On balance, though, it is further evidence that unlimited fishing is no longer a sustainable option.

## Drive out illegal fishing and other criminal activities

One of the most vexed issues relating to fishing is the illegal entry of foreign fishing boats into national EEZs, amounting, in their own way, to acts of international piracy. It is not only that these incursions result in the theft of resources but also that, invariably, fish are caught through unsustainable practices. Additionally, the profits to be gained and the low risk of being caught have attracted the interest of organised crime.

The vulnerability of fishing to illegal activities is not difficult to explain. One is the lure of economic incentives, a second the fact of weak enforcement, and a third reason is to be found in barriers to enforcement.[155] Countries with a large ocean space but without an effective naval force and good coastguard coverage, are easy prey for law-breakers. African nations are especially vulnerable, Somalia being a case in point. With a weak, if not non-existent, central government, its 3,000-kilometre coastline and associated EEZ is regularly encroached on by foreign fishing vessels. It has a case in international law to defend its waters but this is not enforced.

For different reasons, Seychelles is another country which finds itself open to abuse of its fishery rights. With its vast ocean space, there is no realistic prospect of effectively policing it. As a result, small fishing boats from Madagascar regularly operate freely around the outer islands of the small island state, while larger vessels from more distant countries also take their catches in Seychelles waters without challenge. As these incursions are invariably selected by individual skippers or companies, the fact that they might come from friendly states like India and Sri Lanka is incidental.

To date, we still await a breakthrough in cutting back on illegal fishing. The UN's Sustainable Goal 14 includes a target of eliminating the practice by 2020 but that date has been and gone. If there is any room for optimism, it must surely lie in the use of new technologies that can easily enough locate and track the destination of illegal vessels:

> New data and technological capabilities are unlocking innovative ways to monitor activities at sea. For example, A1-powered electronic monitoring systems can reinforce observer programs to increase coverage. Satellite-based data analyzed through machine learning can show when a vessel is likely to be transiting, fishing, or even meeting with another vessel. Finally, databases have enabled detailed inspection of vessels' history, including changes in names and their ownership. All these data combined could be used to provide a comprehensive picture of the vessel's identity and activity.[156]

Nearly ten years have passed since the launch of Global Ocean Watch, an international initiative designed to make best use of new technologies to track fishing and other vessels at sea.[157] There was hope at the time that this would mark the beginning of the end for illegal fishing. Indeed, progress in mapping movements has been made during this period but we are still a long way from achieving what is intended. The technology is there but is the political will? Simply asking for restraint is clearly not enough on its own. Perhaps I am being too impatient as, at last, I can see signs that nations might be ready to take effective action. I take heart, in particular, from collective support for what is known as the IUU Fishing Action Alliance Pledge.[158] It is also indicative of stronger commitment that the US Coast Guard has named IUU fishing as the top maritime security threat.[159]

An international commitment is essential. There is a parallel with the situation arising from piracy off the coast of Somalia earlier in the century, when the situation could only be brought under control through concerted action. Foreign powers responded when they saw that their own interests were being affected. The same could be said of illegal fishing but, so it seems, we are not quite there yet. Only through enhanced coastguard capacity and, if necessary, an international naval presence (as there was in the case of piracy), coupled with the use of existing technologies, is there a chance that present practices will be ended. It can be done.

## Why Has It Taken 10,000 Years to Learn What Comes Next?

Humans discovered some ten millennia ago that there were better ways of assuring a regular food supply than by gathering fruits at random and hunting wild animals (which was always a game of chance). Why has it taken so long to accept that there might also be more reliable ways to catch fish than by braving the open seas? The practice of farming on land did not arrive overnight. Necessity, though, is the mother of invention and, albeit belatedly, cultivating fish in water-borne compounds at sea or in seawater tanks on land offers the prospect of a more sustainable future. The idea is seductive but, as we will see, the difficulties in achieving net gains are not inconsiderable.

Aquaculture (although more accurately for fish-farming in saltwater, mariculture) holds the key to constant supplies to feed an increasing number of people. With an annual growth rate of 8 per cent in each of the past ten years, it is one of the world's fastest-growing industries and stands in contrast with the catch decline in wild fisheries.[160] In principle, it is the obvious answer to the challenge of fish supplies, although, of course, as with any new industry there are problems to overcome. These include the effects of pollution and habitat destruction, especially near the shoreline; various forms of disease and parasites in the growing areas; the challenge of sourcing sustainable and cost-effective feedstuffs; the variable impact, through temperature changes in the sea, of climate change; and a tentative approach by some governments, unsure of where to set limits to development. Added to these is the basic issue of ensuring that fish taken from the sea to feed captive species does not exceed the amount produced for human consumption; there has to be a net gain.[161] Much of the literature on the subject focuses on these difficulties, each of which will be the subject of industry-based and academic research, to overcome them. This is a new industry and I believe that most if not all of the problems identified can be overcome. As a result, my own focus is on some of the more successful

developments that are already evident. There is certainly progress in some
areas and this bodes well for the future.

*The architecture of aquaculture*
*(Top) Industrial tanks in Seychelles are replacing traditional forms of fishing on*
*the open sea*
*(Bottom) In contrast, fish cages can be located in open waters, as in this case in a*
*bay in Greece*

## *Innovation is winning the day*

To mark the occasion of World Oceans Day in June 2021, the winners were announced in a competition organised by the European Institute of Innovation and Technology for the most innovative developments in sustainable aquaculture.[162] They are all geared towards business outcomes and each involves teams from more than one country. For instance, SuSeaPro (Sustainable Seafood Processing) aims to scale up a novel processing technology to improve the quality and safety of seafood used in aquaculture. The process is designed to reduce the presence of harmful pathogens like listeria, with the added advantage of minimising food waste; and the team is drawn from the Netherlands, Denmark and Greece.[163] To take another example, Next Tuna has the ambitious aim of becoming 'the first sustainable European source of tuna by reproducing Atlantic bluefin tuna in a land-based, eco-friendly recirculating aquaculture system'.[164] On that particular occasion, seven awards were made and all demonstrated a basic commitment to sustainability and also to animal welfare.

These are by no means isolated examples and the same pattern of business start-ups based on advanced software and sheer ingenuity is evident elsewhere too. Thus, my attention was caught by another competition for aquaculture breakthroughs, this one located in the Gulf of Mexico. In this case, six 'blue tech' start-ups have been selected because of their focus on improving ocean health, increasing coastal resilience and developing new technology, as part of what is called the Gulf Blue Navigator Programme. As the following table shows, the winning companies illustrate an enormous diversity of skills and applications.

| |
|---|
| **Blue Ocean Gear**<br>Intelligent tracking buoys for aquaculture farms, commercial fishing fleets and ocean observers, saving time while gaining operational insights (California). |
| **Marauder Robotics**<br>Remote work platform that collects critical ecosystem data in near real-time and automates underwater tasks done by divers to restore biodiversity (Georgia, US). |

| **SeaTrac Systems** |
| Persistent, multipurpose solar-powered surface vehicles to efficiently, safely and cost-effectively perform real-time data collection and communications for research, commercial and defence applications (Massachusetts). |
| **BeeX** |
| Advanced underwater vehicles with the ability to swarm targets working in tandem with software tools to help reduce the costs and risks of underwater work at scale (Singapore). |
| **Safety Net Technologies** |
| Solutions that enable sustainable practices in the fishing industry for a world where oceans and people thrive together (UK). |
| **SeaTrec** |
| Energy-harvesting systems that generate electricity from naturally occurring temperature differences in ocean waters to power deep-water oceanographic research equipment (such as floats, gliders and autonomous underwater vehicles) for cost-effective deep ocean data collection (California). |

If one looks for a common link between these various start-ups, it has to be the development of advanced software applications, coupled with the energy and imagination of young people. In contrast to those Jeremiahs who say it can't be done, these examples show that it can. And there is also a sharp awareness that unless the various projects are designed to be profitable, they will be unlikely to see the light of day. What is more, the need for them to be sustainable is now a given.

There is, too, another factor and that is university involvement. The best-known Silicon Valley entrepreneurs turned their backs on formal university programmes and yet Stanford University was always in their midst for those who wanted to share in its opportunities; as such, it became a powerhouse in IT development in its own right. And the same is true in the development of aquaculture. The Gulf Blue Navigator Programme, for instance, with its focus on practical applications in the Gulf of Mexico, has been driven by the University of Southern Mississippi. In the competitive world of modern places of learning, USM is making a name for itself as a pioneer in Blue Economy education and research. Undergraduate programmes in ocean engineering and marine science, combined with shoreside research facilities, are opening opportunities for a new generation of graduates to be a part of the burgeoning Blue Economy. The case for this emphasis is compelling:

> *Thirty-five per cent of the workforce in three Gulf Coast counties – Harrison, Jackson and Hancock – is related to the blue economy, with a contribution of $14.9 billion toward Mississippi's Gross Domestic Product. However, the employed workforce is under-educated for technology-related jobs. The blue economy is projected to be one of the fastest-growing segments of the national economy in the coming years. Students in our program are ideally positioned to make significant contributions in this critical area of ocean engineering.*

> *Waves, currents, high pressure, corrosive saltwater, limited visibility and communications are just some of the hurdles one faces when developing technology for the ocean environment. Ocean engineers understand the particular issues and have developed strategies to overcome them.[165]*

This university in America's south has got it just right. Aquaculture (which is only one aspect of its ocean-oriented work) will be dependent on a skilled workforce at all levels, and this will be a continuing need. As well as first degrees and research programmes, the new industry will call for high-level training and opportunities for practitioners to learn from each other. Progressive universities like USM have a vital role to play. Fortunately, there is an increasing number elsewhere too which have the foresight to see what needs to be done. In contrast with the conditions in the Gulf of Mexico, Scotland's St Andrews (founded in the fifteenth century) is also pioneering education for the industry in the present century.[166] To meet the needs of people already in employment, they have introduced a selection of relevant online courses. As part of a wider network, the university is also associated with an aquaculture information hub, The Fish Site, and with a major provider for health products in the industry, the Fish Vet Group.

With a constantly growing demand for fish, aquaculture has to respond with the development of innovative practices. The very language to describe it illustrates how distant it is from traditional fishing; in the words of one advocate, Ioannis Nengas:

> *In the aquaculture industry, imagine an interconnected network of*

*devices, sensors, computers, tanks, grading equipment, fish counters, pumps within a state-of-the-art fish farm communicating with each other, sending and uploading critical data to a central command station, providing the operator a complete view of the entire facility.*[167]

In the same presentation, Nengas went on to propose 'seven digital farming technologies that will impact the present and future of the global aquaculture market, from Europe to Asia-Pacific to the Americas'. These comprise digital feeding – providing information to enable exact amounts of feedstuffs to be delivered; artificial intelligence – so that fish behaviour can be monitored and remedial action taken in the event of disease; computer vision – so that the condition of each fish is known, while human intervention is reduced; smart sensing – giving the operator an immediate picture of the nutrition, health and environment of the species in question; underwater drone data collectors – where operators can check for mortalities in the cage, monitor feeding and inspect underwater cages for damage (and even to repair nets through specialised drones); augmented vision – which provides actual visual information; and virtual reality, where conditions in a particular fish farm are simulated and interventions applied by the viewer.[168]

If nothing else, the above review of innovative technology applications makes the striking point that a new generation of entrants to the industry will require totally different training opportunities, compared with traditional fisherfolk.

## Northern lights

Norway has emerged as a leading exponent of aquaculture. With the latter still regarded around the world as a new industry, the relatively lengthy experience of this northern nation offers numerous lessons in how it can best be developed.[169]

With its cold, clear waters, stretching well into the Arctic Circle, Norway offers what is probably the best example of a planned national network of fish farming. It is not only geography which gives it a leadership role, although that certainly helps. The unique feature of deep-water fjords, sheltered from the open sea, results in a coastline extending over nearly 100,000 kilometres (second only in length to that of Canada). Fishing has always been a mainstay of the economy, and aquaculture itself has been developed over some five decades – longer than in most countries and now yielding a valuable source of experience.

But that is not all. Norway is a rich country, not heavily populated and with a high level of *per capita* income. As well as fishing and tourism, there are valuable reserves of oil and gas beneath the sea, and a natural landscape that provides timber and hydro-electric power. More than that, as in other Scandinavian nations, there is a respected system of governance, in which people in general have trust in their elected representatives. This level of trust has helped over the years to give public support to the transition from wild fisheries alone to a combination with aquaculture – a transition which has challenged the ways of long-established communities and traditional occupations. In fact, aquaculture now accounts for about three-quarters of the total fish catch. None of this is to suggest that the practice of fish farming in Norway is perfect. Practitioners in that country are the first to acknowledge that there are problems (mainly technical) yet to be resolved. But with their half-century of experience and a commitment to developing aquaculture as a modern, sustainable industry, it would be folly for other countries to ignore this experience. There are valuable lessons to be taken.

One obvious fact is the advantage of having the consistent support of successive governments. Even if funds are not to come wholly from the public sector, this can give private investors the confidence to venture into areas where there might still be a high element of risk. New techniques are regularly being developed and cannot rely alone on the slender resources of start-up businesses. A committed government can also give direction to the development of the industry. In a recent interview, the minister at the time pointed to three priorities:

> *First, to address the impact of aquaculture on local ecosystems and wild salmonoid stocks, we are working to further develop the traffic light system, which was established to ensure that the industry may grow within the confines of ecological sustainability. The industry still faces some challenges regarding sea lice, diseases, and fish health, and also the increasing awareness of fish welfare. Second, to address the industry's need for new localities, we are working to establish a framework for licensing aquaculture production at sea. Aquaculture at sea or 'offshore aquaculture' may contribute substantially to future growth. Third, to address the need to reduce the carbon footprint of the industry, we are working along several dimensions, one of which is the development of more sustainable feed from local sources.*[170]

Each of these priorities should resonate with the aspirations and plans of other countries. Thus, the first priority sets growth firmly within the limits of ecological sustainability. It also identifies a number of scientific and other issues which need to be resolved. Secondly, there is a significant difference between locating farms in the sheltered waters of the fjords, as opposed to the open sea. The latter is a new frontier that calls for different techniques and regulations. And, thirdly, the minister draws attention to a need to develop more sustainable feedstuffs, an issue which is widely recognised in the industry elsewhere too. A situation where smaller species are simply transferred from the wild to aquaculture, resulting in the loss of essential food for the former, is to be avoided at all costs.[171]

In spite of being developed over a 50-year period, aquaculture in Norway is still considered a new industry, with numerous challenges outstanding. To date, salmon and trout have accounted for the main catches, with the former, especially, identified as the icon of the country's output. Constant research and tight regulations have ironed out some of the early difficulties, when questions were asked about the impact of water-borne disease and excessive densities of fish in the various cages. A common criticism has also been that farmed salmon consume more than their weight in feedstuffs made from wild fish, but this is countered by evidence to show that the ratio is much lower and more efficient in the farms than in the wild. In addition to salmon, some farms now specialise in smaller species like mussels, while the prospect of adding to the menu a large fish like cod is encouraging.

*Salmon farming in Norway's fjords is a carefully controlled activity*

Aquaculture attracted a bad name for itself in the pioneering days because of overcrowding in the cages, an excessive use of antibiotics yet also a failure to control the spread of diseases, and polluted waters. As the Norwegian example shows, a sensible and fair system of controls is essential if problems like these are to be overcome and good reputations earnt. In the end, it is the consumers of aquaculture products who need to be convinced. Perhaps this is the most important lesson of all for the development of the industry in other countries. If only for commercial reasons, high standards at every stage in the process are absolutely essential.

Currently, an issue in Norway that is especially topical and relevant to other nations is to extend the practice of fish farming from sheltered waters to the open sea, where conditions are altogether different. There are obvious advantages in doing this, not least of all to extend the space available for new farms but also to reduce the risks of disease and contamination from land-based pollution. In turn, there are natural challenges to face, such as adverse weather conditions and potential difficulties of access, not to mention the higher costs involved. But a start has been made and there is obviously a commitment to find ways to minimise the obstacles.

> *Ocean Farm 1 is one of the world's first offshore fish farms. A full-scale pilot facility, it is located some 5km off the coast of Central Norway, at the same latitude as Alaska. It is the largest such structure in the world, measuring over 100m across and extending more than 40m below the ocean surface. The facility can hold approximately 1.5 million Atlantic salmon in total. The pioneering fish farm also features cameras, oxygen sensors and other digital equipment. By collecting as much data as possible about the farmed fish, operators can optimise feeding, interaction and environmental conditions. The creators have described the facility as the 'world's largest floating laboratory'.*[172]

Nothing illustrates better the innovative nature of modern aquaculture, requiring constant research and development, smart technology and a well-trained workforce, than this new venture into the open sea. It offers an important model of how other countries, too, might achieve a successful transition to the Blue Economy. The example of Norway is being watched with interest.

# Chapter 5

# Lemming-Like Urges
*Managing the irrepressible growth of maritime tourism*

Not entirely unlike the migratory urges of the unfortunate lemming (allegedly unable to change course, even if it leads to its own demise), humans have themselves been drawn *en masse* to the sea. Although the migration of the latter is inherently more benign in intent, there is still a very real danger of falling over the cliff. The lure of the ocean and its environs is powerful, yet resultant tourism is fraught with its own potential for self-destruction. People come to enjoy nature at its best but, in doing so, they endanger the very purpose of their visit. They find themselves in a fragile relationship; like dancing with the devil, one false step and all can be lost:

> *The natural resources that draw tourists to coastal and marine zones underpin the economies of most Small Island Developing States and coastal destinations and provide myriad contributions to economic growth and human wellbeing. Yet, the health and beauty of these ecosystems – the very thing that draws people to coastal and marine destinations – continues to be threatened by tourism itself.*[173]

Such is the dilemma which confronts maritime tourism; although it is one of the pillars of the Blue Economy, it is presently unsustainable. So, what can be done to turn things round? Looking for answers, I start with an encouraging selection of initiatives designed to do just that. It might seem at first an eclectic mix but one thing they have in common is to put sustainability at the heart of a new model. This marks an important step forward, not least of all in alerting tourists themselves to the precarious situation that has been created. But, in my view, it will not be enough. That is why I then suggest that what is missing is substantial funding to achieve sustainability on three fronts: for the maintenance of the natural environment, to ensure that the host communities receive a fair share of the economic benefits, and to create good working conditions and a safe experience for providers and users alike.

Too often in any policy-making, money is glibly proposed as a panacea but in this case my belief is that it really can make a difference. The reason for my optimism is that tourism itself has the spending power to pay for what visitors come to enjoy. There is no such thing as a free lunch. The cost of a vacation is about more than the cost of flights and accommodation. Sustainability comes at a price. Paying for the whole tourism experience, and not just part of it, is the missing link and later in this chapter I show how the deficit can be redressed.

## What Is It About the Sea?

For most of history, the sea was a place to avoid, an unknown world that was feared and left to sailors and fisherfolk to make what they could of it. Yet now it is the number one tourist venue. How was the traditional balance reversed?

*Beaches like this one on La Digue, Seychelles, are ever more difficult to find*

Aristocrats and their entourages in Europe set the pace from the eighteenth century when they established the fashion of salt-water bathing. At the other end of the social scale, industrialisation and the spread of urban living led to 'the masses' (initially in Europe and the east coast of the US) making their own trips on crowded trains to the new resorts. Later, the private car added to the choice of destination, dispersing activity over a much wider area. In turn, air travel from the middle of the twentieth century created a wholly different experience, with no part of the world any longer beyond reach of the intrepid tourist. Not just any part of the world but, in particular, the ocean. Is there a single image that matches more closely a popular idyll of the ultimate vacation than a tropical island fringed with white, sandy beaches surrounded by a turquoise sea?

Numbers have increased, year on year, and even the negative effects of COVID in 2019 seem unlikely to have been more than a blip in the general trend. Given the dependence of different economies on its continuing contribution, there is nothing to suggest that this growth pattern will change. Coastal and offshore tourism is here to stay and must be addressed as an inseparable element of the Blue Economy. The reasons for its inexorable growth are hardly surprising, a product of greater disposal incomes combined with the opportunities afforded by modern means of transport. Yet in some ways tourism is the most difficult Blue Economy challenge of all, seemingly at odds with the essential principle of sustainability. Unlike, say, shipping, where new technologies are already reducing its harmful impact on the ocean environment, or fishing, where a rational and enforceable system of controlled catches could allow stocks to replenish, tourism poses a different order of problems. The sheer numbers of people who make their way to the sea puts immense, if not unsustainable, pressure on the whole maritime environment. Imagine a solitary bay, where for years fish and sea mammals have been left undisturbed and coral reefs allowed to evolve in their own way. And then a modern hotel is built and every day of the year, hundreds if not thousands of sun-seekers trample across the dunes and dive into the hitherto placid waters. Everything changes.

This is not the place for an exercise in statistics but suffice to say that on the eve of the pandemic the total number of tourists across the world reached 1.5 billion.[174] This is close to one in five of the total world population, an enormous number in itself but also portending a much higher proportion in the future; not only a higher proportion, but also greater numbers overall because of more people on the planet. The provenance of tourists will also change, with many coming from countries that are presently only venues. Of course, not all tourists make their way to the sea. Many seek different destinations, visiting cities and antiquities, going on safaris and engaging in alpine pursuits; but even if half of the total were maritime visitors, the impact would still be immense.[175] Transportation and accommodation alone are enormous consumers of resources, not to mention essential infrastructure, water and food supplies, and numerous services. It matters, too, that often the most favoured locations for coastal tourism are also ecologically the most vulnerable, enjoyed for the very fact of their unique features yet unable to withstand incessant use.

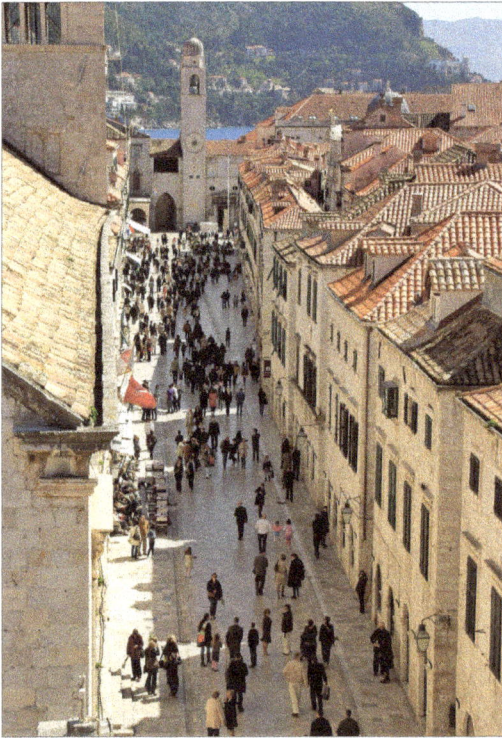

*The Mediterranean draws an unceasing number of visitors to its unique features*

But the whole purpose of this book is to acknowledge where progress is being made. Sustainability is an elusive concept when it comes to tourism but, in spite of the difficulties, there are many interesting and workable projects which give hope that further solutions will be found. It is not so much that there will be a panacea, a magic wand which can make all of the problems disappear. There is an old adage that the excellent drives out the good and, although excellence must be the ultimate goal, the attainment of the good is a very worthwhile interim target. And, fortunately, there is no shortage of examples to report. It is some of these that I will now highlight, showing how they address different challenges, and can be found in contrasting parts of the world.

## How to Keep the Numbers but Reduce Environmental Impact

In spite of being popularly portrayed to the contrary, the eleventh-century Danish king, Cnut, was a wise man, who demonstrated when he stood on a beach and faced the oncoming tide that even a monarch was unable to change the course of nature. Following his example, it is not so much a question of trying to forestall the tide of tourist numbers as finding ways to reduce their impact on the environment. This is no easy task and will often best be done by enthusiastic and inventive NGOs which can exploit niche opportunities for users and local communities alike.

One creative example is the work of an NGO called Green Fins, which has as its aim the protection of coral reefs through sustainable marine tourism. It acknowledges that activities like snorkelling and scuba diving are popular ways to explore the unique environment of coral reefs, but it also knows that, if not carefully managed, these pursuits can do untold harm. The answer, claims Green Fins, is to set standards for marine tourism companies as well as individuals, to ensure that visits to coral reefs are sustainable. It 'encourages and empowers divers, snorkellers, the diving industry and coastal communities to reduce the pressures on coral reefs by demonstrating to marine tourism companies a range of practical, low-cost alternatives to harmful practices – such as anchoring, fish feeding and chemical pollution – as well as providing strategic training, support and resources'.[176] Pioneer projects have been started in various countries, including Costa Rica and the Dominican Republic. Coral reefs need all the help they can get, not only because of visitor numbers but also because of the vulnerability of reefs to temperature changes.

In other cases, governments and international bodies can play the lead role. Another natural feature under pressure is that of coastal wetlands. Too many of these areas, rich in biodiversity, have been wantonly drained, leaving those that remain even more in need of support. That is why I was especially interested in a scheme for the Nariva Swamp Protected Area, an expanse of wetlands of international significance on the south-east coast of Trinidad.[177] It is a transformative project that aims not only to sustain the wetlands but also to bring benefits to surrounding communities. Such projects require investment, in this case from the Inter-American Development Bank Innovation Laboratory and the UN's World Tourism Organization. The intervention of these bodies was part of a wider initiative to support the post-pandemic recovery of tourism through innovative and sustainable approaches. 'Experience Nariva', as it is popularly known, is a good example of how, through thoughtful management, tourism and long-term prosperity for local communities (the natural guardians of fragile resources) can go hand in hand.

When it comes to reducing impact there is probably no single region that has been under greater pressure for decades than the Mediterranean. Traditionally, this is where Europeans flock for their seasonal quota of sun, sea and sand, and, given this relentless pressure, it is remarkable that it has been able to retain something of its original appeal. That is why a recent study which advocates an ecosystem approach to sustainable management deserves to be read.[178] Although much of this publication is devoted to problems that still need to be resolved, my eye was caught by some localised examples of good practice.

For instance, measures have been introduced around the Balearic Islands (in the western half of the sea) to protect invaluable seagrass meadows (so effective in carbon capture). Access and anchorage within designated areas is now restricted. Another example, this one off the coast of Catalonia (also in the western half of the Mediterranean), seeks to limit the number of divers at any one time within protected areas. More widely in its application, the Blue Flag programme urges marina and boat operators, in particular, to achieve high standards of water quality, environmental management, education and safety. Although these examples are, in some respects, encouraging, they also reveal that it so much harder to make radical improvements once inappropriate buildings and infrastructure are in place, as is the case around most of the Mediterranean. Far better, where possible, to apply sustainability principles at an earlier stage of development.

Elsewhere in the world, in popular tourist areas, initiatives follow what is now becoming a well-trodden path. Cox's Bazaar, in the northern reaches of the Bay of Bengal, is the subject of a study which urges the inclusion of all stakeholders in any changes. Measures include a management plan for the area, investment in essential infrastructure, marketing directed at locally-made products, and a levy to assist the protection of specific features.[179] While studies like these are, in principle, welcome, they remain one step removed from direct action; plans are fine but who knows what becomes of them? My heart is with an organisation like Green Fins or a project such as 'Experience Nariva', where one can see from the outset tangible improvements. That surely is where the emphasis should now be put.

# How to Make Offshore Tourism More Sustainable

Most tourists who come to the sea are shore-based, finding accommodation in hotels and guesthouses. But there is also an important element which is based offshore, with vacations spent aboard cruise ships and on privately owned or chartered yachts. A new generation of cruise ships is planned and the order books for yachts are full. Taking to the sea is, in itself, an understandable pursuit, offering a unique opportunity to get away from the crowds and to experience the ocean environment firsthand. Like so many human activities, however, it becomes a question of numbers and social responsibility.

## *Sustainable cruise ships?*

At first glance, one wonders if the idea of sustainable cruise ships – which can be likened to floating resorts – is an oxymoron. On the eve of the pandemic, 30 million cruise passengers shared this experience. The largest ships could accommodate as many as 6,000 passengers on multiple decks (above and below the water line) and the average occupancy was around 3,000. Visiting different ports is included in their itineraries, the massive ships when they dock often dwarfing their surroundings. Clearly, the potential impact on the ocean and along the coasts must be taken into account in any assessment of sustainability in the Blue Economy.

Perhaps it is not surprising that some of the most meaningful attempts to be sustainable have been pioneered by smaller companies, where the problems are more manageable. It is a relatively small Norwegian company that is acknowledged as a leader in this field. Hurtigruten, originally just a ferry service, now specialises as well in expedition cruises in remote far northern and southern latitudes, usually carrying no more than 500 passengers. Through the introduction of battery hybrid systems, they have been able to cut fuel consumption by 20 per cent and further changes have largely eliminated noxious emissions. In 2021, their cruise ships were recognised as the safest and most sustainable in the world. To add to their reputation, they also fund a foundation, with the three main objectives of preserving endangered wildlife, tackling plastic waste and marine litter, and supporting local and global projects in the areas where they operate.[180]

On a much larger scale, recognising their impact and a growing concern amongst their passengers that they need to be more responsive to the environment, some of the leading operators have also started to introduce appropriate measures. In fact, Royal Caribbean, the fourth-largest cruise ship company, has been doing this for some years. Currently, it concentrates on five areas of activity where greater sustainability is the goal. *Icon of the Seas*, the newest ship in the fleet, will be powered by liquefied natural gas, widely considered to be the cleanest-burning fossil fuel available, emitting virtually zero sulphur dioxide and particulates. A second area of management, through its own on-board desalination facilities and reverse osmosis, is to generate 90 per cent of its freshwater needs. Waste disposal is also a major issue and, in an attempt not to add to the ocean's volume of plastics, single-use plastics have been largely replaced. Where possible, food served onboard is from sustainable sources, with 90 per cent of wild-caught seafood and 75 per cent of farmed seafood meeting internationally accredited standards. Finally, shore excursions are also designed to respect local requirements and benefit coastal communities. [181]

*Balancing large numbers of passengers on cruise ships with the goal of sustainability presents a considerable challenge. The Icon of the Seas is a recent attempt to achieve this*

A different way to bring about more sustainable practices is for the authorities in heavily-visited areas to impose their own restrictions on cruise-ship traffic.[182] Thus, in the Norwegian fiords, access is restricted to ships using low-sulphur fuels, with the aim of achieving fully emission-free cruises in these waters by 2026. Off the coasts of the Galapagos islands, restrictions are even greater, with a limit of no more than 100 passengers per ship and designated routes to follow.

## 'I am sailing, I am sailing'

The image of yachts is seductive and generally benign – one may still think innocently of impressionist paintings of white sails against the background of a vivid blue sea – but the potentially harmful impact of their modern use on the marine environment cannot be overstated. As with so many tourist activities, sheer numbers create problems of their own. Most yachts have engines as well as sails, and fuel consumption and unwanted emissions represent a possible threat to ecosystems. So, too, does irresponsible waste disposal, sailing into vulnerable locations, and the damage caused by anchoring.

*Claude Monet, 1882 - Cliffs and Sailing Boats at Pourville*

*Sailing can mean different things to different users*

In spite of the high costs of sailing, it is one of the fastest-growing tourist pursuits. Although susceptible to downturns in the world economy (as it was during the global financial crisis and, later, during the pandemic), it seems to be sufficiently resilient to bounce back quickly. One recent estimate suggests that the 2021 value of the global yacht market, amounting then to $10.8 billion, will increase by some 50 per cent to $15.15 billion by 2026.[183] Most of this will be accounted for by middle-range vessels but, even with the problems surrounding Russian oligarchs and the berthing of some of their exotic craft, as a result of the appearance of new billionaires, the demand for super yachts seems set to rise further. In line with a growing demand, yacht designs at all levels of the market are becoming more environmentally conscious. Take, for instance, the following advertisement for a new-generation yacht:

*Zero 34 is made with entirely sustainable and recyclable materials,*

*both for the hull and for the furniture and interiors. Available with
normal or hybrid engine for environment protection and energy
saving... A diesel electric hybrid propulsion system can provide fuel
savings, lower maintenance costs, higher than average engine load
and lower air and water pollutions.*[184]

The example of the Zero 34 is repeated with variations by other companies
which also promote innovative design and new materials as the best way to
achieve sustainability. One producer explains that it is time to replace fibre
glass, the perennial favourite of the industry, with a new composite which
has many advantages, not least of all (unlike fibre glass) because it can
be recycled.[185] Across the industry, in a sector where, because price is not
always the critical factor, there is room for building in the costs of research
and development for what is still a limited customer base. Thus, the Aquon
One is a state-of-the-art, hydrogen-powered catamaran developed by Swiss
engineers. It is a remarkable example of circular technology, starting with
the use of solar power which is converted by photovoltaic panels into
electricity to drive the motors and other equipment on board. The latter
includes the desalination of seawater into green hydrogen which can later
be converted back to electricity.[186]

Hydrogen-powered craft in large numbers are still largely for the future
but, closer to the present, hybrid engines offer enormous advantages in
terms of efficiency as well as cost. The plans of various shipyards are already
well advanced:

*Feadship wants to only use hybrid energy or to be electric before
2025, while Oceanco wants to use only 100% renewable energy
and produce zero waste by 2030. The NEEL-TRIMARANS teams
also committed from 2018 to develop a more eco-friendly type of
boating.*[187]

At the same time as mechanical improvements, attention is also focused on
more efficient designs which will lower friction between the hull, air and
water, the aim being to reduce fuel consumption. The weight of a yacht
is important as well, which has led to the use of lighter but still robust
materials in place of traditional ones like steel.

If all of this is at the top end of sailing the seas, seemingly of little relevance
to the rest of this branch of tourism, that's not how it works. Those advances

which first appear at this level will in time become the norm. That is why I welcome reports like that of the exclusive Monaco Yacht Show, featuring developments in sustainability. At the 2022 exhibition, the Sustainability Hub was described as 'an incubator for companies that provide innovative or tried-and-true eco-friendly solutions, as well as for budding start-ups working on sustainable alternatives that fit in seamlessly with the yachting world'.[188] This is only the beginning and I am confident that today's innovations will be tomorrow's world.

And, apart from private yachting, when it comes to chartering there is also room for optimism. By no means all operators are sustainability-minded but there are, fortunately, many examples of good practice as well as regulations to limit negative impacts. In fact, some operators now make a virtue of their ecological credentials, appealing to a like-minded clientele. On balance, though, with other operators still on the same wavelength as hunters with an Ernest Hemingway macho-approach to the ocean and its species, there remains a great deal more to be done.

## How to Enlist the Support of Tourists Themselves

Tourists cannot be dismissed *en masse* as unwitting enemies of the environment. The fact is that, increasingly, there is an appreciation amongst the tourists themselves that the unique ecosystems they have come to visit will be degraded if limits are not put on their heavy use. That is why visitors may well choose to be actively engaged in local conservation efforts and even to support these after they have returned to their home countries. Of course, there is a fine balance between their privileged position as paying guests and a willingness to participate in, say, the manual routine of beach-cleaning sessions. Increasingly, though, there are always some visitors who are keen to play their part.

At one extreme, the most obvious source of synergy will occur when tourism is explicitly on the side of nature. This is often referred to as ecotourism, and it embraces two dimensions. One is that visitors will be helped to view and understand particular species of wildlife or natural features, and the other is that the whole experience is designed to avoid damage to the environment they have come to enjoy. There is now a wide range of specialist operators to make all of this possible and ecotourism can be seen as a growing aspect of coastal and marine activities more generally. As an illustration of what this means in practice, one can turn to the example of a catamaran named *Mala*, skippered by a couple of 'eco-warriors', and carrying its guests around the islands off the coast of Croatia. In a published interview they highlight some of the main features which, as more specialists offer this kind of facility, are becoming a welcome norm:

> We like to point out that this is a self-sufficient boat. With solar panels for charging batteries and a water-maker, we have no need to go to ports and marinas, unless the guests particularly want to… Instead of using plastic water bottles (on average a charter for six would use 200 bottles in a week), guests are presented with an attractively-designed glass container at the start of each trip… We do not consume plastic at all and we always recycle glass, paper and other materials. Guests are also given canvas bags with the Catamaran Mala logo for shopping trips… There are plans to provide only natural toiletries, and also to use eco-friendly cleaning materials… At least once a week guests are invited to join in collecting garbage from beaches and coves on the itinerary, an activity which is strongly supported.[189]

To take another example, in the Pacific, across the myriad islands in that vast ocean there is a high degree of economic dependence on this kind of activity. The potential monetary value of marine-based ecotourism activities which focus on wildlife watching has been quantified. For example, shark-diving in Fiji has been estimated to generate $42 million each year, while a humpback whale returning each winter to Tonga may be worth more than $1 million during its lifetime.[190] Figures such as these themselves provide strong evidence that conservation has an economic value beyond its ability to protect a unique environment.

NGOs are often the most effective vehicle to take tourists across the line between traditional visits and a more participative model. Looking to my own domain, Nature Seychelles is an exemplar of innovative conservation with a number of unique schemes and partnerships across the world.[191] It has been active since 1998 and is the largest and oldest environmental NGO in the archipelago. In different ways, the traditional distinction between tourism and active conservation has intentionally been erased. A centre point of its many activities is the responsibility it has been given to manage Cousin Island, a small landform within the inner reaches of the archipelago. Used for years as a coconut plantation, the ground had been cleared and endemic wildlife had virtually disappeared. Nature Seychelles has turned this round and now attracts some 10,000 paying visitors a year, as well as being a venue for education courses. The entry fee goes some way to meeting the costs of conservation. In addition to species regeneration, through a carefully-managed scheme of transfers, and in spite of the large number of visitors, the island nature reserve is now carbon neutral. Nature Seychelles is registered as an education provider in Seychelles and offers a variety of training courses in subjects like mangrove rehabilitation, coral-reef monitoring and reef-revival techniques. Opportunities exist to learn about climate change mitigation schemes.

This single organisation shows just how much can be done to marry the interests of tourists and conservationists. For a different group of tourists, it is now quite common for high-end hotels to demonstrate their commitment to local conservation schemes and, where possible, to encourage their guests to participate. It is proving to be a helpful addition to local conservation efforts, fuelled by genuine interest in what can be done, tinged perhaps by an element of guilt at the realisation of the pressures which tourism places on the environment. In an interesting article on how some of the leading resorts have introduced green initiatives, Lavanya Sunkara covers a wide geographical and thematic spread to make the point.[192] She writes about guests on Nicaragua's Pacific coast who become enthralled at the sight of turtles breaking out of their eggs and then wanting to learn more about the future of these beautiful creatures. In contrast, for all of its reputation as a tropical idyll, Sunkara reveals bad practices in the Maldives when it comes to waste disposal. Exceptionally, one resort has shown the way by developing its own techniques so that 90 per cent of its solid waste is recycled. Meanwhile, on the Canadian Pacific coast, guests at a wilderness resort agree not to fish for salmon or expect it on the menu, in favour of helping to ensure sufficient supplies for the whales in the region which rely on this source of food. In other countries, too, one can find a growing number of examples of projects where tourists can participate in reef regeneration and turtle rehabilitation, as well as weaning users off harmful sunscreen products. Finally, anything to do with Seychelles always catches my eye, which is why I was pleased to read about the following:

> *Hilton Seychelles Northolme Resort & Spa, a boutique resort on the verdant Mahé Island, opened a coral nursery at the nearby Beau Vallon Bay to help protect and preserve the marine life along the*

*island's Northwest coast. Guests can snorkel along a coral trail and visit the nursery with a marine conservation specialist. There's also an opportunity to adopt coral, especially the fast-growing Acropora and Pocillopora, which have been adversely affected by rising sea temperatures.*[193]

Money counts, and finding ways like this to attract long-term funding is a valuable initiative.

*Hotels know that marine conservation projects support their own interests. Coral restoration at Berjaya Tioman Resort, Malaysia*

## How to Make Tourism Safer

Increasing tourist numbers leads, in turn, to a higher rate of accidents, some fatal. Of course, it is the most dramatic events which capture the headlines. In April 2022, it was reported that a Japanese tourist boat with 26 passengers had sunk in freezing waters off the northern coast of the archipelago.[194] Japan (following the pandemic) had not yet fully opened its borders to international visitors, so it was recorded as a domestic tragedy. In contrast, while I was reviewing this information, I read a few months later of another fatal accident, this time involving an international a group of tourists, in foggy conditions high in the Andes.[195] Four tourists were killed and 16 injured after visiting Peru's world-famous Machu Picchu site, when the minibus they were travelling in crashed into a ravine.

These two incidents could not, in one sense, have been more different – one at sea and one on land – and yet a connecting factor was to demonstrate how much trust tourists put in local operators. In one sense, of course, this is the right thing to do as these are the people who know their surroundings and whose communities are dependent on tourism for the income it brings. But in both cases, questions were asked about the competence of the operators and their decisions to embark on journeys in adverse conditions. There followed calls for tighter regulations to guarantee competence and safeguard the interests of passengers. All very well, but this has become a standard response, leaving unanswered the question of why such measures are not already in place?

The fact is that safety remains an often-neglected aspect of tourism, although it is inherently an essential dimension of sustainability. Seeking to discover the ocean is to be encouraged but there needs to be just as much effort and expense put into ensuring that it is a safe experience. In this respect, the tourist authorities and operators have an obvious responsibility but, in reducing the number and gravity of accidents, so, too, do tourists themselves. Insurance companies are well aware of the damage that high-profile accidents inflict on the industry as well as individuals, but they are also in the best position to know that these are not typical of the claims they have to deal with. It is not the dramatic cases which are commonplace but the mundane, some of which are avoidable and others less so. Road accidents rank high in the scale of accidents but so, too, do less obvious incidents like tripping on an uneven pavement, staying in the sun too long and suffering heatstroke, or contracting food poisoning from unhygienic kitchens. These are everyday events but engaging in a sea sport in which one is not fully accomplished can also lead to a serious accident. Even if one is a strong swimmer, being unaware of local currents is an all-to-common cause of drowning – more, say, than the headline-making threat of sharks.[196] There is also the human factor of some tourist venues being dangerous because of the risk of mugging or personal attacks.

Against this background, the issue of tourist safety can be enhanced and there are many common-sense ways in which this can be done. Just to mention a few:

✧ tourists should be confident that local operators for all water transport and sports can show a seal of approval for competence and safety considerations. Ideally, this can develop into something like an international code, rather like instantly-recognisable colours in traffic lights;

✧ local authorities should guarantee that there are no emissions of untreated sewage to contaminate bathing areas;

✧ accommodation at all levels should meet agreed standards, designed to ensure safety as well as comfort;

✧ use of the environment that tourists come to visit should be sustainable and this will be included in all marketing materials;

✧ where there are particular crime hazards, tourists should be made aware of where to avoid and specially designated tourist police should be in evidence on the streets.

There are many other initiatives that can be taken, some of which one can already see. But, while it is important to get the message across, it is also important not to arouse an unnecessary sense of fear amongst visitors, nor to change the character of a natural setting by installing unsightly notices. The simpler the demarcation the better – like the habitual red flag fluttering above beaches where it is dangerous to swim. Authorities and operators can together help to provide a safe framework for the enjoyment of tourists but, ultimately, the users themselves must take responsibility for their actions. Educating all parties in the importance of safety and showing examples of good practice is, I believe, an area where more work needs to be done if people are to continue to discover and enjoy the ocean.

## Towards Transformative Tourism

I remarked at the start of this chapter that tourism presents one of the most difficult challenges in transitioning to a sustainable Blue Economy. In the preceding sections I have highlighted some interesting and encouraging initiatives but I maintain my earlier concern that we still have a long way to go.

An inescapable fact is that the number of tourists continues to grow, adding to the pressures on an already-overworked environment. Each day, more visitors trample on vegetation which plays its part in coastal defences, collect seashells from the beaches as souvenirs, and disturb the fragile ecosystems of coral reefs. In most cases, there is no intent to damage what they have come to enjoy, but that is the inevitable outcome. And there is no sign of this constant pressure easing in the years to come. Faced with this kind of scenario, what is a sensible response? Simply to allow things to roll forward, with tourist venues left much as they are now, but with more users, is not an option; the natural environment will continue to suffer and the quality of the tourist experience will be degraded. Of course, as a result of good management there will be notable exceptions, but the general trend will be adverse. If a better balance between demand and supply is to be found, a radically different approach to tourism is imperative.

In searching for solutions, my mind turned to the exceptional case of Aldabra, within the remote waters of Seychelles. This internationally acknowledged jewel of the ocean deserves all the superlatives that are attached to it, an awe-inspiring environment where rare species flourish largely unmolested. It narrowly escaped development for military purposes in the 1960s but since then it has rightly been cherished. But at a cost. In order to maintain its outstanding qualities, access is strictly regulated and very few visitors are fortunate enough to see it firsthand. Effectively, this means that there is a willingness (or at least an understanding) for most of us to pay a price just to know it is there. Of course, this kind of blanket policy could hardly be applied everywhere but the principle is what matters. It suggests that unrestricted tourism will become a thing of the past. In an extreme case like Aldabra, only a very small number can visit the island but, in other cases, numbers can be more flexibly matched.

A less dramatic example of tinkering with supply and demand can be taken from the Italian coastline, where it has for long been the practice to charge for access to the best beaches. In return, visitors can expect general maintenance and a range of facilities. Investment is essential and, with market forces at work, those beaches that are considered the best ones will attract more visitors. Increasingly, environmental factors are seen as important indicators of what is good, so that providers are keen to demonstrate sustainable practices. According to a recent study, Legambiente, which is one of the most influential Italian environmental NGOs, has devised a certificate for beach clubs. Those which implement a list of specific green practices are awarded with the Legambiente Turismo Ecolabel. At the time of writing, nearly 20 beach clubs were recipients of this award. The important lesson from this is that it seems that visitors are positively influenced by this mark of good practice. It is also worth noting that the work of NGOs in this field can play an important part in raising standards.[197]

I know that the idea of restricting access to tourist venues – whether through the price mechanism or government policy – might seem to run counter to the principle of inclusiveness. It is hard to see how this can be totally avoided, although ways can be found to reduce any unfairness: for example, by granting privileged access for local communities or by transferring a proportion of fees to allow, for example, for schoolchildren to enjoy their beaches as they have always done.

There will always be reasons given to forestall change but in this case, if tourism is not to be a force for environmental degradation, these arguments must be overcome. To create a sustainable future for maritime tourism, the secret will be to capture a proportion of the immense fund of resources it generates and to use this as a force for good. Instead of dwelling on its unsustainability, ways must be found to make tourism transformative. Increasingly, advocates for a healthy ocean are putting emphasis on a positive approach. For instance:

> *...the potential for tourism as a powerful and transformative force for sustainable development is significant. In 2019, the tourism sector was the third largest for exports, one of the fastest growing, the largest service employer and one of the most critical drivers of economic growth through job and enterprise creation, export revenues and infrastructure development... There is no healthy ocean without sustainable coastal and marine tourism at a scale to meet consumer demand. Well-managed tourism can support conservation while contributing to sustainable development and providing income opportunities and a higher quality of life for coastal communities.*[198]

To switch from an exploitative to a transformative approach can be likened to an ocean tanker changing direction; it has to be a measured operation and requires a mix of patience and ingenuity to take account of countervailing currents and winds. Caroline Tippett, the author of a thoughtful report under the auspices of the international NGO, WWF, proposes a threefold strategy to achieve the kind of change that is needed.[199] The first shift of gear is to integrate more closely new and existing developments with the interests of local communities as well as the interests of nature. This includes embedding sustainability and resilience principles within the life cycle of all infrastructure; in order for it to work it has to be a long-term project and not mere window-dressing at the time of its inception. A second shift should move from outdated concepts of mass tourism to what the author calls 'sustainable, restorative tourism'. She provides evidence to show that 'up to 40 per cent of tourism worldwide is wildlife tourism across seascapes and landscapes'.[200] Tourists simply find the sighting of species like whales, sharks, turtles and dolphins irresistible, and the financial value of conservation for local communities can fund not only protection measures but also boost coastal economies. There is every incentive to ensure a healthy population of these species in preference to earlier practices of serving them on a dinner plate. Thirdly, there is a need to align financial mechanisms to the goal of sustainability. This is not necessarily a question of altruism although that always helps too. The real inducement for investors is that nature-oriented tourism is good business, whereas a devastated environment is not. Instead of short-term profits which soon tail off, sustainable development can ensure long-term prosperity and satisfaction for all parties. That would be truly transformative. But how do we reach this promised land?

## Take Heed from Boracay

*Boracay closure 2018: A salutary lesson of over-use. Removing clumps of algae on the first day of the clean-up*

In April 2018, the government of Philippines ordered the immediate closure of its most popular coastal resort, Boracay. Before the influx of tourists, which started in the 1980s, the island is recalled as a stereotype of a tropical paradise, with white sandy beaches and clear blue waters. By the time it was closed, for a period of six months, the then President described it as a cesspool. The focus of attention was on the absence of proper sewage treatment and waste disposal, and closure was ordered to enable the necessary infrastructure to be installed. Prior to this action, the resort was hosting an annual total of 1.7 million tourists, with expenditure in the region of $1 billion. Tourism in its heyday supported an estimated 55,000 jobs.[201]

A combination of weak governance, corruption and a belated recognition that revenues would be endangered if the situation was allowed to continue, led to this temporary closure. Unfortunately, this is not an isolated event and, to take another example, Maya Bay in Thailand was also closed in 2018 to allow the natural ecosystem to recover from overuse. It has recently reopened although (to protect new coral growth and to return the space to an endemic shark population) tourists are no longer allowed to swim in the bay.[202] I believe this kind of situation could so easily be avoided, not just in the worst-affected areas but wherever there is maritime tourism. To make progress I offer a four-point plan.

- ✧ Firstly, any solution must be **international** in scope – but not reliant on bodies like the UN agencies, as their timelines and record in securing agreement for effective measures are not necessarily good. Instead, I suggest we look to a representation of international pressure groups, which can act as arbiters of good practice.
- ✧ Secondly, I would urge the universal introduction of a **Sustainable Ocean Levy** (SOL), representing a charge for the upkeep of what it is that visitors come to enjoy. The charge would be levied at the time of entry to the country in question and would be based on *per capita* visitor numbers and local plans to show how sustainability can be achieved. I know there are already schemes for charging but the important thing is to have an international measure of performance and understanding.[203]
- ✧ Thirdly, the monies received from the levy will be spent on **specific, accountable projects**. These might vary from a planting scheme to restore mangrove forests to projects designed to provide rewarding jobs for local communities, from the protection of endangered sea mammals to monitored procedures to ensure safe conditions for workers and visitors alike.
- ✧ Next, a means will be devised to measure the extent to which sustainability is being implemented. Venues will be graded annually to show how successful they are and the outcomes will be widely publicised. This kind of **certification** will be available to tourists when they choose their destination. The system works on the premise that some visitors will automatically look for sustainable venues, knowing what they can offer. Others will discover through experience that it is worth paying more

for their vacation experience in the knowledge that the sea will be clean, and that host communities will share fairly in the benefits of a popular venue.

Of course, the details of SOL would need to be followed through, but if the principle is accepted – namely that **all** aspects of maritime tourism must be paid for – the rest will follow. One thing is certain: urgent action is needed before unique attractions (whether natural features or local livelihoods) are lost forever. If it is to contribute to the kind of Blue Economy envisaged, maritime tourism cannot be allowed to fall so far short of acceptable standards of sustainability.

As a short addendum, a survey of more than 1,000 visitors to Seychelles in 2019 showed that 80 per cent would be willing to pay an environmental levy. Legislation was framed and the introduction of a Tourism Environmental Levy was planned for the start of April 2023. At the eleventh hour, this was delayed because of objections raised by the industry. That is not the end of it but it is indicative of how new taxes of any kind need to be painstakingly negotiated. At least, if it works in Seychelles, it can then be used to demonstrate the case in other countries.

# Chapter 6

## Cropping at Sea
*Innovative schemes to source food from the ocean*

So far, I have looked at three pillars of the Blue Economy – shipping, fishing and tourism – which are already well entrenched and at the heart of our relationship with the ocean. In each of these cases, the subjects are familiar and it is not difficult to think of ways in which they can become more sustainable. In this chapter, though, it is time to venture beyond what is already known and explore new possibilities. Unless we break into these domains the transition will be incomplete.

One global issue, in particular, is pressing. With most of the planet's surface given over to the sea, are there any ways in which this vast expanse can provide more food? We are already blessed with an essential supply of protein-rich fish but can we now look for a wider range of products? What is the potential for harvesting edible crops in salt water? Against the background of a growing population, food security presents a challenge facing every nation. The problem is sharpened by a diminishing supply of suitable farmland. To what extent can the ocean contribute more than it does already?

In the first section, I will point to an important area of progress, featuring the cultivation and inventive application of seaweed. This hitherto-neglected plant can offer a plentiful and healthy source of food and is the subject of some truly breakthrough developments. Yet, even with the prospect of achieving its potential, if we are to enjoy sufficient diversity, we will need to go beyond this. So, in the second section I look at what else might be possible in the way of growing food in saltwater, and I ask what is presently being done to make this a reality. Finally, I question whether the sea can help with another basic need of life on this planet, as a sustainable source of drinking water.

We already ask a lot of our ocean and, in the interests of sustainability, we need to tread carefully in seeking more. We cannot afford to repeat the mistakes made in developing the planet's finite area of land with little thought for the future. In all respects, the ocean should be seen as the world's new frontier.

## Food for Thought

At first glance, seaweed hardly seems a likely candidate to offer global salvation. Visitors to beaches may think of it only as it appears in rotting piles above the waterline, some of it eventually collected to spread over nearby fields as a natural fertiliser. Children may recall it in a more joyful light, attracted by its lustrous texture when taken direct from the sea and draped around their shoulders like garlands bestowed by Neptune. Years later, the strong smell of seawater will remain in the nostrils. In some parts of the world (mainly Asia), its nutritional value has for long been recognised and seaweed is an essential ingredient in daily diets. Sushi lovers, everywhere, would not be without it. At most, though, it has remained on the sidelines of our mainstream diets, marginalised in our thoughts even by its nomenclature as a weed.

All of this is now changing, and very fast too. At a recent conference in London, I listened to Vincent Doumeizel, a (if not 'the') leading figure in shining a new spotlight on seaweed. He urged us all to think again about this long-dismissed product. Hearing what he had to say was riveting and, inspired by his claims, I was soon to learn that there are many other scientists, too, around the world, who are equally enthusiastic and committed to the cause of seaweed. Doumeizel himself is the Food Programme Director at Lloyd's Register Foundation and Senior Advisor on Oceans to the UN Global Compact. He has recently published a book which brings together the many developments in making the best use of seaweed.[204]

Like all true innovators he is also a visionary, painting a vivid picture of the remarkable benefits that seaweed can offer:

> As a food source, it's filled with protein, nutrients, zinc and vitamins, with little or no fat, and once dried, easy to store and transport. While some cultures and cuisines use seaweed a lot, many people think they do not like seaweed. I tell people if you think seaweed

*is not good, just try to eat a raw potato. If you cook it, then it's good… But looking at seaweed as a food source for humans is just scratching the surface. Rich in protein and with natural antibiotic and antimicrobial properties, seaweed is a good source of animal feed too… More importantly, it makes a dramatic impact on methane emission from livestock. Just the smallest bit of a red seaweed added to the feed of ruminants like cattle has been found to reduce their emission of methane – a greenhouse gas tied to global warming – up to 90 per cent.*

*Seaweed can also be used as a bio-stimulant to improve crop performance and enrich soil, and in the medical field it is being explored in treatments for Alzheimer's disease, cystic fibrosis and some forms of blindness… It's being developed as an edible form of packaging that could be used, for example, as packets for ketchup, oil and other liquids, and a solid version of seaweed is being developed for use to replace plastic straws. It also is being developed for use in making a fabric that is more sustainable than cotton production (the latter which can entail heavy pesticide, land and water use).*

*Seaweed even has a role in empowering women and promoting gender parity. In developing economies such as Tanzania, where seaweed is farmed, as much as 80 per cent of the industry's revenues and jobs have gone to women, while men in the community continue to fish.*[205]

The versatility of seaweed is beyond question, yet there is so much still to discover. To help in tracking where we are on this journey of change, perhaps the best starting point is to go back to basics and to learn a little more about this remarkable organism in its natural state. For a start, seaweed is amongst those algae which flourish in saltwater conditions. We speak of 'seaweed' as if it is a single type of plant but the reality is that there are numerous species, measured in thousands. Importantly (in terms of their accessibility), they are ubiquitous, occurring in all parts of the ocean, from polar to tropical. They will usually be distinguished by one of three colours: red, brown and green. Red seaweeds embrace some 7,200 species, brown about 2,000, and green marginally fewer with 1,800. Unlike land plants, they are without traditionally structured roots but, instead, they are normally tied to the ocean floor through 'holdfasts', which perform no other function than that of an anchor.[206] Generally, they are to be found quite near the surface, to a depth of 8 to 40 metres, but in clear waters they can grow much deeper, down as far as 250 metres. There are also large clumps of floating algae, the best known of these forming the Sargasso Sea, which seem to propagate themselves by fragmentation.[207]

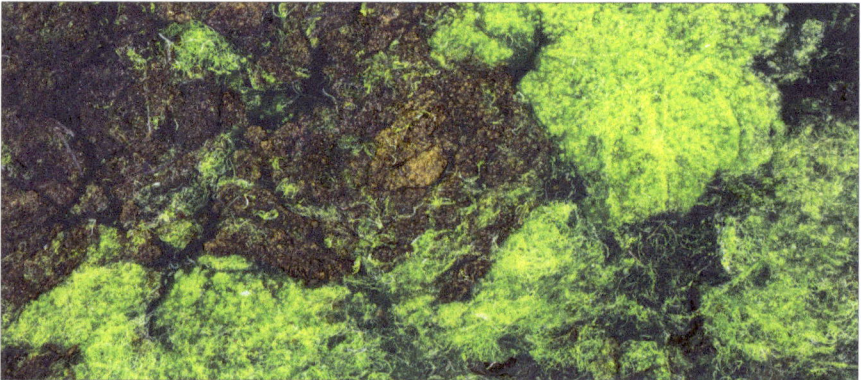

*The number of seaweed species can be measured in thousands, all of which are edible*

As a source of food, all of the thousands of species of seaweed are edible, and not simply edible but highly nutritious. Doumeizel reports on studies showing that a sensible use of seaweed in just 2 per cent of the ocean would be enough to feed 12 billion people, without using any animal or vegetable resources. And, unlike some other plants, it retains all of its nutrients when dried. Seaweed also releases much less carbon than land plants, and it is possible for the carbon it does produce to be sedimented and put 'back where it used to be before we started to take it out of the soil'.[208] Doumezeil also points out that the name of a weed hardly helps in its promotion, and the example of Norway could be followed, where the term 'sea forests' is preferred. That immediately conveys a sense of scale and (in the same way as for forests on land) a need for sound management.[209]

## Long Live the Revolution!

Such is the potential for radical change that Doumeizel likens it to a revolution. So much so that, spurred on by Lloyd's Register Foundation, he has joined with others to produce no less than a seaweed manifesto.[210] Revolutions have taken their place as momentous points of change in history. They have variously been proclaimed under the banner of grand concepts like freedom and democracy, independence and sovereignty. Leaders have been overthrown and new political systems ushered in. But never before have revolutionaries manned the barricades for seaweed. Time will show: it may be different from other revolutions but, also, it may yet prove to be more enduring. In a world desperately in need of change in how we do things, perhaps it will be even more important than its political counterparts too.

The manifesto is rightly described by the contributors as a visionary document.

> *Our vision is an upscaled, responsible and restorative seaweed industry, playing a globally significant role in food security, climate change mitigation, and support to the marine ecosystem, as well as contributing to job-creation and economic growth. The vision goes beyond being sustainable. The aim is to restore abundance to the ocean while solving some of the world's biggest societal challenges. About 50 per cent of the photosynthesis on Earth occurs in seaweeds*

*and microscopic algae floating in the oceans, contributing to the uptake of carbon dioxide and the release of oxygen. The seaweeds provide shelter for marine life and are an important part of the food chain.*[211]

As the subtitle of the publication indicates, it is a manifesto for nothing less than a sustainable future, with direct links to at least 6 of the UN's 17 Sustainable Development Goals. Foremost of these connections is the ambitious but absolutely essential goal of 'No Hunger'. In terms of calories, the ocean presently provides only 2 per cent of the world's food needs, leaving an enormous potential to fill the gap.[212] Seaweed and other algae can make a real difference, offering not only a nutritious food for humans but also a source of feed for aquaculture and farm animals, as well as fertilisers to increase food production on land. In different ways, seaweed can also help in the realisation of the other SDGs too, offering additional income to coastal communities and leading to new opportunities for education and training.

*Women harvesting seaweed in Zanzibar*

As in any good manifesto, the way ahead is clearly marked. There will be obstacles as well as opportunities, and mechanisms will need to be put in place to transform an agenda into action. Nothing can be taken for granted and the very best in research and development will be essential if setbacks are to be overcome. Sustainability is the watchword and lessons have to be taken to learn from mistakes that have been made in land-based farming.

In the final section of the manifesto, milestones are identified to mark the journey. Firstly, there should be a mapping exercise to show the present extent of the market and to identify where there might be gaps. This is followed by a second marker, in the form of a Safe Seaweed Coalition, to ensure that proper regulations are developed, and safety standards applied in all aspects of activity. Thirdly, the new industry must include the restoration of seaweed habitats damaged by, for instance, ocean acidification. World stocks must be kept at a measured level to ensure future viability. Next, one comes to a milestone where a restored ocean and seaweed farming forests assume the role of carbon sinks to mitigate climate change. Further markers include developing a framework for offshore production; integrating seaweed production into the wider realm of aquaculture; and biorefinery systems, ideally located in the ocean itself to minimise the transport costs of wet seaweed.

The final milestone in the manifesto is an especially important one, calling for the establishment of a 'global blue farming platform'. A successful seaweed industry will depend on the combined contribution of different sectors: public and private, the scientific community and commercial interests. There is a lengthy process involving interconnected parts, starting with seaweed as it is, establishing ways to guarantee its health and viability in different locations, and then attracting the interest of investors. Writing a manifesto is one thing, carrying through the revolution another. But a start has been made and the opportunities are too good to miss. From my own perspective, what is interesting is that, when I wrote my first book, I did not include a reference to the potential of seaweed. Seven years later, such is the evidence of progress, this book would be incomplete without celebrating its growing importance. Long live the revolution!

## Changing the Menu

The revolution has barely started but already seaweed and kelp (a different species of algae from seaweed, but with many comparable qualities) have become fashionable additions to traditional cuisines. Kelp is not as ubiquitous as seaweed, being restricted to cooler waters, but is now a favourite amongst health-conscious 'foodies' in the US and Scandinavia especially. If this sounds like the beginning of just another food fad, it must very soon go well beyond that. Revolutions habitually start in small ways, the testing point being whether they then attract a popular following. Fortunately, there are signs that this will be the case. For instance, promoting the cause of regenerative ocean farming, Green Wave is an American NGO which aims to build an active network of 10,000 like-minded farmers over the next ten years, and to see the planting of 1 million acres with sustainable sea crops.[213] Green Wave is far from being an isolated initiative and speaks for a new generation of enthusiasts for sustainable ocean farming.

> *With ocean agriculture in its infancy, we finally have an opportunity to do food right; to build a food system from the bottom up. We can avoid the mistakes of industrial agriculture and aquaculture, farm for the benefit of all instead of just the few, and weave economic and social justice into its DNA – all the while capturing carbon, creating millions of jobs, and feeding the planet.*[214]

The question is whether seaweed and kelp can break through into a mass market, and this depends on whether commercial producers believe the figures. Certainly, the headline statistics will encourage a positive response: a consumer preference for sustainable products, up from 45 per cent in September 2019 to 55 per cent in March 2021;[215] an annual compound growth rate in the industry of 12 per cent through to 2026;[216] recognition of seaweed feed products as the fastest growing sector in aquaculture.[217] By 2026, the commercial seaweed market in the US could be worth $85 billion, as a result of a combination of factors.[218] It is anticipated that there will be high product demand from a widening range of restaurants and dining facilities; brown seaweed, in particular, will be used increasingly in the preparation of soups, salads and sauces; a growing appreciation of the nutritional value of seaweed will stimulate substantial growth in North America and Europe; and the presence already of some of the key manufacturers of commercial seaweed which, apart from their own impact, will encourage others to compete for what is proving to be a lucrative market.

*Seaweed salad, followed by crispy seaweed with Japanese noodles*

As a dietary choice, seaweed has already moved well beyond the image of a portion of fresh greens on the dinner plate, with imaginative applications and products for sale. Emerging as an industry leader, the Norwegian producer, Lofoten, advertises an attractive range of derivatives, including seaweed pasta, truffle seaweed salt, Arctic Ocean greens, an essential ingredient for bread, dark chocolate with sugar kelp, and the ultimate taste delight, Lofoten umami. For visitors to the factory shop, within the Arctic Circle, there is also a restaurant which demonstrates the versatility of its products. What could be more prestigious than a visit to the newest of gastronomic venues?

Even in these early stages of seaweed metamorphosis, opportunities are being seized with the enthusiasm and hopes of pioneers. Apart from its direct use as a food, it has increasing value and use as a nutrient in aquaculture and to enrich soils. A world away from the icy waters of the Arctic, a local company in Seychelles has made its own entry into the market. Seaweed Seychelles, dating from 2019, acknowledges the research and development expertise it can call on from the Commonwealth Scientific and Industrial Research Organisation. There are plans to extend the range of its products but presently the focus is on a plant growth promoter and a soil conditioner. The latter is a pure liquid extract from seaweed, totally organic and free of chemical additives. In turn, the soil conditioner enriches plant growth through a slow-release system which enables the plant to thrive for longer. One main benefit of the soil conditioner is that it also acts as an insect repellent.[219]

It seems that change is very much in the air. At a recent exhibition, I was able to talk to a young man, Yohan Gallet, who explained how he made a dramatic career change: having trained as an airline pilot, he decided, instead, to devote his time to developing a more sustainable form of agriculture.

> *I finally made the choice to join the new generation of oceanic entrepreneurs to preserve the world's marine ecosystems, while playing a key role in combating food insecurity and climate change.*[220]

His homeland, Mauritius, has an unwanted record for its heavy use of pesticides and he wants to change that. The way forward, he believes, is through the use of natural materials from the sea, hence the name of his enterprise, Sealife Organics. Each day, a new supply of seaweed is washed onto the beaches and most is left to waste. Yohan, however, saw its potential to enrich farmland and he set about developing products such as environmentally-friendly compost, potting soils and fertilisers – all rich in carbon, calcium and potassium. Launched in 2020, he has ambitious plans to achieve new markets, matched by a realisation that harvesting what is left on the shore will need to be supplemented by domestic and large-scale seaweed cultures to meet a growing demand. As well as selling direct to farmers, there are targets in Mauritius for households and commercial nurseries.

*Seaweed washed ashore on an Atlantic beach in the west of Ireland*

In reading about various applications, I was intrigued to learn more about how, in the nineteenth century, seaweed provided nutrients for impoverished and starving people along the west coast of Ireland. When the potato crop, on which the country was dependent, failed because of disease, it led to widespread starvation and, in turn, to large-scale emigration to the United States in the hope of better lives. For some at the time, seaweed was a lifeline but later it was dismissed as 'famine food'. Only recently is it back in favour and is now much sought-after:

> One of the most famous varieties of Irish seaweed is Dillisk or Dulse. With its reddish brown colour and smoky vegetal flavour, this variety adds a salty kick and beautiful flavour to any bake or stew. Tasty and versatile, this 'Famine Food' is not only making waves because of its flavour it also has huge health benefits with many containing high levels of vitamins A, B and C, as well as good fatty acids.[221]

With an annual production of some 40,000 tonnes, seaweed is used in Ireland not only in cooking but also in aquaculture and for fertilisers. It is now an industry in itself, giving rise to a number of new companies which, in their various promotions, stress the contribution made to sustainability, with more than a hint of traditional family practices. To take just a few examples, *Bio*Atlantis has the strapline, 'nature working naturally'; another new business, Wild Irish Seaweed, claims its seaweeds are 'hand harvested sustainably' by the Talty family, off the coast of County Clare; in turn, Connemara is described as '*the* organic seaweed company'; Emerald Isle promotes itself as 'a family business producing seaweed as supplements, cooking, gardening and bath products'; and Irish Seaweeds describes its products as 'treasure from the Irish coastline'.

Ireland is opening new markets but it is worth noting that its seaweed output is still minuscule compared with traditional Asian producers like Indonesia. With its numerous islands and long coastline, this was for long the world's leader, producing some 10 million tonnes annually. More recently, its leading position is now challenged by other countries, notably, China and the Philippines. Indonesia's output has declined as a result of poor management of this valuable resource and the loss of natural coastline habitats, a salutary lesson that needs urgently to be addressed.

## Too Much Salt?

Seaweed is our great hope but it would be folly to rely on just one solution to the world's food security problems. Beyond seaweed, what opportunities are there to grow familiar land-based crops in the sea? There is a massive incentive to do this. For one reason, the extent of the ocean far exceeds that of the land, so it would surely make sense to use some of that additional space if and where possible. But there is another reason too: each year, as a result of the warming of the planet and the melting of glaciers and the polar ice caps, sea levels are rising. The effects of this are already widely apparent in low-lying areas. Year on year, seawater seeps beyond the beaches into adjoining fields, at first bubbling to the surface but eventually flooding whole farms. As a result, traditional forms of agriculture become non-viable. It is a loss that cannot be afforded, affecting most directly coastal plains on the edge of large land masses, and small island states. For the latter, where flat land is often at a premium, the problem is especially acute. So what can be done about it? Is there any chance of developing crop strains that are resistant to water-borne salt? And can the surface of the sea be used for floating farms? These are two possible ways forward that need to be explored.

### *Seawater rice*

We can start with the potential for developing salt-resistant crops. An interesting example can be found in China, where the traditional juxtaposition of a very high population and a longstanding dependence on rice as the nation's staple food has, for some years, encouraged research on this topic. Areas where crops have failed because of excessive salt content have been chosen for experiments, extending back over 50 years. It is the growing importance of food security, however – not only for China but, more widely, across the world – which has given this work a greater sense of urgency.

The challenge for scientists is to see if it is possible to develop new strains that can grow on farmland already degraded by a high salt content as well as other areas which are presently experiencing encroachment by the sea. The cultivation of rice normally uses large quantities of fresh water, so it is not so much the threat of flooding which is the problem but the presence of salt that comes with it.[222]

Research into this aspect of rice production has emerged from the well-established development of hybrid varieties, derived from different parent plants which, in combination with other strains, can offer greater yields than any one type on its own. In the experimental stage, scientists have already developed a new species that has double the salinity tolerance of other rice. 'Unlike regular rice, the new rice line can expel salt it takes from the soil into the air through salt glands it has on its leaves.'[223] The breakthrough has come through the successful crossing of two very different rice parents, which scientists had originally thought was impossible to do.[224]

Acknowledging the importance of this area of research, the Sea Rice Research and Development Centre was established in Qingdao, a city on China's north-east coast. The location is within reach of a number of large pockets of salty/alkaline soil where for years any form of productive farming has been unsuccessful. There are now some interesting and relatively recent breakthroughs, based on a programme of experimental planting that was launched in 2018. From small beginnings, the institute has plans to harvest 30 million tonnes of rice from 6.7 million hectares of presently barren land. There are already signs that 'seawater rice' (as it is popularly known) can result in higher yields than some of the traditional varieties.[225] Commercial farming of the new species has still not started although there is optimism that it soon will. If this proves to be successful, it will have enormous implications not only for China but also other nations with rice-growing capacity. A further factor is that it offers encouragement to scientists working in related fields to develop saltwater resistance in other crops that face the same threat of seawater encroachment.

## Mixed fare

An easier way to augment a seawater menu is not necessarily to try to adapt plants which traditionally are vulnerable to salt, but rather to concentrate on species known as halophytes, which grow naturally in salty conditions. These include samphire and sea aster, which can both be used as green vegetables. Innovation and persistence are so important in finding new solutions and it is often left to small start-up companies to show the way. Thus, on the west coast of Scotland, the founder of Seawater Solutions explains the process:

*We take this land, whether it's degraded farmland or flood-affected lands, and we then build an artificial saltmarsh ecosystem where we can extract food at the same time. We'll pump seawater over this area, sometimes we flood it, and then we'll begin to grow saline plants... The salt marshes where they grow protect the coast from flooding and erosion and absorb 30 times more carbon than rainforests do.*[226]

There is already a proven market for these products but the problem with halophytes is that they are very restricted in range. They are useful additions to diets but the bigger challenge of producing a wide variety of vegetables remains. That is why there is interest in experiments being conducted in the North Sea, centred on a farm on the Dutch coast. Under the auspices of the Salt Farm Foundation, work is focused not on pure seawater but on 'medium brackish water', composed of a mixture of sea and fresh water. This has already yielded some promising results.

*With its partners at the SalFar project, the Salt Farm Foundation has set up 16 fields in seven countries on the North Sea to test the salt tolerance of various crops. The researchers found that certain varieties of potatoes, cabbage, tomatoes, carrots, beetroots and strawberries have high salt tolerance. Brackish water was also found to be suitable for irrigating oats, barley, onions and sugar beet.*[227]

The main difficulty to date is to convince neighbouring farmers that introducing brackish water onto their land will not cause long-term harm to their own growing plans.

Even the Dutch experiment, however, is based on using large quantities of fresh water. Growing crops in unadulterated sea water is more complex and awaits successful work with plant DNAs. Scientists, of course, are working on this and the search for change and the prospect of making 'impossible' breakthroughs is beginning to feel a bit like Silicon Valley in its heyday. In 2020, for instance, two young scientists from England set up shop in Waterloo, Canada.[228] As a new start-up, registered as Agrisea, they were given laboratory space to take forward pioneering work they had already started in California. With the aim of finding ways to grow vegetables in seawater, they focused on the genetics of those plants that naturally flourish in such conditions. The secret, they saw, lay in a subset of genes that enabled their sample to thrive in the presence of salt rather than failing to grow. Learning from nature is a sound approach and the task of editing a single gene to increase salt tolerance has already been achieved. But the real challenge facing Agrisea is to successfully edit a whole gene network. If this can be done, whether by this company or others, it will take time to complete the process. The important thing is that a start has been made and no one can doubt the determination of young scientists to reach the common goal.

## Farms at Sea

Rather than confronting the problem of salt content head-on, a different (although possibly complementary) approach is to treat the vast ocean space as an extension of the land and to look for ways to build floating farms on the surface (with or without the use of saltwater). The idea is not especially new but we are still some distance from seeing this kind of unit on the open seas. However, in and around harbours and potentially in estuaries, avoiding rough water, there is no shortage of existing examples, some of which are rooted in tradition. Thus, in Bangladesh, the perennial issue of inland flooding from rivers has for long been turned to advantage with floating farms where vegetables are grown as well as seedlings for sale. What is different now is that, across the world, there is interest in the sea because of the space it offers and, compared with the past, the adoption of smart techniques to make the process more cost-effective.

*Rotterdam  gets much publicity for its two-storey floating farm in the protected waters of the harbour*

*Bangladesh has for long developed floating farms on a large scale to combat flooding*

An interesting prototype is to be found in Rotterdam harbour, where a two-storey structure, completed in 2019, was possibly the first floating farm to accommodate dairy cattle.[229] A lot of emphasis is put on the humane conditions provided for the cattle; animal welfare is claimed to be a top priority. With 40 cows on the farm, 320,000 litres of milk are produced every year, most of it pasteurised and some used to make yoghurt. The diet of the cattle is sourced locally from organic waste: for example, 'our cows are fed brewers' grains from a number of Rotterdam breweries, bran from Schiedam windmills, grass from nearby sports fields, and potato peelings from a local processor'. It is also claimed that 'the beds for the cows are made of flexible and strong materials that can be adjusted to the wishes of the cow'.[230]

In terms of sustainability, perhaps the strongest argument is that the farm is located in the city, within a short distance of many of its customers. Avoiding the transportation of food products for long distances to the market is in itself a good reason for using this kind of space. The company has plans to extend the range of its floating farms, with the prospect of a new facility for 7,000 chickens to produce 2 million eggs per year, and a 2,000-square-metre vegetable growth surface for leafy greens and other products.

Demonstration projects are always of value in helping to spread an idea and, sure enough, the Rotterdam experiment is attracting much attention as a possible prototype. Sponsored by an American company which is already developing vertical farming space for crops, a group of engineering students in 2020 produced a report on the potential for a Rotterdam-type experiment within the boundaries of New York City.[231] To pursue their ideas, they concentrated on tomato-growing, based on the argument that, as New Yorkers presently import their tomatoes from California and Italy, a local production unit would be more sustainable.

Although their report is long on principles and short on ways to achieve early implementation, it nevertheless contains some interesting ideas on how this kind of unit can make effective use of smart technologies. The research team has shown that, with good design, there will be only a limited need for on-site labour.

> As an example, sensors would be installed in the building to monitor operations. There could be sensors present in each plant bed to detect a plant's requirements of water, nutrients and other things for optimal growth. The sensors can also detect the presence of harmful bacteria, viruses or any other micro-organism which is harmful to the plants. A gas chromatograph technology could be used to analyse the flavonoid levels, suggesting the optimal time for the harvesting. The technologies mentioned are not new or yet to be invented...[232]

Through hydroponic growing methods the demands for fresh water for this kind of farming will be significantly less than for conventional methods and, although there is a need for a high usage of lighting, photovoltaic cells can help to reduce calls on the city's electricity grid system. Of particular appeal is the prospect of integrating production, consumption and waste management. Closing the circle so that such farms are fully sustainable marks an important step forward.

It is likely that harbour-based farms of this sort will become more common, the main barrier at present being to make them commercially viable. In contrast, the implementation of floating farms in the open sea still presents more formidable obstacles, mainly because of challenging natural conditions and distances from the shore. In spite of – or perhaps because of – these challenges, innovators are already turning their attention to what might be done. In principle, for ocean locations, one design solution is to tie the prospective farms with waterproof cables which are then anchored to the seafloor. The cables are intended to limit the amount of movement experienced in the growing areas. It is a simple enough concept but enormously expensive to construct and maintain, so that to date there is nothing on the scale required that is commercially viable. Like all new applications, however, it is probable that the costs will come down the more it is adopted and technical problems will be overcome; the use of personal computers, solar power and electric cars offer just a few examples of this kind of trajectory. Ocean-based farms on the scale required still belong to the future but perhaps not so far ahead as to be excluded from this present discussion.

## 'Water, Water'

*Water, water everywhere, nor any drop to drink.*

Such was the tormented memory of the ancient mariner, the subject of Coleridge's poem recounting the fate of a shipwrecked sailor drifting aimlessly across a vast sea under a relentless sun.[233] It would have brought the traumatised seafarer cold comfort to learn that, one day, ways would be found to take the salt out of seawater to make it suitable to drink. But for all the means that now exist, there is still no early prospect of addressing the challenge of providing sufficient fresh water for a growing population. The telling conclusion of a recent UN conference was that '... at the current rate, universal access to clean water and sanitation will not be achieved for decades after the 2030 target'.[234]

At first glance, it might seem that desalination is the answer to providing adequate supplies of fresh water, especially in arid regions. Seawater is plentiful – another gift of the ocean – and the only impediment to using it for drinking is the high salt content. Remove the salt and surely the problem is solved. In principle, yes, but in practice the process cannot yet be regarded as sustainable. One reason is that desalination plants are enormously energy-intensive. Until recently, they relied overwhelmingly on fossil fuels to operate, especially in the Middle Eastern desert kingdoms where oil was cheap and easy to source. New metropolitan centres like Dubai and Abu Dhabi could not have been contemplated without the conversion of seawater. Gradually, there has been a transition in favour of renewable sources of energy, from the sun and wind, but this change is still only partial. One reason is that a regular supply of fresh water is then subject to favourable weather conditions, which cannot be guaranteed. The introduction of hybrid schemes, using a combination of natural power sources, is one way this is being addressed.

Another deterrent to using desalinated water is that costs are still high. Over the past decade they have been reduced quite dramatically, although 'the average price of desalinated water is often two to four times more expensive than for other sources'. What is more, 'cost breakthroughs on major, market-ready technology in the near to medium term are unlikely' and may even rise to match higher prices for energy in world markets.[235]

Price apart, one is still left with other problems, not least of all the harm they inflict on marine life being trapped against the filter screens or sucked into the treatment machinery itself. There is also the problem of fish and other organisms having difficulties surviving in the discharge, comprising brine and wastewater, which settles on the seafloor and harms the seabed habitat. With communities becoming more sensitive to the needs of wildlife, new desalination plants are no longer automatically accepted. For instance, in May 2022 the California Coastal Commission unanimously rejected a proposed $1.4 billion ocean desalination plant in Huntington Beach, partly because of its potential effect on marine mammals and other forms of sea life.[236]

Growing concerns about the impact of desalination plants are leading to two responses. One is to continue to refine the process in order to minimise the adverse effects. Faced with consequences like the Huntington Beach debacle, ways will be found to make it more environmentally sustainable. A different kind of response is to reduce the need for desalination in the first place by greatly reducing the wasteful use of fresh water, especially but not only for agriculture:

> Water conservation, water use efficiency, storm water capture, and reuse, and recycled water expansion are proven effective strategies to increase regional water supplies and often cost less than desalination. In addition, these alternatives provide pollution abatement, habitat restoration, and flood control benefits, which are commonly overlooked during cost/benefit assessments.

Necessity is the mother of invention and what would have been unthinkable a little while back is now becoming central to a more conservation-minded approach. Los Angeles, for instance, with a serious water deficit, has recently announced a multi-billion-dollar project to recycle and reuse its wastewater.[237]

Undoubtedly, desalination has a key role in helping to meet growing demands for fresh water and further efforts will be made to reduce the price where possible, and to make the whole process more environmentally-friendly. At the same time, a parallel approach to make more prudent use of natural supplies will attract its own support. As is so often the case, there is no single solution but rather a combination of measures that together can take us a step closer to a sustainable Blue Economy.

# Chapter 7

## Quest for Power
*Practical ways to harness the energy of the ocean*

The sheer power of the ocean makes a coherent statement that we would do well to heed. In the days of sail, the full force of the wind was enhanced by skilful navigation to make effective use of waves and currents. But that was it. Other than on a small scale, there was no incentive to transfer this experience of using natural power to other situations, as a universal source of free and constantly renewable energy. Fuel was derived, instead, from inland forests and mines, augmented later by oil and gas reserves (sometimes in the relatively shallow waters of the continental shelf). But circumstances are rapidly changing. Now that fossil fuels are out of favour, it is the turn of sources which are neither finite in quantity nor polluting in use to meet the demands of society. Natural power can be captured on land, in sun-soaked deserts and fast-flowing rivers, but – if only because of its greater expanse – it is the ocean that offers the most coveted reserve. This has become the vital frontline for a new generation of clean, renewable energy.

In this chapter, I will look, first, at the main sources that can be found across the ocean – from the space on and above its surface which is open to the wind and sun, and to the constant movement of the sea itself. Numerous options are being explored and I will illustrate this trend with a number of exemplary projects. I will then turn to the challenges for marine engineering and what needs to be done to achieve the full technological and commercial potential of ocean energy. Successful developments in this field will mark an important step in the transition to a sustainable Blue Economy; indeed, I believe that without it the transition will be incomplete. Great progress has been made since I reviewed the subject in 2016, but there is still a long way to go. The question is whether we can take the giant step that is needed, in time to make a real difference.

Recognition of the largely untapped supply of ocean energy has come late.

The potential has always been there but it has been easier in the past to extract and use fossil fuels. It is only with climate change and the global trend to transition to clean, renewable sources of power that new connections are being made between supply and demand. In theory, there is sufficient offshore wind capacity alone to meet all of the world's energy needs and more, but many practical difficulties stand in the way of viable conversion and underwater transfer from afar to join the respective national grids. So, too, in different ways with other available sources, there is no shortage in terms of what the ocean itself can offer but ways have to be found to make recovery both economic and environmentally sustainable. At this stage, some developments are more advanced for early use than others, with offshore wind energy being well ahead of the rest of the field; waves also have enormous potential but the conversion rate is presently much lower. In any case, there will probably, over time, be a place for them all, with niche applications as well as fuels for mass use. The task will be to choose different options from the menu – sometimes on their own, more often in combination with others.

## 'Blow the Wind Southerly'

*Blow the wind southerly, southerly, southerly*
*Blow the wind south where's the bonnie blue sea ...*[239]

Winds have traditionally been portrayed as harbingers of change – carrying one to previously undiscovered lands, to speed the arrival of merchandise or to ward off foreign navies, to reunite families or to migrate to different parts of the world. And still we look to the skies and call on this natural phenomenon to take us forward. Now, perhaps, more than ever.

Of all the ways to produce clean energy, offshore wind is presently the best understood and most widely used. There is great hope that it can do much more. One only has to think of a traditional windmill to understand how this can be. In an ocean setting, energy conversion works on the comparable principle of allowing the wind to turn propellor-like blades around a rotor. The blades are sited at the top of tall masts (higher at sea than on land) and, as they turn, the effect is to spin a turbine to create electricity. Power produced in this way is then conveyed to shore and into the land-based grid. This model is a generalisation and it should be noted that, in addition to capturing energy close to the surface, attention is also being drawn to high-altitude wind. To convert the latter requires floating platforms and a form of kite rather than more expensive turbines. But, to date, this is very much a secondary type of application, a supplement rather than an alternative to what are now regarded as conventional wind farms.

*Numerous windmills along Holland's waterways can be seen as a prototype for modern windfarms*

In the present century, mainly in the past few years, offshore wind conversion has grown from a cottage industry to one of the main ways of reaching the global goal of net zero – replacing fossil fuels with clean energy. As the technology has improved, costs have fallen and output has risen. Refinements continue to be made and floating turbines, which enable wind energy to be captured in deeper waters, offer an alternative to fixed anchoring.

The scale of installations is indicative of the dramatic changes that are taking place. For instance, in the UK's most recent development, each of the blades has a span of more than 80 metres, producing a total rotor width of 167 metres (think of a 100-metre sprint and keep running). Just one turn of the turbine is enough to generate all the electricity a home needs for 24 hours.[240] At COP27, in November 2022, offshore wind energy was singled out as the way forward. Of the nine countries which signed up to the Global Offshore Wind Alliance, seven were from Europe, with the addition of Japan and the United States.[241] China was not a signatory but, as the world's leading producer in this field, hosted its own international event in June 2023.

Clusters of wind turbines form what are usually described as 'wind farms' (although perhaps nothing is less like a farm in a traditional sense), at sea as well as on land. Favoured locations for marine installations are shallow waters within EEZs. Although winds are not necessarily at their strongest close to shore, compared with further out, the costs of installation and maintenance of equipment are greatly reduced. In terms of productivity, the figures compare well with inland wind farms: offshore winds tend to be stronger and more constant, and there is presently the added advantage that the size of installations is generally less constrained by planning regulations. Disadvantages are that construction and maintenance costs are higher in the sea, if only because the means of reaching the various sites and the challenge of working in bad weather conditions is a more difficult process. There is also the fact that the substantial investments required, and consequent involvement of large corporations, tends to reduce any sense of community ownership.[242] This can be countered when governments intervene to ensure that some of the financial benefits accrue locally.[243]

On the question of environmental intrusion, it is fair to say that the jury is still out. As one would expect, politicians keen to demonstrate progress in the transition to sustainable sources, together with advocates from the wind-energy industry, play down the question of environmental impacts. Wind farms at sea, they argue, are less invasive than on land and in some respects that is hard to dispute. Proponents are also right to claim that the introduction of artificial structures can in some cases have a positive impact by creating the equivalent of 'reefs' which attract different species and create biological diversity: 'A habitat for barnacles, sponges, and other invertebrates, which may locally increase fish abundance.'[244] In contrast, the presence of wind turbines near to settlements and in areas of natural beauty is likely to give rise to opposition, by reason of noise as well as appearance.

But it is wrong to suggest that, just because they cannot always be seen, offshore installations are necessarily nuisance-free. Amongst the generic concerns is the harm they present to birds and bats in flight, through the risk of moving blades and the pressure effects of vortices. There is also a chance that avian creatures will be forced to find new habitats which may be less favourable. Likewise, marine life – ranging from a diversity of plants on the sea floor to large mammals, as well as fishing stocks – will be affected by noise and turbulence during construction and maintenance activities, as well as constant noise when they are operating. What is more, objections will vary from place to place: off the coast of north-east America, for example, there is a priority to safeguard the passage of endangered right whales, while in Japan there is a localised issue of protecting the feeding grounds of north Eurasian bittern colonies.[245] At the very least, argue opponents, proposals for the introduction of wind farms should be subjected to rigorous environmental impact assessments and not given a free pass in the otherwise understandable rush to net zero.

The fact is that, while the environmental debate continues, offshore wind farms are proliferating at a remarkable rate. In terms of generating renewable energy, compared with when I wrote my previous book on the Blue Economy, a great deal has been done and much more is promised. Net zero is no longer just an abstract concept. Let me give just a few examples.

## *Farms in the ocean*

Most people will never see for themselves the UK wind farm known as Hornsea Two, although it went into operation in 2022 and was designed to meet the electricity needs of 1.4 million homes in the adjacent region.[246] The reason for its lack of visibility is quite simple: Hornsea Two is located more than 140 kilometres offshore, in a part of the North Sea where only fishing boats and ships carrying freight to and from England, Scandinavia and the Baltic are likely to sail close. With its renowned storms and fogs, and often near-freezing temperatures, it is hardly an area to tempt tourists. But the strong winds which prevail are just what is needed for a successful offshore industry.

For the few who venture a sighting, it is something of an engineering spectacle. Extending over an offshore area of 462 square kilometres, it contains 165 wind turbines, rising to some 200 metres above sea level.[247] The new farm follows an earlier development, Hornsea One (of a similar size but generating less electricity), both of which will be surpassed in size by a further complex, Hornsea Three, where there is already planning permission to start development. There are plans, too, for Hornsea Four, which is still on the drawing board. This modern quartet takes its name from a seaside town on the adjacent Yorkshire coast, which dates back to mediaeval times; the contrast between old and new could hardly be greater. The Hornsea developments are themselves just part of a rapid transition to renewable energy in the UK. Until it was overtaken by China in 2021, the UK was already producing more electricity from offshore wind than any other country, with plans to service every home from this source by the mid-2030s. To achieve this goal, the number of turbines will have to be increased fivefold.[248]

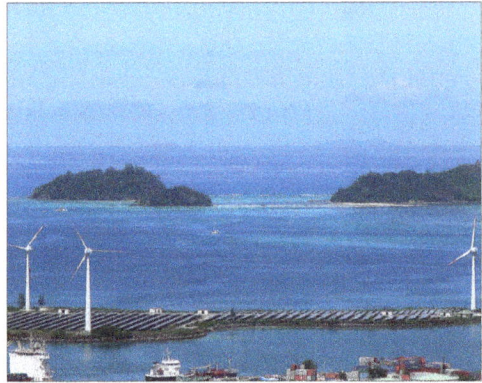

*(Left) Wind farms in the North Sea: the green light was given by the UK government in 2016 for Hornsea 2 to proceed*
*(Right) On an altogether smaller scale, Seychelles benefits from several turbines (donated by the UAE) in Victoria Harbour*

The North Sea remains one of the 'hot spots' in this growing industry – as well as the UK, Norway, Germany, Denmark, the Netherlands, and Belgium have all staked their own claims – but it was never going to be long before China took the lead in offshore wind league tables, notching up a number of 'firsts'. Christmas day 2021, for instance, saw the completion of the country's largest offshore wind farm and its connection to the mainland electricity grid; from start to finish the massive project took just 33 months to finalise.[249] This event occurred only a few days after another 'first', the completion of the largest unsubsidised project of its kind, in the form of the Shanwei Jiazi II offshore wind farm.[250] Triggered by the introduction of a new scheme to allocate ocean space through auctions (less bureaucratic than what it replaced), the growth rate of the country's transition to this form of green energy is nothing short of phenomenal.

> *This policy change led to China's 2021 addition of nearly 17 gigawatts on its own, more than the world had ever added globally in any single year. China is currently home to the world's largest offshore wind industry. From 2010 to 2020, the country's offshore wind capacity growth accounted for 32% of total global expansion. Between 2020 and 2022, one out of every five turbines installed offshore is a model by Mingyang, China's largest private wind turbine manufacturer.*[251]

In a year of worldwide expansion, China accounted in 2021 for 80 per cent of all new capacity, more than quadrupling its rate of growth compared with the previous year. As part of its national growth, Chinese wind-turbine manufacturers took the first four places in the world order.[252]

In contrast with China, progress in America has been slow and, even if present plans come to fruition, the best that can be hoped for is to provide clean energy for 10 million homes by 2030 – a figure that falls far short of original targets dating back to the Obama Administration amidst talk at that time of a Green New Deal. Some of the obstacles to progress (mainly to do with ownership and governance) have now been overcome and development can at last start on five projects on America's Atlantic coast. Meanwhile, a federal auction of ocean space for wind farms off the Pacific coast will lead to new projects there too; in that area, because of the depth of the sea beyond the edge of the narrow Continental Shelf, it is planned to use floating rather than fixed-anchor platforms.[253]

Inheriting a 2030 deadline for net-zero, greenhouse-gas emissions across the nation, the Biden Administration soon pushed the date back to 2050. Even that will probably prove to be beyond reach; a start has been made on the first five projects but their limited scale suggests that the pace and capacity needs to be greatly increased.[254]

| Project | Location | Capacity |
|---------|----------|----------|
| *Vineyard Wind 1* (started 2022) | Off the coast of Massachusetts | Will meet the demand of 400,000 homes in the state |
| *South Fork Wind* (started 2022) | Off the coast of New York State | Just 12 turbines. Will provide clean energy to the 70,000 homes in East Hampton |
| *Ocean Wind* | Close to Atlantic City, New Jersey | Will provide for 500,000 homes by mid-2020s |
| *Revolution Wind* | Off the coast of Massachusetts | Will provide for homes in Rhode Island and Connecticut. Could be operational by 2025 |
| *Atlantic Shores Offshore Wind Farm* | Off the coast of New Jersey | Large-scale development to meet growing demands in the region |

On a very different scale, wind power offers important opportunities for small island states. Invariably, an obstacle to development is cost and supporting infrastructure, but this can be overcome if richer nations offer to help. Such was the case for Seychelles, where I was able to negotiate with the UAE for a cluster of eight wind turbines to be donated. Even with a small number, the volume of power generated can make a difference, in this case amounting to 8 per cent of the energy needs of the country's most populous island. I would strongly urge other nations, where possible, to follow the example of the UAE in reducing global carbon emissions. I return later to the question of financial transfers to support initiatives in less well-endowed countries.

There are few countries with a coastline that are currently not considering or actively pursuing offshore wind generation for electricity. China is ahead of the field but others will emerge with ambitious plans of their own. Progress will be made but the challenge of the global goal of increasing capacity from 60 gigawatts in 2022 to 380 gigawatts by 2030, and then to a figure of 2,000 gigawatts by 2050, cannot be underestimated.[255] The move away from fossil fuels that is needed to achieve net zero is immense; it feels like trying to turn an ocean tanker on its own axis. But the reality is that this is the size of the challenge and if the world is serious about countering the effects of climate change, there has to be a far greater commitment than is currently evident.

## 'Down to the Seas Again'

*I must down to the seas again,*
*To the lonely sea and the sky...*[256]

The sea itself is so obviously brimming with energy yet, compared with the wind, conversion of its various forces is proving more difficult to achieve. Difficult but not impossible, and, through a combination of science, engineering and enterprise, the frontier is constantly being pushed back. Such is the common theme, although each of the different sources tells its own story of how this is being done.

### *Waves*

Anyone who has watched successive waves in a rough sea crash against a seawall or along the foot of a line of cliffs will get an immediate sense of the sheer force at work. Even when conditions at sea are relatively calm, the impact of their persistent flow, one after another, is not to be underestimated. It is the regularity of waves which is one of the attractions for power conversion, in contrast, say, to sources which rely on an unlikely scenario of the wind blowing every day or the sun shining constantly. There is enormous, untapped potential and, theoretically, wave energy alone could meet all the global energy demand. Although waves vary seasonally and even in the course of a day, their behaviour can be predicted using models and monitored with buoys and satellites; and they are considered to be a reliable energy source.[257]

The challenge, of course, is to harness this enormous potential and, to date, the conversion rate is relatively limited. At first sight, the technology required might sound quite straightforward:

*Wave power converts the kinetic and potential energy of the surface wind-waves of the ocean into electrical energy (or some usable commodity, such as desalinated water). Wave energy converters are designed to be deployed in arrays, similar to wind farms.*[258]

*In spite of the enormous power of waves, finding ways to harness this potential is proving an obstacle to providing infinite energy*

Converters, which take the form of enclosed chambers with openings below the surface of the sea, can be likened in their function to power stations. The openings allow successive waves to flow into the chamber and back, leading to changes in air pressure sufficient to drive a turbine which, in turn, is connected to a generator that produces electricity. Even with moderate wave motions, there will be sufficient changes in air flows to turn the turbines.

It might sound simple enough but the process is more complex than it seems and there is no single formula on which all are agreed: 'Many concepts are in development, with little to no convergence in technologies.'[259] Construction and maintenance costs for wave converters and cables are high, and investors fear that as more plentiful supplies come on stream the price of energy units for consumers will fall – good news for consumers but not for those waiting for a financial return. Moreover, as with any intrusive activity, there are environmental implications, including the factor of noise from the arrays of converters.

There is no early sign that wave energy will play a leading role in the move towards clean energy. In spite of working models in Australia and Gibraltar, dating from 2015, the rate of global application has been disappointing. However, the natural potential for global development holds great promise and it is quite possible that research progress and higher prices for electricity in the future will increase the feasibility of wave-generated power. In fact, towards the end of 2022 an important new development pointed the way. In a European-led project with 14 international partners, the aim is to trial and demonstrate a novel floating system to capture and convert wave energy. It is the largest of its kind to date and, apart from its floating feature, it works on the same principles as equipment sited at depth.

> *Floating on the ocean's surface, the device incorporates a trapped air volume, with the lower part open to the sea. Wave pressures at the submerged opening cause the water to oscillate and drive the trapped air through a turbine to generate electricity. This energy can be exported to the grid or used in other offshore applications.*[260]

The experimental project costs some 20 million euros and will be put to the test in Atlantic wave conditions. One of the objectives is to see how unit costs for electricity can be reduced (even though this is not necessarily what investors want to see). But, at this stage, price is not the main driver. If not this particular project, there will undoubtedly be others in different parts of the world: the potential of wave energy is just too great to ignore.

## Currents

Ocean currents – invisible and relatively slow-moving – are less dramatic than waves but its advocates argue that it may yet overtake other contenders to become the third-most-important source of renewable energy (with only wind and solar power ahead). In fact, rather like the fabled tortoise and the hare, its promoters find strength in the steady, predictable characteristics:

> *The waterflows in oceans always move in the same direction, mostly at the same speed. Sailors know the currents for trade routes. The speed may vary from two up to five knots of water speed... Instead of increasing from zero to up to eight knots of water speed and*

*changing direction every six hours, ocean currents are constant and very predictable.*[261]

Japanese researchers have recently completed a three-year experiment to demonstrate that it is possible to generate a sufficient volume of electricity to make a useful contribution to the national grid, even though currents are slow-moving.[262] The main problem is that building and maintaining equipment in the path of a permanent current is very costly. In this particular case, turbines were attached on either side of a generator which, in turn was connected to an anchor line that had to be rooted to the ocean floor. Electricity was generated through the current turning the turbines, with the power then transferred along cables which followed the anchor line, and then into the national grid. An indication of the scale of the challenge is that the floating equipment alone weighed more than 330 tons. Little wonder that the earliest that a commercially-viable scheme might be developed is not before the 2030s.

An associated challenge in using currents is that they have to be located with sufficient accuracy to maximise the effectiveness of the required equipment. Specialist computer modelling offers the way forward and some research centres (like Georgia State University in the United States) are seen as leaders in this field.

## Tides

The great attraction of tides is that they are completely predictable; every port, for instance, will have its manual showing with a high level of accuracy when high and low tides will occur in the year ahead. For investors in renewable energy this is a valuable asset that other sources find difficult to match. Each tide brings with it a change in the water level and it is this which is used to turn strategically-placed turbines which then generate electricity. Against that general background, there are, in fact, three main ways in which tidal energy can be harnessed: through tidal streams, barrages, and tidal lagoons.[263] The first of these is a rapidly flowing body of water created naturally by changes in level, from high to low and *vice versa*; the second results from the artificial placing of a barrier, which forces water to fall to a lower level, turning turbines as it does so; and the third is where water is enclosed (naturally or artificially) and power is generated from the changing level.

An important factor, which limits the application of tidal installations, is that not all coastlines experience high levels of tidal change. In any case, it obviously helps if the location is carefully chosen to maximise the impact of tidal waters that flow through a constricted channel, as, for instance, they might do at the mouth of a river. Like all sources of ocean energy generation, installations are expensive, partly because of the difficulties of engineering at sea and, in the case of tidal equipment, because of the need to provide against the relentless impact of heavy flows of water.

*The pioneering Barrage de la Rance in north-west France*

In its favour is the fact that tidal projects have been attracting attention for longer than most other maritime sources, so that an accumulation of experience has been gained. The French scheme at La Rance, an estuary location in the north-western region of Brittany, dates back to the 1960s and is still going strong. This is based on the construction of a barrage, that was enormously costly to build at the time but which, over a lifetime of use, has come to produce cheaper electricity than from other sources. La Rance was the first but is by no means the only large-scale plant generating electricity from tidal forces. South Korea, Canada, Scotland, China, and Russia can all exhibit their own schemes. But in other locations, costs have been prohibitive. For example, at Swansea in South Wales, a proposal that already had a green light to start constructing a lagoon had to be scrapped at the last minute for financial reasons. Too much had already been invested in the concept for it to be lost altogether and in January 2023 a more diverse scheme, called Blue Eden, entirely financed by the private sector, was announced. The first phase would include:

> ...an electric battery manufacturing plant and battery storage facility, a tidal lagoon in Swansea Bay and floating solar farm within it, a data storage centre, a green hydrogen production facility, an oceanic and climate change research centre, and hundreds of waterfront homes. It would take more than a decade to complete.[264]

The signs so far are that tidal energy can offer niche opportunities but, important though those are, it is unlikely to have universal application.

## Hot and cold

Capturing energy from the sea is all about the movement of water and consequent pressures created, with waves, currents and tides (as above) being obvious examples. A further source is derived from temperature changes, based on the fact that water is cooler at depth than it is at the surface.[265] Known as ocean thermal temperature conversion, it depends on a temperature difference of at least 20°C. This effectively limits possible locations to within a range of 30 degrees latitude on either side of the equator, and with a sea depth of at least 1,000 metres.

A system based on this temperature difference was originally tried in Hawaii but was decommissioned in the 1990s. Currently, larger plants are being developed in Hawaii, South China and France, and less powerful applications are being explored for small island states in tropical locations. At this early stage in its possible application, the installation of suitable equipment remains expensive, but the resulting unit cost of electricity is expected to be relatively low.

## Mixing waters

Another source of power is salinity gradient power, resulting from the mixing of waters with different densities of salinity. The essential process is explained as follows:

> ...by placing a semi-permeable membrane between two salt solutions

*of different concentrations, an electrochemical potential difference can be created as the low-concentration solution penetrates the high-concentration solution until the chemical equilibrium is attained. This principle can be applied to generate a large-scale osmotic pressure by the optimal mixing of ocean water and river water.*[266]

Knowledge of this source of creating energy is not new – and it is acknowledged as being remarkably effective – but the location for installations is limited by the fact that they are largely confined to the limited number of places where there is a natural mixing of fresh and salt water – in effect, through the entry of rivers into the sea. This process imposes obvious geographical limits on where conversion takes place. Also, although the technology is well understood, the means of scaling up operations is still at a developmental stage.

## Sun and sea

A very different use of the sea is to take advantage of the space it offers in order to tap into the sun's rays. The way of doing this is through a method known as floating solar photovoltaics.[267] This works on the basis of solar panels mounted on a floating structure which will, ideally, be located in sheltered waters, such as a bay or harbour. It is especially attractive where availability of space on land is limited or expensive, which helps to explain why the ten largest global projects to date are located within reach of cities in Asia. Of these, the most ambitious is a solar platform extending across 1600 hectares, sited in Indonesian waters but designed to serve nearby Singapore. The second-largest project is in South Korea, with India and China also home to large solar platforms.

In principle, the idea of floating platforms further out to sea is more attractive as they would capture a far greater volume of solar power. They are, however, an unlikely contender to play a large part due to the challenges of maintaining installations in rough seas and deep waters, together with the distance from land-based grids.

*Floating solar plant under construction in 2022 on the Silbersee III in Haltern am See, Germany*

## Time for Some Alchemy

One thing is clear. There's all the energy the world needs within the ocean, now and into the distant future. The challenge, though, is to find more ways to transform this potential into usable power, at a competitive price, and to convince governments that this really is a priority. Crashing waves and strong winds far out to sea are one thing; the ability to convert these to run a car or switch on the lights is quite another. Alchemy is the art (or science) of mixing ingredients in a unique blend that might yield nothing less than gold. Or, even surpassing that in value, the very elixir of life. To fulfil the promise of renewable energy, a little magic is needed.

The stage is set for the best of alchemists to get to work. As I have already noted, there are promising signs that they are on the right track. The sun, wind and water are in the crucible, but who can discover the elusive formula? We have come far enough to know where to look, not so much for the names of individuals but at least their provenance. Talent abounds and I would look no further than to scientists who can unlock long-held secrets; to engineers who can design complex yet also sustainable infrastructure to turn ideas into reality; to innovators who see the possibilities and are prepared to form start-ups; and corporations and other businesses prepared to take risks by investing in what are still largely untested products. Scientists, engineers, innovators and business men and women: these are the people who can make the kind of difference needed to produce clean energy from the ocean and to do so on a global scale.

## Ideas, ideas, ideas

Ideas are always the starting point for change. Think back to the eighteenth century when a thoughtful individual watched steam rising from a pan of boiling water and his creative mind wondered how it might be captured rather than allowed to dissipate. Such a simple thought, yet enough to start an economic transformation based on fossil fuels. Think of a later generation of scientists who understood the idea of electricity, and innovators who quickly saw its amazing potential as a universal source of power. Or, to take a more recent example, all those innovators in Silicon Valley who came up with radical ideas and then changed the way we communicate and exchange information. These were all revolutionary episodes in their different ways. I think this is where we are now, waiting for a new generation of change-makers to turn ocean energy into renewable power. Not just waiting, as it is already happening.

Ideas are sometimes appropriated by governments and large corporations but there is room, too, for start-up businesses to make their mark. The scope for new ways to produce and distribute ocean energy is immense. So it is not surprising that new businesses are offering their wares. World Wide Wind, for instance, is a Norwegian company that believes that radical changes in design can enable much larger turbines than those used at present – up to 400 metres in height – which will lead to a drastic fall in costs.[268] Another European start-up, this one based in Munich, is KiteKraft, which is designing and developing a system of flying wind turbines, which is more sustainable in construction, maintenance and after-use than other systems.[269] A third example comes from Spain, where Alerion uses artificial intelligence drone solutions to identify and fix maintenance problems.[270] Once the wheels start to turn there is no knowing where they will lead. Often with start-ups, the outcome is not for large parts of a process but for individual components – an intricate valve, say, or a form of tubing that can withstand deep ocean pressures. Or, perhaps, making sustainable use of discarded materials. These might seem small contributions but they may well be essential and in line with sustainable goals. Revolutions will often start in small, unexpected ways.

Marine engineering is a fast-moving profession that has extended its activities well beyond its traditional base of shipping and port infrastructure, embracing the whole field of ocean energy. It faces enormous challenges and, if it is to overcome these, it has to design a future that is more sustainable and safer to work in than has been the case in the past. To achieve this, a report published by Lloyd's Register Foundation points to eight steps that have to be taken. The report contains valuable detail that merits closer study but, for the purpose of my own review, I will simply refer to the visionary sections which envisage, in each case, where we should be by 2050.

| OCEAN ENGINEERING 2050 SCENARIOS *(after Lloyd's Register Foundation's Foresight Review on Ocean Safety, 2021)* | |
|---|---|
| *Characterise the ocean and seabed* | By 2050: We will have a similar understanding of the ocean environment to that of the terrestrial. This will allow similar assessment of risks to life and property to that on land. With biodiversity and ecosystems characterised, impact of any developments can be understood, assessed and mitigated against. We will also have a clear understanding of the richness of the earth's oceans and this will provide the public with a scientific basis to grant a social license for ocean use. |
| *Advanced materials for and from the oceans* | By 2050: Widespread use of bio-materials from the ocean in disposable and high-waste applications where rapid breakdown is desirable. New medical applications for marine bio-materials e.g. for wound dressing and anti-infection treatment. |
| *Ocean design methodologies* | By 2050: We will have improved our use of stronger materials and new design methodologies, thereby allowing the creation of larger ships and lighter offshore floating systems. Because of safer designs, deep-water aquaculture will have taken over from world fisheries and hundreds of thousands of renewable wind, wave and tidal energy devices will be in operation. |

| OCEAN ENGINEERING 2050 SCENARIOS |
| --- |
| *(after Lloyd's Register Foundation's Foresight Review on Ocean Safety, 2021)* |

| | |
| --- | --- |
| *Multi-use marine structures* | By 2050: Safe designs, underpinned by understanding of combined physics, will optimise the use of ocean spaces with multi-purposes. More efficient structures will result, as will be proven by higher-level sensors, real-time monitoring and whole-of-life costings. |
| *Whole system economic analysis* | By 2050: A validated and widely adopted process will be in operation. This will allow proposed developments and activities in the oceans to be evaluated on a widely accepted basis with public confidence that all factors are reasonably accounted for. This will reduce conflict and protests associated with ocean activities and developments and provide regulators and governments with a fully rational and accepted basis for decision making. |
| *Remote sensing, ocean data and autonomous marine machines* | By 2050: We will have a world-wide ocean sensor network in place, providing volumes of data yet to be imagined. In fact, these streams of data will be making the oceans as well understood as land. Navies of autonomous drones will be used to build, operate and monitor multi-purpose infrastructure, minimising the ocean as a human workplace. |
| *Ocean cleaning and maintenance* | By 2050: Recovery technologies in second or third generation and able to recover microplastics. Volume of plastic waste in oceans being reduced by 20 per cent, per year. Waste recovery will be taking place in the oceans via vessels for cleaning up plastics and other pollution. |
| *Ocean education* | By 2050: As education is intergenerational, the impact of changing the approach to ocean engineering education will take time. We will see the development of holistic engineers, able to cross disciplines (such as environmental awareness and design), and thereby present complete infrastructure solutions. The public will have a greater understanding of how the ocean can be safely and sustainably developed, providing confidence that scientifically rigorous decisions are being made |
| *Whole system economic analysis* | By 2050: A validated and widely adopted process will be in operation. This will allow proposed developments and activities in the oceans to be evaluated on a widely accepted basis with public confidence that all factors are reasonably accounted for. This will reduce conflict and protests associated with ocean activities and developments and provide regulators and governments with a fully rational and accepted basis for decision making. |

## *Making it pay*

Offshore wind energy is now a global business – a vital source of power and a major employer (often in locations which could previously offer little in the way of economic opportunities). But it has all happened very quickly. Indeed, one of the most remarkable features of the industry is how much has been achieved in a very short space of time.

It was only in 1991 that Vindeby, the world's first offshore wind farm, went into operation off the coast of Denmark. With just 11 turbines and a 4.95 megawatt output it would soon be dwarfed by later developments, but it was then a pioneer and paved the way for an emergent industry. After a quarter of a century it was decommissioned but it had by then already done its job – not only through producing cheap energy but, more importantly, demonstrating that ocean-based wind farms were possible. Such would be the future.

One of the other lessons of Vindeby was that, even then, with its modest output, the development called for major investment by a proven company, in that case, Siemens. Wind farms require constant research and development; a substantial outlay for construction, well before any returns can be expected; and the employment and management of a large and diverse labour force. There is room for start-ups and small businesses to serve different aspects of the enterprise but, at the top of the tree of activities, only the largest and best-resourced can hope to thrive. To illustrate the process, there is the fascinating story of Ørsted.[271]

*The Danish Company, Ørsted, has made a remarkable change in its core business, now setting the international pace for renewable energy production*

The present company originated in 2006 (at first, under another name) through the merger of six Danish energy companies, with the state the majority shareholder. At the heart of the business was power production from fossil fuels, mainly coal but also oil and natural gas, and the growth trajectory was for more of the same. Renewable energy – including the pioneer site of Vindeby – formed only a small part of its profile yet, within two years of the new company's formation, a decision was taken to run down its fossil fuel interests in favour of green energy.

> *We must create a completely different energy system, where the majority of the world's energy comes from the infinite amounts of naturally occurring energy sources, such as the wind and sun.*[272]

In making this decision, account was taken of growing concerns about climate change and public opposition to new coal-generated power plants. A switch on this scale was considered at the time as a high-risk decision – as, indeed, it must have been – but major investments were set in train to turn the company in a new direction. The company bought in to wind-farm development off the coast of England, a deal was struck with Siemens for the latter to build no fewer than 500 turbines (more than existed across the world at the time), and a turbine-installation company was bought so that more control could be exercised over the whole process.

The main challenge to be overcome was that the costs of green energy production were greater than for conventional fuels. It was predicted that these costs would be reduced to a competitive rate as the scale of new operations increased, but what was to be done in the interim? In a game-changing move, Ørsted in 2012 cut its costs dramatically and relied on their predictions for the years ahead. It was a difficult choice but investments in very large-scale farms helped to secure the cost fall; by 2019, the costs of producing electricity from offshore wind was well below that using natural gas, coal or nuclear power.

When the company set out on its new venture it was expected that it would take a generation to complete. In fact, it achieved this within a decade – inverting its own activities and internationalising its reach: 'Harvard Business Review ranked the Ørsted transformation as one of the top business transformations of the decade.'[273] It won deserved acclamation for a milestone project and a significant boost for efforts to reduce the impact of global warming.

Such are the fortunes of a single company. There are other ways, too, in which the offshore wind industry is making its mark, not least of all through stimulating growth in ports that can provide new services. Take, for instance, the case of Hull, on England's north-east coast, close to the major wind-farm developments in the North Sea. Once Britain's busiest fishing port, with the decline of that activity its economic future looked bleak. Instead, in an unpredicted reversal, Hull has emerged as a hub for the new industry of offshore energy. As one of the major investors in the city, Siemens explained why the area was chosen for its manufacturing operations:

> *The Humber [on which Hull is located] is an enormously attractive river because of its sheer scale. There are no height restrictions, we can take the towers out vertically, and there was lots of space and good access to the sea. Hull offered the neatest solution for us. The UK's offshore wind programme is mostly down the east coast too, and some of the largest projects in the world lie adjacent to the Humber Estuary.*[274]

The implications of this choice are many – ranging from the manufacture of components for the hundreds of wind turbines required, specialist shipping services to transport them to offshore locations, restructured storage and loading facilities, not to mention training for the numerous new jobs on offer. Flat land is not in short supply on either side of the Humber Estuary, where Hull is located, and the Able Marine Energy Park has beenbuilt on the south bank to cater for specialist needs. As with any thriving industry, there are indirect as well as direct benefits, with the parallel growth of a range of support services including cafes and hotel accommodation, real estate and transport.

Too often, the costs of net zero are overstated at the expense of the benefits, but the story shows the folly of being too cautious. For one thing, the unmistakable trend is that, as the industry scales up, so one sees a steady and sometimes dramatic reduction of costs. A second reason is that, quite apart from the central objective of supporting the move to net zero, there are numerous other benefits that can accrue in communities like Hull, where traditional sources of employment have declined. I am not always optimistic about the prospect of development as it undoubtedly has its costs as well, but this is one case where I believe that it is leading to beneficial change.

# Chapter 8

# Hidden Treasure
## *Can seabed mining be sustainable?*

Beneath the vast expanse of the ocean surface lies another world. At first, around the shores, the continental shelf is little more than an extension of the adjoining landmass. But then one reaches the edge of the abyss and, with the sudden drop that follows, everything changes. Remarkably, in view of what is known about the rest of the planet, and even outer space, most of the ocean floor remains largely undiscovered. The scientific consensus is that only 5 per cent of the deep sea has been explored in any detail.[275] When a passenger jet was lost somewhere in the Indian Ocean in 2014, rescuers floundered without definitive maps of the maritime space and its currents at different depths that might have helped in their search.

*(Above and overleaf) The deep sea is a fascinating but still largely unknown part of our planet*

At least we have a broad impression of the most prominent features of the seabed. There is an average depth of some 3,800 metres before one reaches the ocean floor, a surface every bit as diverse as the terrestrial landscape. Here, one finds mountain ranges and peaks that match and even surpass the height of those on land; a mid-ocean ridge that wends its way over a length of 40,000 kilometres between continents around the globe; seemingly endless plains and deep ravines; unexpected gradient falls that plunge, in one location, to more than 11,000 metres below the surface; scattered eruptions of warm waters (known as hydrothermal vents) emanating from the earth's interior, which create their own ecosystems; as well as much larger, active volcanoes capable of upsetting the rhythms of the sea far beyond their own points of turbulence; and, in contrast with hydrothermal vents, cold methane seeps which also give rise to their own (albeit very different) micro life systems. Underlying these individual features is a dynamic platform of tectonic plates, responsible for varied geological formations in the past and still capable of causing further movement.

Such is the remarkable physical backcloth for a new era of underwater activity – mining for an array of metals – that is currently high on the commercial and political agenda for ocean development. There is growing pressure from multi-national consortia working with individual countries, small as well as large, to go beyond the present limits of exploration, with a view to widespread excavation. In the face of these forces, this is highly likely to happen, in one form or another, in the near future. But is there any chance that the kind of activity, on the scale contemplated, can be reconciled with the Blue Economy goal of sustainability? I have great concerns about the advent of deep-ocean mining, which I believe can only be seen as an inherently intrusive form of development. And I am not alone in fearing for the future. We are at a turning point in the exploration and use of the ocean; we only have one chance to get it right. So, in this chapter, my aim is to review the arguments, for and against, and see if and how the potential impact of seabed mining can be restrained, if not totally prevented. The very integrity of a sustainable Blue Economy is dependent on the outcome.

## The Last Frontier

What treasure is it that exists on the seabed that justifies an expensive, risky and difficult set of operations to extract?[276] To answer this, first of all a distinction needs to be made between what can be found on the continental shelf, in relatively shallow waters which are within the jurisdiction of individual countries, and the great expanse of the deep seabed that lies within the High Seas.[277] In the former areas, one form of extraction is a well-established activity, with oil and natural gas the prize. So long as mining by the respective countries is contained within the boundaries of their EEZs, they are legally free to undertake their own operations (albeit within recommended international guidelines). The new frontier, however, is beyond the continental shelf, in the abyssal reaches of the ocean floor. In the past, the technical difficulties and levels of investment needed to operate in these conditions have deterred potential operators from seeking permission to excavate. More recently, especially over the past decade or so, the sheer volume of minerals that seems to be available and high market prices, coupled with the advance of robotics and extraction technologies, has brought even the deepest stretches of the ocean within the realms of commercial viability. As an illustration, a Chinese explorer who plumbed the depths of the world's deepest trench in an advanced submersible reported that he could see for himself abundant evidence of minerals, adding that further dives would reveal a 'treasure map' of the previously inaccessible and unknown seabed.[278]

On the basis of a series of explorations in seas around the world, the list of minerals to be found in the deepest parts of the ocean is becoming irresistible for countries and corporations alike. The potential costs of extraction will be enormous but so, too, the returns. Gold, platinum, copper, cobalt, nickel, manganese, lead, lithium, titanium and zinc are amongst the treasures that might soon be brought to the surface.[279] More descriptively, with an indication of their practical value:

> *Copper, nickel and cobalt can all be found at high concentrations, in mineral deposits, as can the so-called 'critical' metals. These include the rare earth elements used in a range of new technologies such as memory chips, LEDs and batteries for electric vehicles. It is thought the mountains of the Pacific alone could contain about 22 times more tellurium – which is used in solar panels – than the known land-based reserves combined.*[280]

Paradoxically, some of the identified seabed minerals are used in products designed to reduce dependence on fossil fuels, such as car batteries and solar panels. One set of environmental goals is, therefore, potentially in conflict with another. In the understandable rush to develop renewable energy, little thought seems to have been given to the hidden costs of extracting essential minerals from the ocean floor. If sustainability is to be achieved, the potential balance between means and ends still needs to be assessed.

Historically, the world's frontiers were there to be crossed, the only constraints being the limits of human vision and endeavour. In the present century, however, there is a belief that decisions on a global scale should be regulated by international bodies, so that benefits can be enjoyed by all of humanity. In the case of the inter-related ocean, the agency of the UN charged with this responsibility is the International Seabed Authority (ISA). To date, this body has so far allowed exploration in the High Seas but has not issued licences for excavation. But the pressures to relent on the latter are immense and it is unlikely that these will be resisted for much longer. Indeed, the clock is already ticking, in the face of an application for seabed mining by a member nation (in fact, the smallest nation in the world), namely, the Pacific island of Nauru. With its environment and social structure devastated by a long history of phosphate mining, it is now seeking to take its chances through another form of excavation.

Backed by international investors, Nauru has pressed the button to initiate a whole new process. Finding a loophole in the ability of the international authority to forestall development, a bid was made to allow the mining of a vast area of the Pacific, most of which lies well beyond Nauru's own jurisdiction. Thus, in June 2021 the President of that country lodged a letter with the International Seabed Authority, claiming the right (in the absence of agreed regulations) to begin development within two years. The letter proclaimed 'the intention of Nauru Ocean Resources Inc (NORI), a subsidiary of a Canadian company called DeepGreen (*sic*, renamed the Metal Company following a merger in 2021),[281] to apply for approval to begin mining in July 2023'. It chose as its venue an area known as the Clarion-Clipperton Zone (CCZ), in the North Pacific Ocean between Hawaii and Mexico.[282]

Nauru, of course, was just the 'front' for the consortium as it is only sovereign nations which are permitted to make an application in this way. But it was clear that all parties to the application were drawn by what lies on the floor of the ocean, while being dismissive of what critics claimed would, inevitably, be adverse impacts. In the words of a recent article:

> *DeepGreen is looking to extract polymetallic nodules from the seabed. The nodules, which resemble potatoes and are thought to take millions of years to form, are rich in manganese, nickel, cobalt and rare earth metals, key components of batteries for electric vehicles. DeepGreen argues deep-sea mining is a less environmentally and socially damaging alternative to terrestrial mining, and is crucial for transitioning to a greener economy.*[283]

This cameo is, of course, only an early example of a process which will progressively spread across the ocean floor. In spite of DeepGreen's contention that it would be less damaging than mining on land, it is hard to make a comparison between one activity which is well-tried and documented and another which is still a largely unknown quantity. All one can say at this present juncture is that environmentalists are overwhelmingly opposed to the prospect of large-scale ocean mining. Why is this so?

*The simple form of a nodule conceals its value as a source of coveted minerals*

## Opening the Treasure Chest

One only has to see how the various seabed minerals are distributed and the different ways in which they will be extracted to understand why environmentalists are so concerned. On the basis of our present knowledge (which, significantly, remains partial, in spite of the gung-ho claims of potential developers) there are three forms of mineral deposit on the ocean floor: polymetallic nodules, polymetallic sulphides *[sic]*[284] and cobalt crusts. To describe these (and to indicate how they would be extracted), I can do no better than call on the respective descriptions provided by Pew's scientists.[285] Thus:

> *Polymetallic nodules contain rich concentrations of manganese, nickel, copper, and cobalt. They are found in abundance in a few ocean basins, most notably the Clarion-Clipperton Zone (CCZ), a great abyssal plain as wide as the continental United States, that lies 4,000 to 6,000 meters below the surface of the eastern Pacific Ocean. Billions of the potato-size nodules are scattered on top of or half-embedded within the muddy bottom of the CCZ. Their exploitation would probably involve scraping 5 to 10 centimeters (2 to 4 inches) off the top of the abyssal plain, separating the nodules from the mud,*

*pumping the nodules to a surface ship by means of a giant tube, and returning the entrained water and fine particles through another tube.*

**Poymetallic sulphide** *deposits are found in areas of underwater volcanic activity and seafloor spreading, usually at depths of 1,000 to 4,000 meters. Deposits are often located near tectonic plate boundaries. Hydrothermal vents release superheated, mineral-rich solutions. As these solutions cool, the minerals precipitate out, forming towers on the seafloor with high concentrations of valuable minerals. Deposits formed by these eruptions, along with shallow subsurface deposits, could provide rich but moderately sized areas for mineral exploitation. Operations would remove the sulfide-rich deposits and return water and fine particles through a tube.*

**Cobalt crusts,** *[where] concentrations of valuable minerals are often found on the sides and summits of underwater mountains. The richest deposits are found at depths of 800 to 2,500 meters as crusts of seamounts in the western Pacific. Crust thicknesses can reach 25 centimeters (almost 10 inches), but more typical deposits run to 10 to 15 centimeters (4 to 6 inches). The basic mode of exploitation would be to remove the cobalt-rich layer on the seamount surface while leaving behind the less valuable rock beneath it.*

Each of three types of mineral reserve will require different methods of excavation, all of which will be highly destructive of the seabed environment.[286] Thus, in the case of polymetallic nodules, scattered in large quantities across the abyssal plains, the process of extraction can be likened to a vacuum cleaner that sucks up the mineral-bearing nodules (which is what is intended for the Clarion-Clipperton Zone). It is an indiscriminate process that takes no account of what is believed to be a vast range of existing suspension feeders and sediment communities on the ocean floor. Those which are not destroyed at the time of extraction will likely be covered with resultant sediment that returns following disturbance to cover the floor. Nor is the method used to extract polymetallic sulphides – a potential source of gold, silver, copper and zinc – from hydrothermal vents, any kinder to the environment. The pockets of warm water where these occur are recognised as havens that support some of the most unique and important ecological communities on the planet, yet all will be at risk. Finally, a different method is used to strip and scrape cobalt-rich crusts that encase seamounts.

This, too, will be a destructive process, especially as seamounts are recognised as biodiversity hotspots, supporting complex ecosystems from peak to base.

The volume of minerals retrieved in any one of these ways is likely to be considerable and, so the developers argue, of widespread benefit to humanity, but there is no doubt that each of the extraction methods is intrinsically destructive. Habitats that will be removed in a matter of hours may have taken eons to evolve and (as current and recent explorations show) contain species not previously known to science. It is obvious, in general terms, that the impact of extraction in each of these situations will be damaging but, while this cannot easily be denied, developers claim that the potential benefits outweigh environmental costs. It is all very vague and the fact is that, in each of the three clusters, there is a whole new world yet to be discovered. To allow mining to start without fully understanding its implications would be a travesty.

> Of the three habitat types vulnerable to mining – abyssal plains with polymetallic nodules, hydrothermal vents with massive sulphides and seamounts with cobalt-rich ferromanganese crusts, the last – especially in the Prime Crust Zone (an area in the West Pacific identified as of the greatest economic interest for mining cobalt-rich crusts) – are the least explored, hence their biodiversity has not yet been characterised. Even in polymetallic nodule zones, thought [only 40-50 years ago] to be bereft of life... four decades of research by contractors and scientific organisations in the nodule-rich CCZ (Clarion-Clipperton Zone) show that environments and associated biodiversity remain largely undiscovered or unidentified. And while hydrothermal vents are the most characterised and understood of the three habitats, many species at vents appear to be rare... and poorly known.[287]

Not enough is known about how extraction will affect the immediate areas of mining, regardless of wider implications. Thus, the direct removal of minerals will also displace and probably destroy faunal communities in the delicately-balanced ecosytems at depth. In other ways, too, the seafloor will be changed, for instance, as a result of sediment plumes caused by disturbance, with adverse effects on living organisms. There will be temporary increases in sound, vibration and light, the effects of which remain unknown. So, too, contaminant release will have its effects and water properties will be changed. In the scheme of things, these might all seem like relatively minor intrusions that in some circumstances could be accommodated, but the one thing that is known is that the recipient ecosystems are extraordinarily fragile and may be unable to recover.[288]

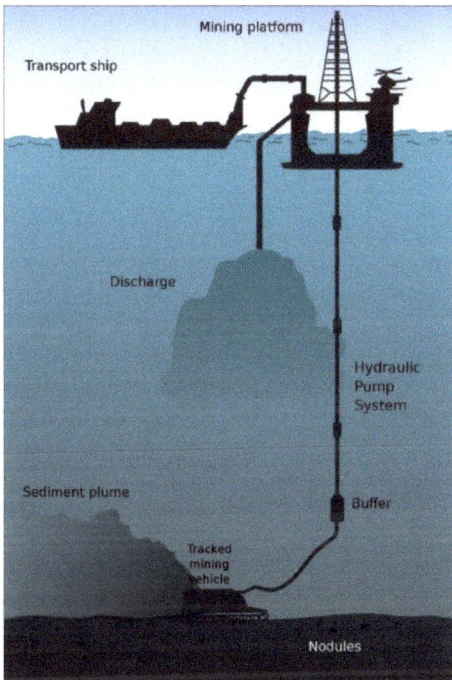

*Methods of deep-sea mining will vary but the essential principle of drawing minerals to the surface is a constant*

Little wonder that the message which aptly expresses the concerns of environmentalists is 'delay until we know more'. There is simply too much at stake to risk irreversible damage to a unique part of the planet that has, in places, taken millions of years to evolve. Not surprisingly, the call for a moratorium has come from many quarters, one of the most effective voices being the DeepSea *[sic]* Conservation Coalition, which has brought together more than 90 NGOs, fishing representatives, and law and policy institutes. The most consistent argument for deep-sea mining is that it is essential in providing a future supply of minerals on which the world has become dependent. But this is not true, counters the Coalition, arguing that, instead, 'we should be concentrating on reforming terrestrial mining practices, choosing materials with least environmental impact, developing the technology and systems for reducing the use of raw materials, improving recycling and transitioning to a circular economy'.[289]

The point of a moratorium is that it offers an opportunity for collaborative research so that the environmental, social and economic impacts of this new form of development are better known. It also enables studies to identify ways in which deep-sea mining can be managed 'in a way that protects the marine environment and prevents biodiversity loss, habitat degradation and species extinction'.[290] Additionally, if some mining does go ahead, there are social implications with a consequent need to ensure that local communities are not excluded from any benefits by consortia with their own commercial priorities. And (as we will see in a later section) the regulating authorities themselves need to be examined to ensure they are fit for purpose. In short, as many experts warn, to rush ahead without more knowledge of the process is to take needless risks, with irrevocable consequences, yet for no good reason. Quite simply, 'the rush to mine this pristine and unexplored environment risks creating terrible impacts that cannot be reversed'.[291] So, the question is asked, why not pause until the science can provide responsible guidance for our actions?

## Into the Abyss

There is nothing like practical experience to demonstrate what is involved, and so it was that an early test case brought many of the issues surrounding deep-sea mining to the fore. In this, the impoverished nation of Papua New Guinea saw what it thought was an easy opportunity to change its fortunes. With the prospect of retrieving massive sulphide reserves from a swathe of the ocean floor between the Bismarck and Solomon Seas, within its own jurisdiction, the government awarded an exploration licence to a Canadian mining company, Nautilus Minerals Ltd. As well as numerous voices of reason from the scientific world, calling for restraint, there were also concerns amongst small island states in the region, like Fiji and Vanuatu, which could see the potential downsides of too hastily embracing the process and uncritically accepting the arguments put by potential developers.[292] Immune to criticism, however, permission granted by its own government to explore was soon followed by consent to allow mining to start, even though, in practical terms, this awaited the completion of a specially-designed ship with bespoke equipment. Bedazzled by the figures, the PNG government went further than the role of enabler by itself opting to purchase a 30 per cent stake in the project. Clearly, in doing so the signatories had not heard of the old adage, 'if you choose to sup with the devil be sure you use a long spoon', for it was soon apparent that they had taken on more risk than could be supported and were out of their depth in the world of high finance.[293] In the following years, the project floundered and by the end of 2019, before the new ship had been delivered, the Canadian company was declared bankrupt. That left the PNG government exposed to debts amounting to $120 million.

Opponents of the scheme – globally and from local communities which had also been opposed to development – rejoiced in its demise, claiming not only that they were in the right in this case, but also that the collapse of the project heralded the end of deep-sea mining in general before it had even started. The euphoria, however, was short-lived as it proved to be the particular project that had failed and not necessarily the bigger programme for mining that was still gathering momentum. Being first in line is a risky business as there is the question of funding invention as well as paying for the application of tried-and-tested products. Nautilus clearly tried to do both at the same time and sunk under the weight of its heady ambitions. But it was certainly not, as its critics had hoped, the end of deep-sea mining. Far from it. Economic historians will know that industrial transformation is littered with similar stories, of businesses lured by the prospect of early profits that get ahead of themselves and fail in the process. Those that follow them, however, can learn from mistakes made and are better placed to succeed.

Into the space left by Nautilus, larger companies like DeepGreen (also Canadian) were quick to bid for new opportunities, especially in the Pacific High Seas. By early 2022, the ISA had issued 31 exploration contracts across different parts of the world. Grant-holders, in the form of state-backed enterprises and private companies, were given exclusive rights to explore what lay within their allotted territory and to study the marine environment therein but not at that stage to extract minerals. Nineteen of these contracts are located in the Pacific Ocean, where polymetallic nodules are especially abundant, allowing exploration (in most cases until the end of this decade) across vast zones.[294]

The environmental case against the activities of developers is powerful but so, too, are the reasons advanced to go ahead, driven by financial facts and projections. Business analysts point, not to the micro-organisms in the sea floor that survive in seemingly impossible conditions against all the odds, nor to the thousands of years it takes for sediment to accumulate even by as little as a millimetre, but, instead, to prices for minerals on the stock markets. In the words of one such analyst: 'Experts expect the global metals and minerals market to have a compound annual growth rate of more than 8 per cent between now and 2026 as the energy transition accelerates.'[295] And in this expectation lies the main incentive to invest in such a high-risk industry: 'The anticipated growth of the mining industry has encouraged Wall Street analysts to bet big on the commodities market.'[296]

To support their case, the main players are quick to claim that the new metals will be used to counter the rate of climate change, as a result of enabling the production of equipment for renewable energy generation and to enable mass production of battery-powered vehicles. In a wider sales pitch, the case is made for new generations of mobile phones and exciting breakthroughs in communications technology. Although these are sweeping claims that can be picked apart, the fact remains that, on the face of it, they have popular appeal.

Proponents can also point to advances in equipment that will make even the deepest operations a reality. An important aspect of this is to perfect ways in which seabed mining can take place remotely, creating a safer process than has traditionally been the case with terrestrial mines. Submersibles, for instance, are being used at the exploration stage, and these can be controlled remotely or through a human presence. One example is the Alvin:

> ...a human-occupied submersible that can carry two scientists and a pilot to a depth of nearly 5,000 metres. It allows researchers to observe and collect data for more than two-thirds of the ocean floor.[297]

Some of the new developments are specifically designed for the actual retrieval of minerals and these will constantly evolve as more experience is gained. In contrast, many of the technologies are already in use for other applications, with or without modifications for this particular activity. For example:

> Several technological innovations are expected to drive innovation in metals over the next decade from 3D printing to artificial intelligence and big data analytics. The use of drones in mining projects is also expected to make operations more efficient thanks to better monitoring, surveying, and mapping techniques to repair faults, manage inventory, and enhance site safety.[298]

In turning a vision of deep-ocean mining into a reality, the major powers are leading the way. Take, for example, the case of India. Although it cannot at this stage begin to engage in mining, it is investing heavily in the means to do so. Engineers at the National Institute of Ocean Technology have developed a deep-sea excavation machine, Varaha-1, which has already been successfully tested in a central stretch of the Indian Ocean to a depth of more than 5,000 metres.

> *The 9.5-tonne machine was carefully lowered into the ocean waters using a high strength umbilical cable. It weighs 3.5 tonnes in the water due to the buoyancy. The descent of the mining machine to the seabed generally takes about 3.5-4 hours. This spot, where the large machine was lowered, is part of the 75,000 sq. km. area allocated to India by the International Seabed Authority (ISA), for conducting exploratory deep-seabed mining.*[299]

The attraction of this venture is the plentiful supply of polymetallic nodules in the Indian Ocean, which will meet India's demands in this field for the foreseeable future. With successful tests to date, the country is geared up for an international agreement that will enable mining in the region to begin as soon as permission is given.

One can be sure that if either India or China is making plans, the other major Asian power will be monitoring the situation and doing likewise. China is known for its long-term perspective in geopolitical matters and has been patiently building its presence within the International Seabed Authority itself. With its own permanent mission in Jamaica (where the offices of the ISA are located) critics say it is in a strong position to influence decisions.[300] Led by state-owned enterprises, China's approach is 'long-term, strategic and politically orchestrated'.[301] With five exploration contracts, it has more than any other country and clearly aims to reinforce its dominance in markets for rare metals and rare earth elements. Like India, China has been active in developing its own technology to enable extraction when permission is given, with successful tests of a prototype machine termed Pioneer 1 carried out in the South China Sea.

Nor is it just the major powers which are committed to deep-sea mining exploration, as the case of Nauru has already shown. Other Pacific nations with a strong interest in this activity include Kiribati, Tonga and the Cook Islands. Elsewhere, in the Indian Ocean the small island state of Mauritius has also declared its intent, reinforced with the preparation of legislation to regulate how the new activity can be managed within its own waters.[302] Beyond the limits of its EEZ boundaries, there is also the possibility of aligning itself with larger nations and consortia that have identified the mid-ocean area as a rich source of ocean-floor minerals. It can be no coincidence, too, that Mauritius stands to gain from the probable transfer from Britain of the mid-ocean Chagos archipelago, another potentially rich location for seabed minerals, into its own domain.

## An Uneven Contest

If ever there were an uneven contest it must be this. On the one side, all the might of the major powers – aided and abetted by lesser ones too – with the practical involvement of international consortia with the 'know how' to excavate and the backing of the world's money markets. Previously unimagined machinery, the stuff of science fiction, has already been designed with the capacity to descend thousands of metres to the ocean floor, pre-programmed to vacuum and scrape, drill, and remove living organisms and innate particles before propelling the treasured harvest through vertical pipes to the surface for further processing. In contrast, on the other side, are those who urge the protection of an ecosystem that until now has been left for millennia to evolve undisturbed.

*The sheer bulk and mechanics of deep-sea mining equipment is incompatible with the fragile ecosystems at depth*

The arena for this contest is the deep sea, where neither side really has a full picture of what is there. But we do know enough to visualise the tiniest creatures and plant life defying all expectations of life in the cold, dark conditions of the deepest stretches of the ocean. It has been a long, slow process of evolution but the reality is that each area that comes within reach of seabed miners could disappear overnight. Which side of this uneven contest will 'win'? What will be the outcome? Even by the time this book is written it is probable that crucial decisions will have been taken but, at present, one can only point to possible scenarios.

At one extreme, let us imagine that the outcome is a permanent veto on any deep-sea mining across the High Seas. Experts from the High Level Panel for Ocean Sustainability argue that this option is only feasible if it is accompanied by a search for alternative mineral sources and lifestyle changes: 'Refocus on initiatives that enable transition to circular economies with emphasis on metal demand reduction through reuse, recycling, alternative materials, extended product lifetimes and behavioural change.'[303] I for one, would favour a permanent veto but, with the experience of a lifetime in politics, I fear the chances of achieving this in its entirety are slender. The immense political and commercial pressures for development will not so lightly be cast aside. Preventing deep-sea mining would be a victory for the environment and integrity of the planet but one only has to look at the annual climate change conventions, where convincing arguments are not enough to win the day, to see how unlikely such an outcome will be.

At the other extreme, is it possible that the pendulum will rest in the opposite direction, opening the High Seas to seafloor excavation with only a minimum of restraints. China, India, Russia, the United States, and other major powers are ready to take advantage of what would simply become a race to extract the most, with, one might fear, no account taken of the consequences. Retrieve what is needed to supply batteries for electric vehicles and renewable energy equipment (perhaps worthy causes in themselves) and leave it to future generations to count the immeasurable costs:

> Biodiversity and its ecological functions in the areas impacted could be lost, possibly irreparably. The scale and ramifications of those impacts – as well as the extent to which the mining will lead to overall benefit for humankind – are hard to predict on current knowledge.[304]

Or is it more realistic to be looking at other scenarios, somewhere between these extremes, where there are opportunities to compromise? Taking a lead from the new practice of marine spatial plans within national jurisdictions, why not designate parts of the ocean floor for development, with the rest left undisturbed as permanent sub-marine sanctuaries? From the viewpoint of the Blue Economy this would be far from ideal – the areas where mining could take place being vast (one of the exploratory areas is as wide as the landmass of the United States) – but it would be preferable to allowing a total 'free for all' akin to a nineteenth-century gold rush.

Over and above different scenarios, there is the simple expedient of extending the period of the moratorium to allow not only more information to be collected about the impact of deep-sea mining but also to explore alternative ways of meeting global demand for metals. Significantly, it could also encourage the involvement of a wider range of stakeholders, rather than leaving crucial decisions in the hands of an international organisation which seems far from fit for purpose. We have waited for millennia to reach this point; surely a few more years would not be too much to ask for. Time itself is a precious resource which should not be squandered in needless haste.

*Exploration licences have been granted but there is widespread opposition to going beyond these to the point of excavation*

## Is the Arbiter Fit for Purpose?

In the face of the above, what attempts are being made to create an orderly process? Can we rely on an international regulator to do so? There is, indeed, such a body but, as I have pointed out in earlier chapters, international regulators are only as strong as their member states allow them to be. Lines of authority are by no means always clear or effective. Thus, whereas globalisation remains a concept, nation states are real, and the fulfilment of the former depends on the agreement of the latter.

The regulating body in this case, the International Seabed Authority, has been negotiating for years to bring a semblance of order to development across the High Seas, so far without conclusive outcomes. Faced now with the challenge of providing ground rules for ocean-floor mining, and then ensuring their enforcement, the prospects are even more uncertain. While no one could reasonably disagree with the mandate of the Authority, being 'to protect and preserve the marine environment', the machinery of governance is cumbersome and often opaque. With its 167 member states (plus the European Union), it has to find a way through a maze of widely divergent interests, in the context of a system where decisions are made more difficult by various rights of veto. Another weakness is that a key committee with a membership of 30, designed to provide expert advice on applications for licences, contains only three members with specialisms in marine ecosytems.[305] The major powers are not easily persuaded to ignore their own priorities, while lesser nations (especially some small island states) see in deep-sea mining an unprecedented opportunity to strengthen fragile economies. The situation is not helped by the United States, which has not ratified the United Nations Convention on the Law of the Sea and is thereby excluded from ISA membership. In principle, this leaves it free to evade regulations and conduct its own operations.

At one point, the ISA planned to produce a code for deep-sea mining by 2020 but this has repeatedly been pushed back. The significance of the Nauru intervention is that it sets a deadline of July 2023, by which time either the ISA provides a set of agreed rules or that particular consortium (and by implication, within another two years, all of the others with exploratory licences) will be free to move to the next stage, which is actual excavation. That will signal the end of arguments to delay until more is known about the effects on the marine environment, even though, by the end of 2022, more countries were pressing for an extension to the moratorium. Only France was calling for an outright ban, 'while Germany joined Palau, Fiji, Samoa, the Federated States of Micronesia, New Zealand, Costa Rica, Chile, Spain, Ecuador and Panama in calling for a precautionary pause, precautionary delay or moratorium' to allow more research.[306]

Few observers seem to believe that suitable regulations can be finalised before the 2023 enforced deadline. But, equally, all the signs are that unless changes are made to the decision-making body itself, it will not be too long before exploitation, more widely, will be allowed. The scenario tells its own story, with some nations still wanting to slow the process while key powers like China and India have completed their preparations and are ready to start. At the root of concerns, assert critics, is the suspect role of the supposedly-neutral decision-making body. First, Greenpeace in 2019 launched an attack on the ISA, pointing to its undemocratic structure and failure to take proper account of scientific advice.[307] Since then, in the absence of a positive response, confidence has waned and further criticism was never far below the surface. The unsatisfactory state of affairs was all-too-evident when, in April 2022, an inflammatory article appeared in the LA Times, basically accusing the CEO of the Authority of being too closely associated with the deep-sea mining industry and of enabling the ISA to fund a training business that it was itself supposed to regulate.[308] Rejection of the claims was not helped when a senior marine geologist (formerly working in the organisation) declared that 'the ISA is not fit to regulate any activity in international waters'. This was supported by another former employee (a marine biologist who served as the authority's scientific affairs officer for five years until late-2018), claiming 'that the current secretariat is very much in favor of deep seabed mining, and it's no secret that it perceived that environmental conservation would be more hindering than helping mining'.[309]

*Responsibility to grant permission for deep-sea excavation rests with the UN International Seabed Authority*

## A Question of Ethics

In the very deepest reaches of the ocean, new species are yet to be found. It was only in 2018, for instance, that in the Mariana Trench, the deepest point in the ocean, scientists discovered the existence of snailfish. These are quite widespread in shallower waters but it was not previously thought that any fish could survive in such hostile conditions. Somehow the snailfish has managed to do so. Described as 'ghostly white', it has no scales, large teeth and (contrary to other species in the deep ocean) does not create its own light. As far as presently known, it offers no material value to humans and poses no threat. So would it matter if mining operations led to its rapid demise? After all, humans have managed quite well so far without encountering this deep-water creature and have not even known about it until now.

To my mind, it does matter. The continued existence of species cannot be judged according to their material value, nor even to whether all but a few deep-sea scientists will ever witness them. Who are we to decide whether one component or another of the planet should be removed for all time? Ethics must surely come into the reckoning and the snailfish is as much a part of our universe as anything else. In fact, it should be seen, not as an isolated example but as representative of the many thousands of other species that inhabit the ocean, largely out of sight and out of mind. Thus, very recently, scientists discovered another five thousand previously unknown species in one of the very areas in the Pacific that has currently been granted an exploration licence.[310]

In determining the particular case of seabed mining – whether to develop or not to develop – there is the essential question of doing what is right or wrong for the world. For me, it seems inherently right that the last frontier of our badly-scarred planet should be spared from further ravages. I know that simply to assert this is not enough but it surely has to be a weapon in the environmentalists' armoury. Ethics is by its very nature based on an abstract set of concepts and arguments, but even these are based on a view of reality. Perhaps the best way to make this particular case is to remind ourselves of the hidden wonders of the deep ocean. Ideally, everyone should have a chance to experience for themselves the breathtaking transition that happens beneath the surface of the sea. Each zone passed through in the long journey down to the seabed is home to completely different ecosystems. To offer a succinct portrayal of the changes,

I will borrow from an illustrative article by a scientist at the Smithsonian in Washington DC:

> *Most are familiar with the surface layer, which extends down 650 feet (200 m) and receives the most sunlight, allowing photosynthetic organisms like phytoplankton to convert sunlight to energy. It is the home of pods of dolphins, schools of fish, and shoals of sharks. Scientists refer to this highly productive area as the epipelagic zone.*
>
> *But the majority of the space in the ocean is a dark world. Dive below the epipelagic and you will enter the mesopelagic zone. Also known as the twilight zone, this area receives only faint, filtered sunlight, allowing no photosynthetic organisms to survive. Many animals have adapted to the near-darkness with large eyes and counterillumination.*
>
> *Beginning with the bathypelagic zone, the ocean is completely void of light from the sun, moon and stars. Animals create their own bioluminescent light and, if they haven't lost them, have highly light-sensitive eyes to see the light produced by other animals. The water temperature is near freezing. Travel deeper and you will find the abyssopelagic zone – the abyss. And finally, the deepest reaches of the ocean are found at the bottom of precipitous trenches. These locations venture into the hadalpelagic zone, places so deep only a handful of humans have ever travelled there so far.[311]*

It is a world in itself and not to be dismissed for short-term gain. To reinforce the point, I take account of the views of a few of the best-known ocean scientists, who are as one in opposing any new exploitation of the 'blue' that characterizes our planet. In my search for inspiration, I first revisited the seminal works of the pioneer marine biologist and conservationist, Rachel Carson, whose writings, long before the present debate, remain as apposite as ever:

> *It is a curious situation that the sea, from which life first arose should now be threatened by the activities of one form of that life. But the sea, though changed in a sinister way, will continue to exist; the threat is rather to life itself.[312]*

Another great champion of the ocean, Sylvia Earle, also trained as a marine biologist and has been active throughout her life in speaking for the ocean as an existential element of human life:

> *The ocean is large and resilient, but it is not too big to fail. What we are taking out of the sea, what we are putting into the sea are actions that are undermining the most important thing the ocean delivers to humankind – our very existence.*[313]

Likewise, the widely-respected voice for global conservation, Sir David Attenborough, has been tireless in his efforts to show the world the wonders of the environment and also the urgent need to give it greater value:

> *The rush to mine this pristine and unexplored environment risks creating terrible impacts that cannot be reversed. We need to be guided by science when faced with decisions of such great environmental consequence.*[314]

Elsewhere, he gives his support for a moratorium so that the issues can be better understood. Everything he says rings true. But who is listening? Certainly, he has a worldwide following but is that enough? Attenborough is now in his nineties and not in a position to actively campaign. Fortunately, like a relay team, there is always someone else to carry the baton and, in continuing the good work, I am a great admirer of National Geographic's Explorer in Residence, Enric Sala. His views are unequivocal:

> *There is a clear moral argument for protecting more of the natural world. There is an even stronger human survival argument, because the loss of all ecosystem services would mean global human extinction... Thus, the value of the natural world must be infinite.*[315]

But is it enough to have to rely on individuals, no matter how remarkable they are? Where are the nations and commercial organisations prepared to find other solutions to the unsustainable demand for precious resources. Where is a universal state of consciousness that the planet cannot simply be swept along well-worn tracks? Where is a deep understanding of the ocean to match the threat of proposed mining? Where else can we look for answers?

Can the world's religions – which claim mass followings – help to turn the tide? In fact, it is not difficult to find religious doctrines which support the cause. The teachings of Buddhism, especially, are closely matched to the aims of conservation.[316] They pin the blame for environmental destruction on human selfishness and greed, arguing, in turn, that only by changing the human mind will true solutions be found. A consequent belief is that people should consume less, limiting their demands to those things which are necessary for living. These, of course, are words that will resonate with every conservationist and, in different ways, one can see that there are aspects of other religions, too, that offer hope that things could be better. The reality, however, is that such doctrines have not acted as a brake on needless development in the past and, if they remain as words alone, there is no reason to expect that they will be able to do so now.

Likewise, in search of the missing link I have referred to the works of some eminent philosophers from the past, yet here, too, their teachings can be read in different ways. Jeremy Bentham, for instance, the nineteenth-century philosopher, wrote about governments being guided by actions which bring the greatest happiness for the greatest number. At first, such propositions seem to make good sense, that is, until one probes further. Who, for instance, is the arbiter of happiness? Will it make most people happy if ocean minerals are excavated to enable the production of more mobile phones and associated products? Or will the balance lie on the side of those who take satisfaction from saving micro-organisms which no one would, in any case, be likely to see? In the absence of a transformation of values, it is not difficult to see where the balance of public opinion will lie. But how would such a change happen?

Or should I interrogate economists to find the magic formula? The difficulty, I soon found, is that, from the time of the classical economists like Malthus, Ricardo and Mill, the 'dismal science' is better at determining price than value. I have yet to find an effective way to put a price on a seabed creature not previously known to science. And even if I take the advice of modern pundits, who glibly urge me to 'follow the money', my quest would only end in the accounts of mining investors. The real value of the environment is left unspecified.

But it *does* have a value, to me and countless others who care about the future of the planet. The snailfish *does* matter, as do all of the other species in the deep ocean which would be threatened by oceanic mining. The irrecoverable loss of any one species would be a loss to all. I believe that is something we constantly have to bear in mind. As you will see, I stand firmly on the side of those who argue, at the very least, for a moratorium to enable a more informed debate. Only then can we hope to come to a reasoned decision on a subject that is fundamental to all of our futures.

# Chapter 9

# Wasteful Ways
*Consigning waste to where it belongs*

One of the best-known facts about the ocean is that it has become the world's largest trash can. Whether it is the sight of assorted litter strewn along even the remotest beaches, or collecting far out to sea to form floating islands of garbage; whether it is the spreading of untreated sewage close to the shore, or tragic pictures of sea mammals and fish ingesting discarded plastic – these scenarios are all now in the public domain. Nothing demonstrates better the ways in which a once-pristine ocean has been despoiled by humans. Not just at present but for centuries past it has been treated this way, the difference being that today the sheer volume of waste is many times greater than it used to be and it contains modern products, especially plastic, that do immeasurable harm and never completely disappear.

My immediate response is one that so many of us share: disgust that we can do this to our precious planet, shame that we have so little respect for our marine ecosystems, and disbelief that we are consciously degrading a major source of our own salvation. Quite apart from ethical concerns, clean seas can contribute in so many ways to providing essential food for growing numbers of people; instead, through contaminated fish and other marine life, we find ourselves at risk of consuming poisons of our own making. In all respects, the state of the ocean is an affront and a major barrier to a planned transition to a sustainable Blue Economy.

Once again, though, my aim is not to dwell unduly on the evident problems that plague the ocean but to use these as a launch pad for constructive strategies to reverse the situation. To make lasting progress, I am suggesting that the issue be tackled in four stages. Firstly, I am using as my compass the principles of the circular economy, so I will start by explaining this. Then, in practical terms, there is an urgent need to turn off the tap: to prevent the further entry of unwanted materials into the open seas. Thirdly, although in an ideal world we would be designing out the creation of new waste, we are not there yet: in the meantime, we need an active and targeted programme of recycling to turn waste into value. Finally, there is the outstanding task of finding ways to clean up the residue of past neglect, an enormous challenge in itself. Tackling any one stage on its own will not be sufficient.

## Going Round in Circles

In writing this book, one of the most heartening experiences is to come across some luminary figures – outstanding people who are dedicated to making a difference. And it is with one of these individuals that I will start.

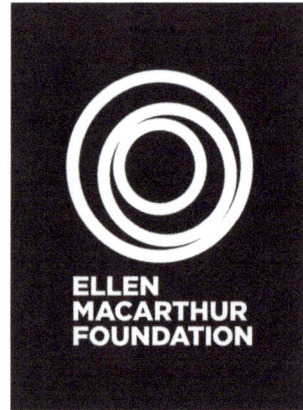

*Formerly a world-beating sailor, Ellen MacArthur now heads a successful foundation which promotes the idea of the circular economy*

Ellen MacArthur is a remarkable individual. Born in a village with the improbable name of Whatstandwell, in a part of England which, in relation to the small size of that country, is far from the sea, she knew from an early age that more than anything else she wanted to sail. Nothing would stop her and she learnt her trade the hard way, not only discovering how best to use the wind and sails to advantage but also through understanding the fine details in the design and construction of her super-efficient yachts. For a while, she worked in a boatyard in France and accompanied experienced sailors in races, until she was ready to set out on her own round-the-world ventures. The highlight came in 2005 when, not yet 30 years of age, she broke the record for the fastest circumnavigation of the planet. Honours and fame quickly followed but five years later she retired from competitive sailing in favour of new activities, amongst which was the establishment of her own foundation. She is now known for many things, including her fervent advocacy of the 'circular economy'.

It is not hard to imagine where the idea for this new chapter in her life came from. Weeks alone on the ocean, pitting her wits against the elements but also with time to reflect on what it all meant: the breathtaking beauty of some of the remotest parts of the earth but also unwelcome glimpses of rubbish floating by. What impressed her most of all, though, in her loneliest moments, was a sense of how the world was misusing its finite resources.[317] Once they were gone, what then? For MacArthur it was not a question of trying to solve individual problems but of looking holistically at the management of the world as a whole. In her own words:

> *In our current economy, we take materials from the Earth, make products from them, and eventually throw them away as waste – the process is linear. In a circular economy, by contrast, we stop waste being produced in the first place.*[318]

The circular economy goes beyond recycling as that in itself is based on the existence of waste; the secret is to find ways to eliminate the end product itself. If applied to energy, for example, it would not be a question of recycling what is left behind from production using fossil fuels so much as favouring alternative, renewable sources which do not generate waste in the first place. The idea of the circular economy can be applied to different issues and it is something I keep in my mind when exploring other aspects, too, of the Blue Economy. It is relevant, for instance to the way that food is grown and managed, to biodiversity and the model of nature, and to cities which are presently voracious consumers but, with smart designs, could be more sustainable.

In any situation, there are, asserts MacArthur, three basic principles that drive the circular economy. The first is to eliminate waste and pollution altogether; to do this, design and foresight are necessary, so that thought is given at the outset to what will eventually happen when the initial use of a product is completed. A second principle is to circulate products and materials at their highest value; in other words, to use them as intended for as long as possible and only then to disaggregate them so that the component materials can be used in other ways. There is no room in this approach for a 'throw away' culture. Finally, focus needs to be shifted from extraction to regeneration; taking a lead from nature, when products have no further use, they should be fed back into the earth to ensure continuity without waste – a modern application of 'ashes to ashes'.[319]

The circular economy makes good sense, not least of all because it does not require impossible technologies and utopian aspirations to put it into practice. But it does require a new way of thinking, and that is the biggest challenge of all. It is one thing to discuss the concept with like-minded people and quite another to convince nations at different stages of development. This can be illustrated in relation to, firstly, plastic in the ocean, and then to a wide variety of other pollutants.

## Turning Off the Tap

There is no point in digging a hole in the sand if the tide is still coming in. Likewise, to seek to remove the accumulation of past waste while new deposits continue to fill the gaps would be a fool's errand. Nor, unfortunately, does it seem enough simply to call on the better side of human nature to change the habits of a lifetime. Although many people would be willing to do so, it is unlikely that this would be enough on its own to reverse the flow of unsustainable practices. Instead (or, ideally, as well), the first step must be to actually prevent the further accumulation of waste, most of which emanates from activities on land. This can be done in one of two ways – by reviewing whether the offending materials need to be produced in the first place and, if they do, by stopping them from entering the ocean.

Waste materials – when they are generated on land – will mainly enter the ocean in one of two ways: either from being carried by rivers and outwash down slopes, or through deliberate dumping. Theoretically, both can be stopped, the main practical obstacles being a lack of political will and the allocation of resources.

### *Plastic is the bête noire*

Plastic waste in the ocean is the most extensive challenge by far. Not one to mince his words, before he became Britain's king the then Prince of Wales described it as 'a growing ecological and human disaster' which needs an urgent solution.[320] Each year, a further 13 million tonnes finds its way into the sea, or, to put this more graphically, 'that's the equivalent of a garbage truck emptying a load of plastic rubbish into the sea every minute'.[321] And, year on year, the volume is growing, with an expectation that it will increase threefold over the next 20 years if nothing is done to stop it.[322] Unfortunately, many people make a profit from this harmful process and it is not in their commercial interests to stem the flow. In contrast, a growing body of opinion now sees this as the kind of threat it is, to the ocean ecosystem and to the world at large, and there is a high level of support for remedial action. Thus, since I wrote my first book on the Blue Economy there has been a surge of interest in finding ways to change things, to drastically reduce if not (as one would wish) completely eliminate the damaging environmental impact of plastics.

*(Top) Plastic waste in the ocean threatens wildlife and symbolises the modern threat to a sustainable planet (Bottom) One of various ocean cleaning systems to remove accumulated garbage*

Realistically, whether we like it or not, plastic is here to stay, at least for the foreseeable future. If we were starting now, with the benefit of hindsight, we would not choose to put so much dependence on a material made from fossil fuels and with so many legacy problems. But we don't have that luxury and must respond to the world as it is. The fact is that plastic is a remarkably versatile material that can be used in numerous ways, most of them highly effective and often beneficial; the medical world, for instance, would find it difficult to manage without it. In these circumstances, the best we can do is to prevent further waste and, at a subsequent stage, to clean up as much as we can of what is already in the ocean. Taking a lead from the idea of the circular economy, the essential problem is that plastic waste is presently the end product of a linear process: it is made, it is used, and then it is discarded. How can we change this so that the process becomes more circular? In other words, how can we eliminate waste so that nothing is lost?

For the Ellen MacArthur Foundation, because of its specific impact, attention is focused on plastic packaging. This is, after all, the biggest single source of waste in the process and, because much of it comprises small, disposable items, it will often find its way into the sea. Amongst the various prescriptions from the Foundation, ways must be found to remove all unnecessary plastic packaging through redesign, innovation, and new means of distribution; there should be no more single-use products; all plastic packaging should be 100 per cent reusable, recyclable, or compostable; and it must be free of hazardous chemicals.

MacArthur's circular economy provides a valuable template and other think-tanks, too, agree that solutions are technically within reach. But, at root, it is not a question of whether it makes good sense (which it so obviously does) so much as acknowledging that it is an underlying absence of political will which is the major obstacle to progress.

> Although the technical solutions exist, the incentives are not always in place to scale up these changes fast enough. A reduction of plastic production – through elimination, the expansion of consumer reuse options, or new delivery models – is the most attractive solution from environmental, economic, and social perspectives.[323]

Solutions are available but it seems that these will only work if delivered in a cluster; there is not a single panacea that can solve on its own all the related problems. Thus, indicative of different approaches that are now under discussion, an expert panel convened by Pew Charitable Trusts offers (in the table below) the following combination of strategies:

| ACTIONS TO REDUCE PLASTIC POLLUTION |
|---|
| ✦ Reduce plastic output at source. Like most products, a more efficient assessment of use and a willingness by manufacturers to change can achieve positive outcomes. The more progressive producers themselves would stand to gain most from a modern, socially-oriented industry, and they would undoubtedly be able to enhance their reputations in the process. |
| ✦ Substitute plastic, where possible, with alternative materials like paper and products that are compostable, a move which would drastically reduce the present volume of waste. |
| ✦ Design and forethought could increase the ratio of economically recyclable plastic from an estimated 21 per cent to 54 per cent. |
| ✦ Increase waste collection rates in middle and low-income countries to 90 per cent in urban areas and 50 per cent in the countryside, and to support the informal collection sector. This can be matched by reducing plastic waste exports to countries with low collection and high leakage rates.*<br><br>✦<br><br>* In fact, my own view is that plastic waste exports should be banned with immediate effect. |
| ✦ Attention should also be paid to recycling, with mechanical facilities to be doubled; with an increase of plastic-to-plastic conversion; and more opportunities to dispose of plastic that cannot be recycled economically. |

Through this combination of changes, it is estimated that waste could be reduced by up to 80 per cent of annual plastic leakage into the ocean by 2040. Currently, the sum total of waste reduction to be achieved will amount to no more than 7 per cent annually; the rate has to be drastically increased.[324]

Because of the scale of the problem, its effective resolution is unlikely to come about without international authority. This is now possible (at least in formal terms) through the UN's Basel Convention, originally formed to address the wider problem of transportation of hazardous materials between countries. Significantly, an amendment in 2019 to its earlier brief extended the scope of the Convention to include not only the movement of plastic waste but also its sound management in the source country.[325] The amendment has the support of 190 signatories, the notable exception being the United States. In spite of this omission, the Basel Convention offers the only globally binding powers to specifically address this problem. In addition to its regulatory functions, it provides technical assistance to help countries meet their obligations within their own jurisdictions.

Also with an international reach, there are some influential NGOs which are adept at reaching the corporate world as well as foreign governments. For instance, one of these campaigning bodies, Greenpeace, has focused since 2018 on the role of large corporations. The logic for this is sound, as packaging required by global brands accounts for some 40 per cent of plastic production, much of it being single-use.[326] Although not necessarily a direct result of the Greenpeace initiative, as there were various other campaigns in the same period, within a few years some of the world's largest corporations were announcing significant actions to reduce waste.[327] Coca-Cola, for instance, is committed to a 'World Without Waste' plan, which includes 50 per cent recycled material in all its packaging by 2030, developing new bottles made out of 100 per cent recycled materials, and either using again or recycling 60 per cent of its packaging. McDonald's, another major brand with a past record of colossal waste, has signed up to the principles of the circular economy, with goals to source 100 per cent of its packaging from renewable, recycled or certified sources, and to recycle all of its packaging in restaurants by 2025. A different type of response comes from the IT leader, Microsoft, which has ambitious plans to operate carbon negative by 2030, and by 2050 remove all the carbon it has ever emitted since the company's founding in 1975.[328]

It is as if the floodgates have finally opened and some of the largest corporations are vying to take the lead. The oil and gas giant, Shell plc, is another big name to do so, on its website unambiguously aligning itself with the circular economy.

Theirs is a broad-based environmental strategy which includes tackling plastic waste specifically:

> We have an ambition to use one million tonnes of plastic waste a year in our global chemical plants by 2025. Using a technique called pyrolysis, we use plastic waste to produce chemicals, which can be used to make plastics again. We want to expand the use of this technology at our chemical plants in North America, Europe and Asia.[329]

The intervention of the private sector is not simply a question of altruism but also good business sense, as their actions can be used to promote their reputations as responsible organisations. Additionally, 'as well as being the right thing for a responsible business to do, we believe a focus on the circular economy and waste can bring opportunities to create new business models, drive innovation and respond to customer expectations'.[330] For whatever reason, anything that can be done to reduce the amount of plastic pollution is to be welcomed.

Practices are changing and there is plenty which is encouraging, but it would be remiss to suggest that positive outcomes are as yet anywhere near sufficient. Perhaps unexpectedly, I can see more signs of progress coming from the corporate sector than from national governments. World surveys show that China and India are especially resistant to change, along with much of South-East Asia, Brazil and parts of Africa, all of them countries which claim a higher priority for unrestrained development.[331] True to form, the northern European countries come out best, a result of having the resources to do so but also because of a tradition of social enlightenment – factors which themselves might be explained historically as resulting from earlier progress at the expense of poorer nations.

It is not so much that other countries around the world are opposed to better management of plastic waste, as the fact that their various interventions are often ineffective. Many countries, for instance, have signed up to ban plastic bags and incidentals like drinking straws but too often there are loopholes and insufficient enforcement. The Basel Convention provides a framework for more effective action but it lacks effective powers to compel countries to make full use of them.

Understandably, if they cannot persuade their governments to act more forcefully, then individuals and communities will step in to fill some of the gaps. Since I wrote my earlier book, there has been a huge upsurge in awareness and actions at this level. Is there a school now where young people are unaware of this wider problem? Can there be many individuals who would not think twice before using plastic bags? And is there not a wider understanding of the social value of recycling? There are numerous actions taken locally and by individuals, all designed to make a difference and to spur governments to match these at a higher level.[332] There is still a long way to go but in just a few short years the issue has risen high on the environmental agenda. That in itself is a mark of progress.

## *Waste goes well beyond plastic*

Plastic is on everyone's agenda but, unfortunately, it is by no means the only waste problem to be addressed. The ocean is also a recipient for numerous other materials too: including human waste and oil spills, chemical effluents from farms and manufacturing, and even something as seemingly innocuous as sunscreen (just one of the adverse by-products of tourism in environmentally sensitive locations). Restrictions are in place to limit if not altogether prevent some of these pollutants but, whether intentionally or by accident, a great deal of harmful substances still reach the sea.

Remarkably, it is only within the past 50 years that prevention of waste has been codified, and it was not until 1993 that indiscriminately dumping radioactive materials was banned by international treaties:

> *Before 1972, there were no laws that prevented dumping into the oceans, and this allowed people around the world to dump trash, sewage sludge, and hazardous wastes into the ocean without a second thought. According to National Geographic, millions of tons of heavy metals and chemical contaminants, along with thousands of containers of radioactive waste, were purposely thrown into the ocean.[333]*

To make it worse, richer nations have often taken to transporting their unwanted waste to poorer countries, a case of simply removing the problem from one part of the world to another.

Clearly, indiscriminate dumping and the goal of a sustainable Blue

Economy are sharply at odds. But, it is so often the case that world opinion is divided between those nations which support international action to prevent bad practices, and those which choose to pursue their individual interests regardless of the harm they might be inflicting. Thus, lines have been drawn between the different factions, in relation to what is known as the London Convention and the later London Protocol, the two landmark treaties designed to end illegal dumping. Through the latter, the disposal of all but a few forms of waste materials in the ocean is now banned. What is more, these blanket measures are supported by other forms of international and regional legislation.[334] On paper at least, the situation seems to be under control. Sadly, however, this is not the case:

> *Banning ocean dumping is, unfortunately, not enough to eliminate it. Ocean dumping is tightly controlled and regulated in some countries but not in others. Some countries have not ratified the London Convention and Protocol. Some regional agreements are more robust than others. This has led to an uneven application of and adherence to the ocean dumping regime, and the various international and regional instruments it entails, resulting in a piecemeal approach to ocean dumping governance.*[335]

It is rather like attempts to regulate the High Seas, to put a halt to deforestation, or to limit the rate of global warming. Countries are pleased to send representatives to international conferences, and may well pay lip service to what is proposed, but when it comes to delivering on what needs to be done it is a different story. Time and again, there are exceptions, of countries which ignore requirements or of clauses removed, which render attempts to reach a comprehensive agreement ineffectual.

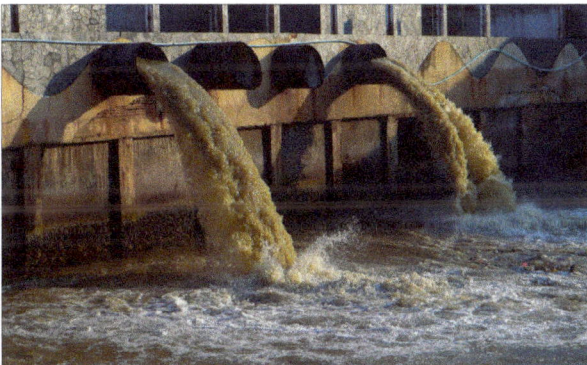

*Raw sewage and other effluents are regularly discharged onto the beaches and into the sea. Richer countries are culpable of doing this as well as poorer ones*

So where is the good news? Well, one can take comfort from the fact that at least the problem of dumping waste in the ocean is now widely recognised. There is more awareness of its harmful effects than there used to be. And there are some law-abiding countries which do their best to conform with international law. But it has to be admitted that good news is hard to come by. One reason is that some countries simply cannot afford to put in place expensive infrastructure to deal with waste that can more easily and cheaply be deposited in the sea. The issue of human waste is a prime example of this. With a growing global population, it follows that there will be more human waste. A popular notion is that the sea has the capacity to absorb sewage so that no harm is done. This is, indeed, a myth, and the problem is exacerbated by the fact that in many parts of the world there is still a near-universal absence of treatment facilities in coastal locations to mitigate the impact. This need not be the case, and in a report on the incidence of untreated sewage off various islands in the Pacific, Greenpeace showed that sustainable, low-cost solutions are possible.[336] In the interests of all, it is a price which richer nations should be prepared to pay to assist poorer counterparts.

A second reason to explain the lack of progress is more technical. Apart from plastic, which is now widely understood (if not, necessarily acted upon), these other forms of waste cover a wide range of materials, each of which demands a different approach. It is not realistic to think that one remedy will cure all of the problems. Instead, multiple forms of waste need to be matched to their own bespoke solutions. Whether the problem is farm slurry or industrial effluents, oil spills or sewage, the same kind of focus given to plastic waste needs to be devoted to each of these contaminants. Training courses, student dissertations with new ideas, research and development, NGO campaigns and, especially, business start-ups can all play a significant role.

For all the differences in types of waste, however, I believe there is a common set of principles which should inform the various responses. The challenge is urgent and my own suggestions in relation to each form of waste disposal are presented in the table opposite.

## MULTIPLE STREAMS DEMAND MULTIPLE SOLUTIONS

✧ Each stream of waste demands its own scientific solution.

✧ A directory of all waste materials presently destined for the ocean should be prepared by a respected international body e.g. UN Global Compact Action Platform for Sustainable Ocean Business.

✧ The approach in each case should be holistic, starting from the need for the product in the first place to the elimination of waste at the present end of the process.

✧ An emphasis should be placed on designs for whole-life use of products. This will require specialist scientists with a common interest in ocean waste.

✧ The concept of the circular economy – as advocated by the Ellen MacArthur Foundation – should provide the basis for a common approach.

✧ Initiatives should be led by dedicated bodies which will include international trusts like Pew and the Ocean Foundation, as well as consultants such as NLA International.

✧ Each exercise cannot be regarded as cost-free. There must be a willingness to transfer resources from richer to poorer countries, and for corporations to build extra costs into their calculations, on the basis that all parties will benefit from a cleaner ocean.

✧ Nations and corporations which 'drag their heels' and refuse to conform to international treaties should attract adverse publicity, in an effort to encourage them to change their ways.

✧ In turn, there should be incentives for nations and corporations which do conform and which become champions of waste prevention.

## A call for more magic

Recycling has a touch of magic about it; put a handkerchief in the hat and pull out a rabbit. Just as I called for a dose of magic to help with an earlier topic, I think something comparable is due for recycling. Often presented as a panacea, that's not what it is at all. It thrives on waste, and can be part of the problem rather than a solution. After all, who wants to lose a handkerchief in exchange for a rabbit?

Returning to the theme of a circular economy, good design at the outset of production eliminates the creation of waste itself, and that should surely be the aim?

> In a properly built circular economy, one should rather focus on avoiding the recycling stage at all costs. It may sound straightforward, but preventing waste from being created in the first place is the only realistic strategy.[337]

One cannot argue with the logic of the argument that 'in a properly built circular economy' waste would be eliminated at the design stage. But we are far from achieving this ideal and, in the world as it is, the assertion that it is 'the only realistic strategy' has to be questioned. It is an ideal to aspire to but we are not there yet. In which case, recycling has a valuable role to play and, in this interim stage, we are undoubtedly better off with it than without – so long as it is treated just as critically as any other aspect of waste management. If all it achieves is to convert waste into products which then find their way onto landfill sites just a few years later, then its potential value is obviously limited. Further, if recycling is to attract investors, it must at least pay its way. This is why there are various studies that focus on the relative costs and benefits of recycling. Different products and locations where this process might take place, quite rightly come under the microscope.

Investors will want to know, quite simply, whether the costs of recycling can be justified. To illustrate this, one of many recent studies examines whether it is cheaper to mine fresh reserves of minerals as opposed to recycling what is contained in previously used products. Answering this question, a group of researchers in China conclude that recycling offers cheaper options than virgin mining.[338] In their study, they focus on just two minerals, copper and aluminium. Their arguments are convincing and yet one can reasonably expect that comparative costs and benefits will vary between different minerals and in different parts of the world where the recycling takes place. With the same purpose in mind in mind, another study also points to the competitiveness of recycling.[339] In this case, the location is a sorting and treatment plant that serves the city of Barcelona for both light packaging and bulky waste materials. The authors of the study argue that recycling can be targeted to ensure that materials are used for as long as possible. Such research is to be encouraged, although always to be received with a degree of caution, given the sharp difference of circumstances in which recycling takes place.

In contrast with decisions based on a detached analysis of costs, recycling can also come into its own when there appears to be no other use for waste materials. Rather than leave them as they are to pollute the ocean, they can attract a value simply by removing them and finding other uses. In this kind of situation, environmental factors can be costed as a good enough reason in itself for recycling. As an example, the fishing industry has been responsible for depositing all kinds of used equipment, either direct into the ocean or in growing piles abandoned on quaysides in various ports. When at sea, as well as being unsightly and yet another example of waste, the entangled nets pose a direct threat to marine life. For inventive minds, discarded materials can be seen as a business opportunity as well as a chance to help in cleaning the ocean. In searching for examples, my attention was soon drawn to the windswept peninsula of Cornwall, in south-west England. There, I discovered a small company which exhibits all that is best amongst people who care passionately about the environment and are committed to making a difference. For centuries, the coastal villages in the region had been home to their own fleets that ventured into the once-flourishing fisheries. This artisanal fishing has since been joined by industrial fleets, which have led not only to greater competition for a scarce resource but have also upscaled new problems of waste.

Waterhaul is the brainchild of a marine scientist, Harry Dennis, who was initially working for a charity concerned with plastic pollution and decided there was more to what is known as 'ghost gear' than simply clearing up. With entrepreneurial zeal, he set up his own company and brought in other young enthusiasts, with business as well as scientific skills. Their activities, as they say, are 'anchored in purpose' and, as a social enterprise, 'we exist to deliver our mission; to tackle ghost gear in oceans by transforming waste to valued resource'.[340] Different products were considered, the preferred option being to manufacture fashionable and resilient sunglasses from recycled materials, with the first of these being marketed in 2018. The magic in the process was that the very qualities which created problems in the first place were also those which lent themselves to conversion to new products:

> *The properties which make ghost gear such a threat in our oceans; the size and abundance of net, the quality of the high-strength polymers used, and the urgency to remove the plastic from harm's way, all make fishing nets a desirable recycling resource.*[341]

*Waterhaul is a small company in Cornwall, UK, which collects and recycles abandoned fishing nets*

This is a small example but I believe, increasingly, that the transition to a sustainable Blue Economy will result not from the deliberations of government committees or international conferences where delegates arrive in private jets, but from the energy, expertise and enterprise of young people like Harry Dennis and the team he has gathered around him in faraway Cornwall. Nearer my own home in Seychelles, I am pleased to see a local attempt to do something similar. Because of the scale of tuna fishing in the western Indian Ocean, along with other fisheries on an industrial scale in the region, there is a prodigious amount of discarded equipment. Unwanted rope and nylon nets, buoys and steel chains, are dumped in heaps around the port of Victoria and are also washed ashore on the islands of Seychelles. Brikole is a recent start-up business dedicated to clearing the residue of a giant fishing industry and putting what is presently waste to good use. The new venture has come about as a result of cooperation between the government, major fishing companies, and NGOs. As always, though, with innovative businesses, little would come about without the drive of particular entrepreneurs.

A regular supply of materials is now guaranteed through an agreement with fishing companies, which provide Brikole with unwanted equipment. Presently, this is sorted locally and then sent overseas to specialist recycling units. The aim, though, is to provide its own recycling plant in Seychelles. In the words of one of its founders:

> *Maybe in one to two years, we will be able to establish our own recycling facility in Seychelles. By introducing recycling in Seychelles, we do not want to focus only on nets. Nets will only be a start and once we know the ins and outs, we will then move to everyday plastic. We will be able to see the different types of plastics being brought to Seychelles and how we can reuse and recycle them.*[342]

Another example of plastic recycling, in this case with very positive outcomes, comes from Tanzania. EcoAct is a young company which has developed its own process to convert discarded plastic into a useful commodity. Its durable product, 'plastic lumber', has a variety of eco-friendly applications in construction, furniture-making, fencing and other uses.

> *We use chemical free and energy conserving plastic extrusion technology called 'Waxy 11 Technology' to recycle and transform post-consumer waste plastics, packaging materials and agricultural waste*

*into durable and environmentally friendly plastic lumbers. Plastic lumbers are an affordable alternative to wood timbers.*[343]

Through a network of collection points, EcoAct offers opportunities, for women and young people especially, to supplement limited incomes. A novel social twist is that payment can be made in the form of medical insurance vouchers to enable members of the community to receive healthcare which might otherwise be beyond their reach.

## The Party's Over

*The party's over,*
*It's time to call it a day.*[344]

Even with effective measures to slow down or, ideally, prevent further ocean pollution there still remains the problem of what to do with the present legacy of waste. The answer to this is twofold: remove the present mountains of rubbish, and then recycle what is possible. Simple enough, it would seem, but not so if only because of the enormity of the task.

Science-fiction images of garbage trapped in vortexes in the Pacific, the greatest sea of all, cannot be passed on to future generations. Nor can the sight of many beaches in developing countries, knee-deep in rubbish, any longer be regarded as acceptable. For the sake of the planet's future, there is an overriding imperative to clear the enormous residue that has been bequeathed to (and partly caused by) present generations. But the task is daunting, to say the least. Given the need for commensurate resources to remedy the situation, I ought to start by looking at what an international body like the UN is presently doing. Instead, I am going to turn the spotlight on the work of an individual, a young Dutchman named Boyan Slat.

I have been following his progress for some years, since he came to my notice with the claim that he knew how to collect the endless mass of waste in the ocean and that he, himself, would make a start. It was an outrageous claim for a young man to make, barely in his twenties at the time, and yet he clearly meant every word. When I first read about his plans, he was taking a generic view of rubbish but he has since focused mainly on the component which is plastic waste. Although he is still the driving force,

Slat now works within an organisation of his own making, Ocean Cleanup:

*Our aim is to remove 90% of floating ocean plastic, which requires global initiative. With the help and support of individuals, corporations and governments all over the world, we aim to realize the mission and work towards a future where plastic no longer pollutes our oceans.*[345]

This seemingly impossible task is based on a sound premise, namely, that most of this form of pollution reaches the sea through the earth's rivers, so the first step should be to intervene at those points where the one meets the other. To narrow the task further, it is estimated by his organisation that 1,000 of all the world's rivers account for 80 per cent of ocean-bound pollution. And so it is this culpable 1,000 that is specifically targeted. The second step, once further prevention is reduced if not totally eliminated, is to concentrate on the gyrating clusters of rubbish in mid-ocean. This can be achieved through specially-designed floating systems which concentrate the waste so that tiny pieces of plastic as well as large objects can be collected. Basically, these systems comprise giant booms that float with the prevailing currents while they ensnare the rubbish, which can then be towed ashore.

As with any innovation, there are those who will argue that these worthy aims are simply not possible to achieve.[346] For one thing, plastic waste degrades into fine particles that cannot easily be captured; for another, the scale of the task is simply too large to overcome at a rate that will save the ocean. As sceptics will often say, if something seems too good to be true, it's because it's probably not true. In response, Ocean Cleanup presses on regardless: concentrating on refining the design of its booms so that they can better withstand the force of rough seas and adverse weather conditions, and matching ocean retrieval with enhanced efforts to prevent pollutants leaving the rivers. Of course, their efforts would be better supported if every nation invested in its own collection and recycling facilities, rather than leaving it to volunteers; surely this is something which should be higher on the world's list of environmental priorities. In the meantime, I am thankful that there are teams of individuals who are at least trying to stem the flow, and the likes of Boyan Slat have my wholehearted support.

Garbage, of course, comes in many different forms, some of which require highly specialist operations to remove. Around the ocean, for instance, there are numerous installations resulting from offshore oil and gas mining, and, more recently, in connection with renewable energy. Susan Gourvenec is an engineer with expertise in the subject, who is aware of the high costs associated with decommissioning, as well as the need to take account of environmental and other impacts which result.[347] Whether to clear non-renewable or renewable, the process is much the same, except for the important fact that in the case of the latter there is no extra financial provision for plugging the wells. Gourvenec predicts that the number of installations will grow and that there will be consequent demands over time for decommissioning.

In contrast with the removal of heavy equipment, expensive to undertake and accessible only to specialists, the task of beach cleaning is cheap and open to all: schools, community enterprises, dedicated NGOs, and individuals who care about the environment. Beach clean-ups are stimulating, because at the end of a session sack-loads of rubbish will be removed, but also dispiriting because one knows that, unless the problem is tackled at source, more rubbish will float ashore on the next tide. In spite of the knowledge that a pristine beach is only temporary, enthusiasts around the world are determined to make a difference. Wherever they are, they need to be supported.

To take just one example, Seychelles has regularly supported beach clean-ups, not only along the most popular stretches of coastline but also in the rarely-visited outer islands. In 2019, for instance, a group of 40 volunteers spent ten days in some of the most remote reaches of the archipelago.[348] These are places that are far from neighbouring countries and with few if any permanent residents. And yet, simply by trawling deserted beaches they collected more than ten tonnes of rubbish, comprising, most commonly, plastic drink bottles, flip flops, along with ropes and fishing nets, all of which had been carried ashore on the prevailing currents and tides. In the same period, a similar clean-up operation was taking place on Aldabra, treasured above all as a world heritage site but yielding no less than 25 tonnes of debris. In both cases, most of the waste had come from distant countries around the Indian Ocean and, tellingly, details of specific brands revealed the provenance. Locating the source of the problem can then become an important basis for campaigning for tighter controls in those countries and companies. And that, in turn, will often lead one back to the perennial issue of inadequate treatment facilities in poorer countries and the urgent need to address this. This illustrates how the problems are inter-related and, as a result, why only integrated strategies will suffice.

*Debris on the beach of the remote island of Farquhar, Seychelles*

# Chapter 10

# The Life of the Sea
*Championing biodiversity, changing direction*

*The sheer beauty and biodiversity of the ocean must surely be protected at all costs*

The ocean should be celebrated for its magnificent qualities, a natural arena of boundless biodiversity. Instead, it is cruelly abused, and what used to be a sea of plenty – a marine cornucopia – is now in many parts struggling for survival. Its waters are polluted, not only near the shore but far out to sea; overfishing has reduced once-plentiful stocks, in some cases to extinction; marine mammals in all regions are at the mercy of harmful (even if not always intended) human practices; and tiny, deep-ocean organisms, sometimes not yet even named, face the threat of decimation if seabed mining goes ahead. And this is not even to mention the pervasive impact of global warming. If further deterioration is to be prevented, radical changes are urgently needed; a new approach is long overdue. The Blue Economy would be a misnomer if the ocean itself were to be left in this parlous state. To coin an apt phrase, we must create 'clear blue water' between a legacy of malpractice and a more sustainable future.

## Finding Common Cause

It was a happy coincidence for me that I was at the stage of writing this chapter when I heard news from New York of an agreement to better manage the High Seas. Had the outcome been different, there would undoubtedly have been a deep sense of disappointment amongst campaigners, including myself. In the event, we can all rejoice that an historic step forward has been taken. But seasoned campaigners also know that this only marks the start of what may yet prove to be a long journey.[349]

The High Seas, extending over most of the ocean and nearly half the area of the planet – the source of most of the biodiversity the sea has to offer – are fundamental to the very future of the world. This is why I start by recognising how significant it was that in March 2023 a gathering of nations under the auspices of the UN finally brokered an agreement that will lead to a new set of international regulations. There is plenty still to be negotiated (and the devil is invariably in the detail) but the stakes are high. Very high. Without a treaty that binds all nations, biodiversity will remain a chimera, lost in its own mist. There are at last grounds for hope that a healthier ocean is possible. But no room for complacency. Even as I write these words, there will be a constant stream of garbage trucks around the world continuing to tip their loads into the sea, untreated sewage flowing into hitherto clear waters, ships belching noxious fumes into the atmosphere, and the clearance of mangrove swamps to make way for new resorts. Biodiversity (not only in the High Seas but also within national jurisdictions) remains seriously at risk; it needs all the support we can offer. It is hard to be overly optimistic. The challenges across the ocean as a whole are too formidable for that. Yet, while one can hardly ignore the many continuing threats, the treaty can be seen as an important milestone.

*At last, it seems that the life of the ocean will be given a chance*

This breakthrough has come none too soon. In the session which opened in February 2023 and continued for 14 days, there was a feeling that progress might at last be possible. But even at the eleventh hour there were still stumbling blocks to overcome.[350] Once again it was argued that the ocean beyond national jurisdictions is a common heritage, belonging to the world as a whole. That is something which has been repeated over the years. This time the argument was focused on one issue in particular, namely, that of how genetic resources might be used in medicines and cosmetics. Why, it was asked, should the richer nations and large corporations, which are in a position to afford substantial exploration and development costs, benefit most (financially and otherwise) from what might be discovered? What about the interests of the rest of the world? These are good questions that underpin all aspects of the transition to a Blue Economy.

The issues were discussed at length and the outcome remained uncertain to the very last. It looked as if the convention might once again fail to reach agreement. In the event, reason prevailed and a treaty was agreed, 'which places 30 per cent of the world's oceans into protected areas, puts more money into marine conservation and [may yet lead to] new rules for mining at sea'.[351] The outcome will bring benefits to many aspects of the High Seas but it is significant that it is formally known as the Biodiversity Beyond National Jurisdiction Treaty. As such, it represents a major triumph for the cause of ocean biodiversity, as well as related issues. In the words of the Secretary-General of the UN, the long-awaited treaty will prove 'crucial for addressing the triple planetary crisis of climate change, biodiversity loss and pollution'.[352] Whatever the difficulties that lie ahead in securing effective implementation, the treaty undoubtedly represents substantial progress:

> *The High Seas Treaty includes an agreement to impose strict protection of the ocean outside national borders and rules for the sustainable use of its resources. It's not about putting nature in a bell jar to remain untouched – but rather, applying a precautionary approach to using marine resources responsibly in this 'Wild West' of the high seas, to ensure that we are not depleting ocean ecosystems and leaving nothing for tomorrow... The new High Seas Treaty stipulates that environmental impact assessments must be completed before any new exploitation of marine resources in areas beyond national jurisdictions. It also features provisions to allow for the equitable sharing of knowledge, technologies and benefits from marine genetic resources. These elements may be used in products ranging from food supplements and cosmetics to life-saving medicines – with ongoing research potentially leading to as yet unknown benefits to humanity in the years to come.*[353]

The formal process of ratification in the months ahead will be time-consuming but the steps to be taken are clearly charted.[354] First, although the essential message was agreed in the final session in New York, the precise wording of the treaty has to be carefully drafted, checked and counter-checked. Once that is done, the treaty needs to be formally adopted by member states and then ratified by at least 60 countries before it can come into effect. There will also be further questions to be clarified in subsequent meetings, such as how marine protected areas will be managed and by whom. Indeed, in which parts of the ocean will these areas be designated? And how will the rules be enforced?

While meanings are still fluid, governments will be strongly lobbied by corporations which resent the prospect of any kind of profit-sharing, which is embodied in the treaty on the basis that the riches of the ocean should be shared by all nations. Conversely, poorer nations which cannot themselves invest in exploration will continue to negotiate for a larger share of the dividends. And, as well as specific points such as these, there will always be international rivalries and 'point scoring' to prevent one faction or another from gaining kudos. In other words, there is still a long way to go.

But these concerns should not be allowed to obscure the significance of the agreement to date. It really is a vital landmark on the road to a more sustainable future.

One ocean expert, Lisa Speer, responded quickly to news of the agreement with the view that it has four main objectives.[355] The first is that it paves the way to create large-scale marine protected areas, which have been likened to the ocean's equivalent of a Grand Canyon or Yellowstone National Park. Ideally, this will mean that damaging activities like commercial fishing and mining will be prohibited in these areas. A second objective is to ensure that the commercial benefits from extracting genetic resources will be fairly shared between nations as they represent a common good. Thirdly, Speer takes the view that the treaty is aimed at making research conducted in international waters more accessible and inclusive, especially for developing countries. Finally, the treaty aims at setting global standards for environmental impact assessments of proposed commercial activities in the ocean.

Another ocean expert (originally from Seychelles) is Angelique Pouponneau. She is in no doubt that the outcome in New York marks progress and is a cause for celebration.[356] Pouponneau highlights the fact that, after numerous international failures and periods of inaction, this is a welcome victory for multilateralism. Rich and poor nations alike finding common cause is itself an achievement to be noted. It is also a win for sustainability, with measures in prospect that are based on sound scientific principles. At the same time, Pouponneau believes that protected areas might well take longer to achieve than hoped and some hard negotiations are in prospect. She asks four questions, each of which will open further areas of discussion: What about enforcement? Who will pay? How can we ensure equity? And what does this mean for science, academic and research institutions?

Finally, she concludes with what I regard as a sensible balance between hope and caution:

> *In short, this is progress. Is it revolutionary? Probably not. Is it incremental progress that has enough to help us build our way to a healthy environment? It's definitely a step in the right direction. Should we feel content? No! There is much work to be done. So now that the cheers have died down – read the agreement in principle, keep an eye out on the date for adoption, cross your fingers that it all goes smoothly, and then think about your role in the uphill struggle that is to come!* [357]

## The Promise of MPAs

Marine protected areas offer the most exciting means to turn words into action. The purpose of an MPA is simple enough, namely, to designate sections of the sea where protection is regulated. And the logic which underpins this approach is incontrovertible. The case rests on the fact that, within these areas, ecosystems are allowed to flourish as nature intended. Even where harm has been done in the past, most species are remarkably resilient and recovery is usually possible. What is more, the proliferation of healthy species within the protected zone will invariably spread beyond the boundaries to benefit the surrounding sea too.

As a Pew Bertarelli Ocean Ambassador, I am keenly aware of the work that has been done, over more than a decade, to promote the cause of MPAs. In the words of Dona Bertarelli: 'The science is clear, marine protected areas are an effective tool to help protect and restore biodiversity, enable the ocean to be more resilient to climate change and recover from the impact of extractive activities such as overfishing, improve carbon sequestration, and secure the food and livelihoods of billions of people who rely on a healthy ocean.'[358]

The cause of ocean sanctuaries is vigorously pursued by other bodies too, such as National Geographic. As the Explorer in Residence of that body, Enric Sala is himself making an exceptional contribution to the cause and, in the process, turning ideas into practice. His passion for the ocean has already enhanced the case for biodiversity, mainly through securing the designation of extensive protected areas.

> *I think of the ocean continuously, and agonize when I see marine life disappear – knowing that most marine life is disappearing without us seeing it. But I cannot stop fighting because I have seen the ocean bounce back when we give it a chance. I have seen fishes, lobsters, and entire underwater forests come back- spectacularly – when we give them space.*[359]

I can also acknowledge the work of other scientists who give credence to the idea of protected areas. Carlos M. Duarte, for instance, is a distinguished professor of marine science who lends support to our understanding of ocean resilience. Amongst his many publications I have recently read a seminal paper (co-authored with a team of like-minded scientists) in which he shows how, if the will is there, all is not lost.[360] As his own starting point, Duarte is only too aware of the damage that has been done:

> *Currently, at least one-third of fish stocks are overfished, one-third to half of vulnerable marine habitats have been lost, a substantial fraction of the coastal ocean suffers from pollution, eutrophication, oxygen depletion and is stressed by ocean warming, and many marine species are threatened with extinction.*[361]

Nevertheless, he continues:

> *…biodiversity losses in the ocean are less pronounced than on land, and many marine species are capable of remarkable recovery once pressures are reduced or removed. Substantial wilderness areas remain in remote regions, and large populations of marine animals are still found, for example, in mesopelagic (200-1000 m depth) ocean waters.*[362]

The logic of his approach is that when relentless pressures caused by humans are removed, or even reduced, ocean species show a remarkable capacity to recover. Not in all cases, as there are tipping points beyond which extinction will be the only outcome. And, even where recovery is still possible, it may take a long time to achieve; in the case of large whales, perhaps as long as a century to return to previous numbers. But the general direction is unmistakable and, in some cases, recovery can be very rapid.

One can add to Duarte's findings, various sources of evidence. After the First and Second World Wars, for instance, when normal fishing activities were curtailed, it was noted that once peace was restored the sea yielded record catches. In more recent times, the coronavirus epidemic had comparable effects, not only on fishing but also, for instance, as a result of a drastic reduction of coastal and marine tourism. Closure was hardly good news for businesses but, in the absence of constant use, fragile environments were given a chance to recover. There is also the case of Chagos, a disputed archipelago in the Indian Ocean, from which the inhabitants were relocated in the 1970s and visitors to the islands prevented from entering. The dispute has continued for the best part of half a century, allowing species in the surrounding sea and on the beaches to flourish.[363]

The most productive MPAs are those which cover very large areas, and even more so if they are connected, one to another. As well as these, there is also a variety of smaller regional and local initiatives. Across the world, these protected areas can now be numbered in thousands (anything from 5,000 to 15,000 depending on the criteria used), but, at most, according to Pew Bertarelli, the proportion of the ocean protected was in the region of 7.5 per cent in 2020.[364] Of this total, 1,000 alone are attributed to the US, including the notable examples of the Papahanaumokuakea Marine National Monument and the Pacific Remote Marine National Monument.[365] There is enormous variety in what is being protected and different MPAs have their own objectives.

> For instance, a group of small islands and the waters around them are protected by the Galápagos Marine Reserve, which is located roughly 1,000 kilometers (600 miles) off the west coast of South America. This reserve contains various habitats, from coral reefs to cold ocean currents to mangrove swamps where trees grow directly in saline seawater. More than 3,000 different plant and animal species, as well as rare ones like the marine iguana, the only seagoing lizard in the world, can be found in the waters around the Galápagos Islands. [366]

While it is encouraging to see examples from a wide range of countries, pursuing many aspects of ocean biodiversity, the reality of protection is sometimes questionable. To be meaningful, each has to be defined by more than lines on a map; they must be effectively managed and patrolled to prevent illegal intrusion. All of which is to affirm why the binding agreement for the High Seas is absolutely essential. Without this, experience shows that guidelines will be ignored and the purpose of designating these large areas (and small areas too) will remain unfulfilled.

The ideal, of course, will be to achieve the commonly recognised target of actively protecting 30 per cent of the ocean by 2030 (the 30/30 formula).[367] But it is not, in any case, just a question of numbers. As is so often the case with designated areas at sea, the crucial question is whether laudable aims are supported with enforceable restrictions. But even here there is a paradox: the more they are protected and fish stocks are allowed to recover, the more vulnerable they are to illegal encroachment. Currently, it is fair to say that MPAs are by no means as effective as they should be.[368] They are still at an evolutionary stage in terms of implementation. But the concept is sound and the full realisation of MPAs could yet represent the greatest contribution to the achievement of a sustainable ocean. A valuable endorsement comes from a recent finding in a protected area of the Pacific Ocean, west of Mexico, where it is shown that the fears of the country's fishermen that catches outside the area would fall were unfounded.[369]

As a realist, I never lose sight of what we are still doing wrong, but as an optimist nor will I believe that a radical change of direction is not possible. To use a sporting metaphor, there is everything to play for.

## Recovery Hot Spots

Sanctuaries, in the form of MPAs, offer the best hope to restore biodiversity for three reasons: leaving nature alone to do the work is a proven remedy; the sheer extent of protection is a factor in itself; and the areas in question are the home of a wide variety of species. At the same time – even if protected areas reach the 30 per cent target – there is a case for supplementary initiatives to tackle particular issues. Regional conditions and the plight of certain species may well call for their own interventions. Additionally, overshadowing the whole issue, the perennial issue of overfishing – the greatest cause of loss of marine life to date – cannot be allowed to continue; the designation of more MPAs alone will not be enough.

*Marine life can flourish in protected seas*

The restoration of healthy populations is a common goal for any initiative but it has to be accepted that this will not be possible in every case. Sometimes, a tipping point might already have been reached, so that it becomes impossible to prevent extinction.

Even when recovery is feasible, the remedy will not necessarily be easy or quick to achieve, and any progress has to be carefully guarded; things can

slip back as well as forward. Moreover, different species require different methods and timescales. In such cases, local knowledge and species expertise can make an important difference. Let me illustrate some of these points in relation to different examples of ocean biodiversity: marine mammals, mangroves, seagrass, and coral reefs.

## Take heart from the humpback whale

It is hard to imagine that, just a few generations ago, books told proudly of the bravery of whalers, of the adventure of hunting whales and the gory experience of harpooning these majestic creatures, breaking their resistance until they could be hauled on board the pursuing vessel and hacked into pieces by their captors. In contrast, whales are now a keenly protected species and worth much more when sighted by tourists than the value of the oil they once yielded or their meat for consumption. A few countries have not yet shaken off the habit but an international consensus led in 1982 to a global moratorium on commercial whaling. Greenpeace rightly takes credit for its own part in triggering a U-turn in public opinion, pointing to its action in 1975 when a team from the campaigning organisation confronted a Pacific whaling fleet and sited themselves pointedly between the harpoons and targeted whales. It was a decisive action and, within just a few decades, Greenpeace could report some dramatic rises in whale numbers.[370] More recently, Duarte cites interesting evidence to show that 'humpback whales migrating from Antarctica to eastern Australia have been increasing at 10 per cent to 13 per cent per year from a few hundred animals in 1968 to more than 40,000 currently'.[371] Nor is it just this single species of whale which is flourishing; different whale species and other marine mammals, too, are in many cases increasing in number:

> For marine mammals, 47% of 124 well-assessed populations showed a significant increase over the past decades, with 40% unchanged and only 13% decreasing... Northern elephant seals recovered from about 20 breeding individuals in 1880 to more than 200,000 today, and gray seal populations have increased by 1410% in eastern Canada and 823% in the Baltic since 1977. Southern sea otters have grown from about 50 individuals in 1911 to several thousand today. While still endangered, most sea turtle populations for which trends are available are increasing in size...[372]

Statistics, however, are notoriously subject to bias and, while the above can be verified, other observers have emphasised at the same time a continuing decline in numbers in certain kinds of whale and in other marine mammals too. More ships at sea and an increased risk of being accidentally hit, the constant danger of bycatches for smaller creatures, hunting for sport, as well as depletion of suitable food sources (krill is now harvested in vast quantities for aquaculture), take their own toll. Positive trends are, therefore, by no means absolute but all are agreed that a general transition from commercial hunting to a conservation-led approach has, undoubtedly, been beneficial.[373] Apart from its impact on whale populations, evidence shows that targeted legislation to protect other marine mammals too – supported by a watchful population and global campaigns – can be an effective means of conservation. Along the west coast of the United States, for example, endangered species legislation has led to favourable outcomes: 'More than 75 per cent of marine mammal and sea turtle populations have shown significant signs of recovery after being protected by the U.S. Endangered Species Act.'[374]

Sea turtles offer a good example of how downward trends in numbers can be reversed. These beautiful creatures have a hard enough time to reproduce on the beaches and escape predators at sea. When they were regarded as a delicacy for consumption their very survival as a species was at stake and, indeed, there are still perennial problems of losses resulting from bycatches, pollution and getting tangled in discarded nets. In spite of all this, the over-riding lesson is that they are remarkably resilient and, if they can be offered protection over a number of years, there is a good chance that their numbers will rise again. This is well illustrated on the Seychelles island of Aldabra, where protective measures were introduced in 1968 and since then have had very positive results:

> *The latest estimates showed more than 15,000 egg clutches on the beaches of Aldabra Atoll per year from 2014 to 2019. Based on the average of three to five clutches per female [it is estimated that] between 3,000 and 5,000 green sea turtles are visiting the beaches of the atoll every year to lay eggs. That represents a roughly 500 per cent increase since the 1960s.*[375]

The case of sea turtles on Aldabra shows that local conservationists can make a real difference in protecting species. But it also shows that there are counterforces at play, which can only be tackled through national agreements between stakeholders and international regulations. The one cannot be fully effective without the support of the other.

## *Who needs sea walls?*

Like so many actions affecting the ocean, a relatively short but critical period of human destruction is followed by reflection and realisation that wrong has been done. The mangrove is one such case. With 80 different sub-species, as a shrub or tree it grows naturally in saltwater and on wet soils, hugging the coastline between sea and land. Typically, mangrove 'forests' are characterised by vegetation growing from a dense tangle of roots which are exposed at low tide and then submerged when the water rises. The species grows best in tropical and sub-tropical conditions (sometimes extending into warm-temperate zones) where it has for centuries been a natural feature of those coastlines. Then, for one reason or another – to make way for tourism and other development, or simply because it was not seen as having any particular value – great swathes were progressively cleared. Much of this change has been quite recent. In conversation with a pilot who regularly flew from Seychelles to South Africa, he recalls that, when he first followed that route, the long, eastern coast of Madagascar was lined with a thick belt of mangrove. Gradually, though, he noticed how the view was changing, with little now left between the sea and farmland beyond.

Radical changes to the natural habitat are quite likely to have adverse consequences that were not anticipated. The effects are soon obvious to local communities, who can see firsthand how things are changing, and it was not long before scientists added their own measured observations. The National Oceanography Centre (based in the UK), for instance, recently concluded that mangroves are 'effective at reducing the water level during extreme events, such as heavy storms or typhoons'.[376] Even if mangroves cannot totally prevent the ingress of high waters, they certainly reduce the impact and likelihood of flooding on the land beyond. In short, they offer a natural form of sea defence. This is a major reason why it is folly to remove them but there are other reasons too. Coastal communities also know that mangroves provide a natural habitat for juvenile fish and other forms of marine life, which take advantage of the protection offered by the tangle of roots. Additionally, there is the food value from catches of oysters, crabs and shrimps, used in local diets and as a source of income. In response to global warming, mangroves have an added attraction for their effectiveness in capturing large quantities of carbon that would otherwise escape into the atmosphere.  Compared with terrestrial forests, they are four times more effective.[377]

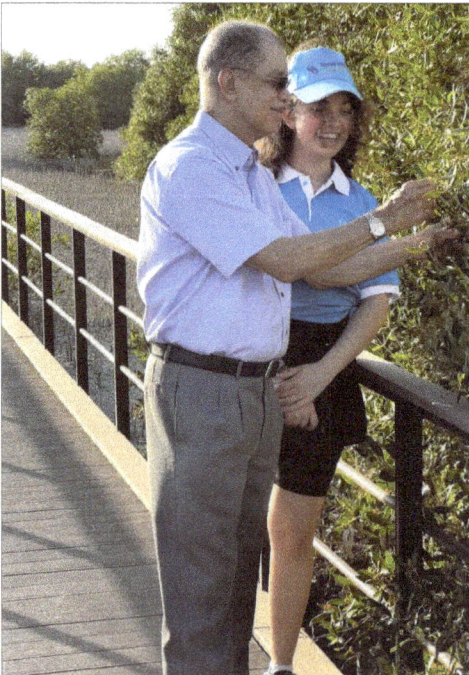

*(Top) Mangroves provide added protection to the coastline. After years of clearance, replanting schemes are now underway (Left) I recently visited, with my daughter, an example of mangrove restoration in Abu Dhabi*

For all these reasons, the further loss of mangrove forests is strongly opposed by conservationists. In an attempt to reverse the trend, replanting is encouraged, although it is recognised that timing is important; it is better to rejuvenate such areas before the rich soils where they grow best are lost. The distinctive roots play a vital role, literally, in holding things together and it takes valuable time to create new ecosystems. Even if there is a consensus in some parts of the world in favour of doing so, the political and practical challenge is formidable. But not impossible, thanks to the work of dedicated groups around the world. To illustrate what is being done, I can turn to the exemplary work of the Global Mangrove Alliance. Under a shared banner, the Alliance is a clearing house for ideas and a common voice for the cause. The Alliance estimates that an area of more than 8,000 square kilometres is suitable for replanting where previous mangrove forests have been lost. The process, however, is by no mean straightforward and much of the work of the Alliance is to provide technical advice for the various projects that are underway. The many islands within Indonesia were found to offer the largest potential restoration area, with over 2,000 square kilometres available for replanting. There is also considerable scope in Mexico, Australia, and Myanmar.[378]

I should also mention the dedicated work of another organisation with a global reach, Mangroves for the Future.[379] And on a smaller scale, Seychelles offers an interesting example of attempts to recover past losses of mangrove plantations. As much as 90 per cent of the original cover has disappeared, due to the usual reasons like land reclamation and development but also the impact of invasive alien species. In response, there are various replanting projects around the islands,[380] and a national commitment to protect all of the remaining clusters.

Additionally, my own foundation was in 2019 the recipient of a research grant, awarded to find out more about carbon capture in Seychelles from natural sources like mangroves, seagrass and wetlands. Best estimates suggest Seychelles is endowed with approx. 2.1 million hectares of seagrass meadows and mangrove forests spread across the inner and outer islands. In announcing the project, I explained that: 'Seagrass meadows and mangrove forests are indispensable for the Seychelles Blue Economy: they provide coastal resilience against storms and sea-level rise, enhance coastal biodiversity and support local livelihoods.'[381] Under the direction of Ameer Ebrahim, working with a team of scientists from Deakin University, the researchers undertook a survey of present sources and produced a road map to guide future policies. Seychelles scores highly as a provider of carbon capture but clear guidelines are needed to avoid incremental losses as a result of development and natural causes. Public awareness is a key factor and Ebrahim explained that: 'Children and local communities are increasingly involved in educational and on-ground restoration programs as a strategy to raise awareness and connect them with coastal wetlands.' [382]

## Idyllic meadows

Meadows are held with particular affection in the historical literature of pastoral life, a romantic portrayal of a segment of the landscape that is timeless and inherently green. But it is only recently that comparable images can directed to the seabed. Seagrass has become an ocean feature of importance, and unique in its own right:

> ...they are the only flowering plants that can live underwater. More closely related to lilies and gingers than to true grasses, they grow in sediment on the sea floor with erect elongate leaves and a buried root-like structure (known as rhizome).[383]

Collectively likened to meadows, seagrass is to be found over a wide extent of the ocean, in temperate as well as tropical regions, although not in water temperatures above 40°C.[384] The meadows are habitually close to the coastline and within a depth that allows sunlight to trigger the essential process of photosynthesis.

Seagrass is hardly a newly-discovered nor a single species (in fact, it contains 60 varieties), but its place in the ocean ecosystem has for many years been largely taken for granted. As such, its continued existence was not valued and, like so much of the ocean, it has suffered degradation. Fishing methods that rely on scouring the ocean floor, land reclamation schemes, and coastal developments including infrastructure for renewable energy, have all taken their toll. Belatedly, this is changing and its true worth and exceptional beauty is at last being recognised. For one thing, seagrass meadows can serve as nutrient sinks, buffering or filtering harmful substances before they reach the open sea. More than that (if one includes algae concentrations as well), the meadows are ranked as the third most valuable ecosystem globally for their nutrient cycling and for the raw product they yield, preceded only by estuaries and wetlands.[385] The meadows are also a wonderful habitat for fish and marine mammals, which can find shelter as well as food amongst the delicate fronds. Prawn and fish species, as well as green turtles, flourish and the benefits of healthy populations extend well beyond the boundaries of the meadows themselves. Significantly, too, it is realised that seagrass (like mangroves) is an effective source of carbon capture – their capacity to store carbon is 35 times faster than that of rainforests.[386]

Statistics are important but sometimes there is a particular story which best illustrates their value to society. I refer in this case to the habitat of the beleaguered dugong, which lives mainly in the Indian Ocean and western Pacific, and the closely-related manatee which is found elsewhere in tropical waters. They can be seen as an essential part of the underwater ecology found close to shores in these regions. For good reason the dugongs and manatees are sometimes described as sea cows which, like their terrestrial counterpart, thrive on a diet of grass. They can grow to a very large size (typically weighing 400kg and above) and can be expected to live to the age of 70.

*The manatee (or dugong): enormous but defenceless creatures in need of protection*

So why single out the example of these extraordinary, defenceless creatures? The answer is that, like so many aspects of the Blue Economy, their survival is threatened by relentless hunting (in spite of restrictions) and the same threats (like being hit by ships or getting caught up in fishing nets) that affect whales. Because of their long life-span and slow gestation period, they are particularly vulnerable to the threat of extinction (and are already declared so in the sea off China). It is a scenario that has become all too familiar – and, yet, I find hope in the fact that there always seems to be a dedicated group of people who actively resist these negative trends. One does not have to look far in this case to find a global project, with its mission 'to stop the loss of dugongs and their seagrass habitats across the Indian and Pacific Ocean basins'.[387] At a national scale, the Australian Government refers to legislation designed to protect a range of species, including dugong. Or, at a more localised level, I can read of a marine reserve off the Tamil Nadu coast of India where it is hoped that declining numbers of dugong can be stabilised.

The scenario is always the same – the natural features of the ocean under threat from human activities, with a rearguard response to try and save the day. I applaud the efforts of those who resist these many pressures but it seems a tenuous way to protect the ocean. There must be a better way and I return with some ideas on how to find a new direction later in the chapter.

## *The jewel in the crown*

In any discussion about ocean biodiversity and adverse effects of global warming, the fate of coral reefs comes high on the agenda. Although they cover no more than 1 per cent of the ocean floor, their impact in terms of colour, variety and clustering of different species is out of all proportion. Much of marine tourism is based on the magnetic attraction of what they have to offer. And at the heart of it all is no more than a small polyp:

> *Coral polyps are tiny, soft-bodied organisms related to sea anemones and jellyfish. At their base is a hard, protective limestone skeleton called a calicle, which forms the structure of coral reefs. Reefs begin when a polyp attaches itself to a rock on the sea floor, then divides, or buds, into thousands of clones. The polyp calicles connect to one another, creating a colony that acts as a single organism. As colonies*

*grow over hundreds and thousands of years, they join with other colonies and become reefs. Some of the coral reefs on the planet today began growing over 50 million years ago.*[388]

*Coral reefs are not only stunning in themselves but also a magnet for diverse marine life*

In spite of their natural longevity, in the face of a changing external environment they are also prone to sudden decline. Pollution, sedimentation and, most widely in the present context, higher sea temperatures and acidification can all lead to their demise. Faced with all this, the coral ecosystem is damaged, sometimes without any chance of recovery. The polyps themselves are translucent but reefs are built over time through the aggregation of, maybe millions, of limestone skeletons and it's the reefs which attract myriad marine plants renowned for their bright colours. These, in turn, are visited by a wide variety of fish and other species, forming distinctive coral ecosystems. In the face, especially, of global warming, the plant life which once flourished is detached from the reefs, the result being a barren environment typified by 'bleaching'. This is the situation that now prevails, with once-flourishing coral reefs no longer resembling how they were in the recent past.

Ocean biodiversity depends in no small measure on their recovery but is this any longer possible? Studies have shown that, even when coral dies or bleaches, so long as local conditions improve then recovery is possible.[389]

Reducing harmful run-off from agriculture and avoiding over-fishing are ways in which this can be supported. In other words, coral in a state of decline needs a helping hand and, fortunately, as with mangroves and seagrass, there are organisations with a major engagement in the process. The Nature Conservancy is one such body with an international reach, incorporating coral recovery in its global conservation activities. Focusing on the Caribbean, its 'multifaceted approach aims to restore the long-term health of coral reefs, increase their resilience to a changing climate and address the threats that have caused their deterioration'.[390] A feature of this body's work is the creation of a number of Coral Innovation Hubs, where laboratories have been established to grow types of coral that can be expected to grow best in affected areas.

Elsewhere, the Australian Coral Reef Society dates back to 1922 and is essentially a scientific forum, with extensive knowledge of coral in different conditions. There are also agencies and actions such as the Coral Reef Alliance, the Coral Reef Foundation, and the American Coral Reef Restoration Program, just a few amongst a growing number of activists finding ways to keep coral as a feature of ocean biodiversity. I have already referred in this book to the innovative work of Nature Seychelles, which has tackled a variety of conservation projects, including coral restoration. In 2020, it launched a new project which is a regional collaboration between Seychelles and Mauritius, designed:

> ...to restore reefs using ocean and land-based nurseries, as well as to bolster regional scientific advances and exchanges. The 'reef gardening' concept will continue to be used, aiming at cultivating at least 50,000 coral fragments to restore at least 1ha. of degraded reef around Cousin Island Special Reserve. The project will also look at novel techniques from overseas in coral genetics and reproduction.[391]

And so it goes on. For every setback and news of further degradation, there is also hope embodied in the efforts of coral enthusiasts. It is a fine balance between negative and positive forces, something I will pursue in the concluding section of this chapter.

## Can There Be a New Synthesis?

Clearly, not everyone thinks ocean biodiversity is important. Experience shows that a common respect and love for a profusion of marine flora and fauna will not simply happen because a few people say it should. My own belief, of course, is that it does matter and I take heart from the fact that this view is widely shared. Not just by avid conservationists but by all kinds of people who instinctively know that a healthy sea is what we should strive for. We all have a responsibility to care for what we have inherited and to pass it on to future generations. It is not acceptable to passively witness the disappearance of the dugong, or the wanton removal of mangroves and seagrass. Everything has a place in the universe, sometimes for very practical reasons – like providing coastal protection – and sometimes for the more abstract notion that every loss, no matter how small, takes something essential away from the whole.

So why is it that not everyone believes that biodiversity matters? Is it because humans are inherently selfish? Is it because not everyone is aware of the effects of their actions? Or is it because we have simply abrogated responsibility and fail to exercise the choice we have? And how should we deal with so many different perspectives? Ethically, I would prefer to be able to rely on rational argument to achieve a consensus around sustainability, but I know that persuasion alone is not enough. To illustrate this in a different context, it would not be sufficient simply to ask every user of the road to drive carefully and leave it at that. One could barely imagine the chaotic outcome if there were not enforceable rules as well. Suffice to say that, for whatever reason, we all seem to need firm guidelines, if not the rule of law, to manage human behaviour. And this applies in the case of the environment just as much as for controlling traffic or paying our taxes – just so long as there is a common good in sight and sense of fairness. In the case of the High Seas, it has taken years of negotiation to get to where we are, and this is itself only the beginning of a continuing journey. Persuasion itself failed to work and our faith now is in the rule of law.

In earlier chapters, I have voiced my reservations about the effectiveness of certain international organisations to make a difference. The success of the UN to broker a treaty on biodiversity might encourage me to change my mind but, if I do, it will not be yet. Let us wait to see if the international body can withstand the undoubted pressures that will be put on it to relent on essential details. In the meantime, once again I admire the tenacity and single-minded purpose of NGOs, which can focus on different issues and are often able to make a difference in the sea. Dugongs and mangroves have good reason to be appreciative of their work.

The fact remains that, even with the law on our side, ways have to be found to understand, if not totally to accommodate, different perspectives. This is not a question of conceding points that would run counter to the goal of sustainability. If, for instance, a fishing community has always hunted whales, the practice should be stopped but, in its place, perhaps investment can be provided to enable alternative activities. Karl Marx was wrong about many things but he was right when he described constructive change in terms of opposing ideas – thesis and antithesis – yielding, through their confrontation and fusion, a new reality in the form of a synthesis. It is this third reality that we should now be looking towards. Sustainability cannot rely on an enduring clash between thesis and antithesis; if we want to overcome this, we must put our minds to finding a synthesis, for which both sides can be signatories. This would not weaken sustainability but, through wider backing, strengthen it.

Moreover, it would be a creative process, inviting new ideas and innovative projects. In earlier chapters, I have spoken about the circular economy as one way to tackle waste; I have questioned whether we can rely on a never-ending supply of fish (whether farmed or in the wild) to feed the world's burgeoning population; and I have questioned whether the value of a new generation of mobile phones justifies the practice of deep-ocean mining. I would question, too, whether we can support the present rate of increase of tourist activities without undermining wider goals of ocean sustainability. Somehow, we have to square the circle, to create new ways of doing things where sustainability is no longer jettisoned at the first sign of competing claims. This is no easy task but we have to be equal to the challenge. Nothing comes easy, let alone the prospect of a better world.

# Chapter 11

## Coastal Watch
*Dealing with rising sea levels, better seaboard planning*

In the planet's gallery of great works, the ocean is the star of the show. But, like an exceptional painting, it calls for a suitable frame to complement its inherent qualities. When both are in harmony, the one enhances the other. Presently, though, there is discord: the reality of rising sea levels is one reason, a string of inappropriate development around the edge another. Restoring a balance between 'picture' and 'frame' is essential if there is to be a sustainable transition to the Blue Economy.

It is no easy task. Geography poses its own challenges. The meeting of sea and land is a place of remarkable variety and there can be no single formula to produce what is right. In the polar regions, for instance, the line between the two is lost beneath great swathes of ice, changing all the time because of a rapid rate of melting. In other instances, the line could not be sharper, like the 3,000 kilometres of uninterrupted coastline where Somalia meets the Indian Ocean. Or, in contrast, the Norwegian fjords, where past glacial action allows the sea to intrude inland along what resemble deep ravines. Elsewhere, one finds sunken coastlines where the sea shares the space with clusters of islands. And deltas, a complex mingling of fresh and salt water, of mud flats and low islands, seemingly chaotic but, in fact, an inter-related system that serves its own ecological purpose. Sometimes, too, as one approaches the shore there is an intermediate zone of marsh or mangrove swamps, creating an ecosystem in itself but also performing a protective role for settlements beyond. Cliffs and sand dunes, white sandy beaches fringed by palms, receding coastlines and reclaimed land, the presence of cities and ports, a venue for tourism or just a popular place to live: all add to the intricate diversity of the ocean fringe.

So, for all of its differences, how can one achieve a good balance between sea and land? Of the possible scenarios, I believe that three are especially important to the goal of sustainability. One is to recognise the impact of climate change and rising sea levels, and to see what can be done to limit or at least manage encroachment; a second is to put the spotlight on ports and harbours, crucial shoreline features which must meet the needs of shipping in a sustainable way; and the third is to acknowledge the intensity of coastal development but also to cast a critical eye on its design and relationship to the sea. These are each different, one from another, but bound together by their common function as the ocean's picture frame.

## Rising Tide

The various impacts of climate change are too well known to repeat in full.[392] When in office, and since then, I have personally campaigned for countries to unite in reducing the rate of temperature increase that is directly due to human development. While the earth's history has been marked by natural climatic cycles (the most extreme being successive ice ages), there is no doubt that industrialisation and urbanisation over the past two centuries have accelerated the present process. So much so that the term 'anthropocene' has been coined to describe the change brought about, not by natural processes but the direct intervention of human actions.[393]

Year on year, gases released by the unremitting use of fossil fuels have accumulated to prevent the natural escape of heat from the sun. The effect is likened to a greenhouse in which the sun's rays are trapped, causing temperatures on the earth's surface and in the lower atmosphere to rise. Carbon dioxide is the main offender (it can remain in the atmosphere for a thousand years) but other gases like methane and nitrous oxide have comparable effects. By now, although the process has gone too far to reverse, efforts are being focused on at least trying to restrict the rate of temperature increase. It seems that the best that can be hoped for is to limit the global figure to 1.5°C. Yet, even at that level (which is itself proving an elusive target), the adverse effects will be considerable.

Higher temperatures will have different impacts in different parts of the world but the one which is most relevant to this particular study is through changes to the ocean, in the form of higher tides and a rising sea level. This will be mainly a result of two factors: one is that, as the temperature of the earth increases, the warmer conditions will lead the ocean's waters to expand. The other factor is that the melting of the polar ice caps and mountain glaciers will add to the volume of the sea. Precise effects will vary, depending on the actual temperature rise and also the particular features of the affected coastline. But one thing is clear: every coastal nation will be directly affected in one way or another. What is more, the process is already underway.

Clearly, countries most at risk are those which are barely above sea level to start with. Maldives is often cited in this category, where its 1,200 islands lie at an average of just a metre above sea level. Small island states in the Pacific, like Kiribati, Marshall Islands, Tokelau and Tuvalu also fear for their future, although they are by no means alone. The situation is replicated across much of that region, where there is a preponderance of low-lying coral atolls and reef islands. Some parts of the Solomon Islands have already disappeared beneath the sea.

Nor is it just a question of islands and whole nations which are vulnerable. Coastal plains of large land masses are also on the frontline. This can be especially important for small island states, where the low-lying coastal strip is often the most productive area for farming and settlement. Mahé, the largest island in Seychelles, for instance, is characterised by tall granitic mountains which rise sharply from the sea, so in that sense most of it is protected from flooding. However, it is the coastal plain on which the economy is most dependent and each year there are more signs of the sea encroaching.

Coastal plains are crucial to the wellbeing of larger nations too. In the United States, projections suggest that the sea level could rise by as much as 30 centimetres (equivalent to a foot) by 2050. Without mitigation measures, this will result in the loss of urban as well as rural land. Some parts of the nation, like Florida, the southern states along the Gulf, and New York will be especially prone to flooding. So, too, in China, the security of coastal plains, where an estimated 20 per cent of the population lives, is crucial to the economy, contributing as much as one third of the nation's GDP.

Elsewhere, the future of whole countries, which are barely above sea level as it is, will be most at risk. Bangladesh is already no stranger to heavy flooding from the sea (as well as rivers, augmented by melting glaciers in the Himalayas) and this will only increase. In Indonesia, Jakarta is a special case as the city is sinking (not as a result of climate change but excessive groundwater depletion) leaving it open to severe flooding in the future – so much so that a new location has been found in a different part of the country for the nation's capital.

And, in the same vein, stories can be told from all parts of the world of threats that have to be faced. But in this book I am looking not so much for problems as for positive initiatives, showing what can be done to live with a rising sea level. The world cannot wait while international leaders say the right words and then do the opposite. We have to dig deeper to find answers. The immediate future will depend on the success or otherwise of mitigation measures – where changes in the ocean have to be accepted as a given, while at the same time finding ways to reduce the impact.

## *Learning from Cnut?*

As already shown, the myth about the Danish king of mediaeval England, Cnut, is popular but wrong. He was not so misguided to believe that he could stand on a beach and exhort the incoming tide to stop before him. Instead (at the expense of getting very wet), he sought to demonstrate to his sycophantic courtiers the reverse, showing that such a mission was impossible and that the powers of a monarch were limited by a greater authority.[394] There is an enduring lesson in this simple anecdote, one that world leaders who flock each year to the latest climate change convention would do well to take. In the end, the sea is largely unstoppable and should be given the respect it deserves. We cannot turn back the tide but at least we can find ways to live with it.

Solutions are not always the most obvious. They require more invention than simply building a barrage or a seawall. In the words of one expert:

> *Fundamentally, there is an issue with the concept of building walls to stop flooding. We should not be thinking that we can stop every flood.*[395]

We cannot stop every flood but we can stop some and, in the course of doing this, we can adopt sustainable methods. Seawalls and other hard infrastructure solutions have their place but often all they do is deflect the power of the waves from one location to another. If used at all, it might be more effective if they are combined with greener solutions, referred to as 'living shorelines':

> *The components of a living shoreline are site-specific. For shores with relatively calm waters, the best bet is often a water-absorbing salt marsh, possibly fortified with sill-like ledges made of rocks, oyster shell bags, or 'logs' made of coconut fiber. Alternatively, a shoreline may benefit from the planting of mangroves, which develop hardy root systems firmly anchored in mud.*[396]

In some cases, creating a living shoreline is simply a question of preventing the loss of natural barriers and restoring the area to how it was before development. The more that is replanted the better chance of dissipating wave energy, and the sooner it is done the more likely it can outpace the rate of sea-level rise. Natural solutions can be relatively easy and cheap to create and are quite dramatic in their effects: just 15 horizontal feet of marshy terrain, for instance can absorb 50 per cent of incoming wave energy.[397]

In fact, the green options to counter flooding are numerous and best matched to specific conditions along the shoreline. As an example of what is available, the Environmental Resilience Institute at Indiana University has produced a useful menu for a living shoreline:

⬦ Create dunes along backshore of beach; includes planting dune grasses and sand fencing to induce settling of wind-blown sands
⬦ Increase shoreline setbacks
⬦ Plant submerged aquatic vegetation (such as seagrasses) to stabilise sediment and reduce erosion
⬦ Redefine river flood hazard zones to match the projected expansion of flooding frequency and extent
⬦ Remove shoreline hardening structures such as bulkheads, dikes, and other engineered structures to allow for shoreline migration
⬦ Replace shoreline armoring with living shorelines – through beach nourishment, planting vegetation, etc.
⬦ Use natural breakwaters of oysters (or install other natural breakwaters) to dissipate wave action and protect shorelines.[398]

In contrast with dealing with localised stretches of coastline, the potential loss of whole nations calls for a different scale of solutions. What, for instance can be done to enable the Maldives archipelago to survive? The root problem, of course, is the warming of the earth and, while this small island state can reduce its own emissions, that will make little difference unless there is a unified global response. There is no high ground to retreat to, and one scheme where sand is dredged from a lagoon to create four new islands, has met with fierce resistance from conservationists, on the grounds that it threatens the biodiversity of a site of international importance.[399] Another scheme for Maldives is for a floating city, an idea that has its origins in the Netherlands.[400] In other words, in this latter case, if conventional development is not possible why not use the sea itself as a building platform? It is claimed that 'the hexagon-shaped floating segments are, in part, modelled on the distinctive geometry of local coral'. These are, in turn, 'connected to a ring of barrier islands, which act as breakers below the water, thereby lessening the impact of lagoon waves and stabilising structures on the surface'.[401]

*Natural barriers are a more sustainable way of countering rising sea levels. Planting on sand dunes (Left) and seagrass restoration(Right) can both help to stabilise the coastline*

It is no coincidence that both schemes – the four islands and the floating city – are the work of Dutch engineers, well-versed in flood prevention from their country's experience of learning to live safely and well for centuries below sea level. There are two immediate lessons one can take from this unique history. One is that, for all the attractions of natural solutions, that country has been saved by a continuing programme of well-engineered and expensive infrastructure: seawalls and flood barriers to thwart heavy seas, coupled with an elaborate system of pumps and drainage channels to keep the land above water. The other lesson is that this approach requires constant investment. Holland could afford this because of its successful mercantile past, and now through its status as a modern industrial nation. But many countries in the world would not be able to match this level of investment.

I am reluctant to prescribe money as a panacea, when sometimes it can obscure the need for innovative thinking, but in this instance I believe it is crucial. How else will heavily populated delta regions like the Ganges-Brahmaputra, the Mekong and the Nile be able to afford what is needed? Or those tiny Pacific islands which have very little income? Walls and other forms of defence have to be built, roads raised, pumping systems installed and numerous buildings and installations relocated. At the very least, I believe this degree of change calls for a huge transfer of resources from richer to poorer nations, including commitments for maintenance and future upgrades. This is a global problem that needs a global solution. Coming to terms with the rising level of the sea, a product of years of mismanagement and avoidance on the part of more developed nations, is not a cheap option. In fact, I would say it is not an option at all; it has to be done. One cannot speak of a sustainable Blue Economy unless it is inclusive.

## Safe Havens

Scattered along the coasts are small, sometimes natural, inlets, which provide shelter for artisanal fishing boats and leisure craft. Such places offer the traditional facility of safe havens for seafarers. In contrast, there are major ports, on an altogether different scale more akin to large industrial complexes, catering for national and international shipping. As well as lengthy quaysides and numerous berths, they are characterised by tall cranes and extensive storage space where containers are piled high, with busy road and rail traffic connecting to factories and consumer outlets, associated refineries for oil and bulk goods, tight security arrangements and bright lights keeping watch on 24-hour operations. To achieve the goal of sustainability across such a wide range of activities, there is much that needs to be done. But there is an incentive to do so, ensuring that ports are as cost-effective and efficient as possible while also meeting higher global standards; new ports for a new age of shipping.

In an earlier chapter, the case was made for safe and sustainable shipping, with a growing number of initiatives described to illustrate the various efforts being made to achieve this. It is not only the ships themselves, however, which are in need of change but also the fixed infrastructure that serves international trade, most notably ports and harbours. They, too, must introduce and dovetail new practices so that they meet the same standards for safety and sustainability as the ships themselves.

*There is a natural symbiosis between small boats and the coast; a mooring rope is all that is needed to forge the link*

The fact is that modern ports occupy a major role in globalisation; they are too important to leave to chance. Their operations are essential to the timely delivery of imports and exports, and to the sustainability of shipping. This was vividly illustrated in the aftermath of the coronavirus pandemic, when supply lines were seriously interrupted because ships and containers were in the 'wrong' place. It was to take years rather than weeks to put right. In normal circumstances, the intricate networks have to be synchronised like the interconnecting parts of a finely working machine. Achieving sustainability is now seen as central to this requirement, partly because of new regulations for cleaner shipping but also because, as in any industry, good management and maintenance is essential.

At a macro-level, a widespread problem is that, by reason of their low-lying location, ports are especially vulnerable to rising sea levels. To ensure their survival and future viability, remedial measures have to be taken in good time, a message that is now recognised by international bodies like UNCTAD:

> Given the critical role of ports in the global trading system and their potential exposure to climate related damage, disruptions and delays, enhancing their climate resilience is a matter of strategic socio-economic importance for the global economy and society as a whole. It is also key to enabling Small Island Developing States and other vulnerable coastal and island nations to explore and harness the full potential and benefits of the blue economy for sustainable development.[402]

The shipping industry is setting a good example in devising ways to become more sustainable and there is evidence that ports are following suit. For all that, apart from the challenges facing ports *in toto*, the various functions within them are diverse, each requiring a different set of solutions to become more sustainable. Moreover, there is a sizeable backlog of unsustainable practices that have to be tackled. But a start is being made and standards are being set by new regulations for shipping, which have consequent implications for ports.[403] Cleaner fuels, for instance, will require complementary refining and storage facilities, as well as associated skills and training.[404] There is progress but the incidence of bunkering spills in harbour waters and the sight of black smoke from cargo ships that still use some of the most polluting types of diesel fuel are not yet a thing of the past.

Unsustainable practices have to be dealt with in different ways, although it must be recognised that actions taken are interconnected. Thus, economic sustainability is essential if there is to be much-needed investment; profitable ports are in a stronger position to bring about improvements. Likewise, environmental sustainability has consequent effects. For instance, in the words of a recent review by UNCTAD:

> While ports are vital for economic development and crisis response, the associated maritime traffic, handling of goods, and road and

*rail transport take a toll on the environment through air and water pollution. This is caused by fuel-powered cargo handling equipment, ships, trucks, trains and the power plants providing the energy needed to run port operations. The emissions include greenhouse gases such as carbon dioxide and particulate matter, which cause respiratory infections such as bronchitis and pneumonia, and chronic lung and heart diseases. Reducing port emissions would cut air and water pollution and improve the health of over 3.5 billion people while helping curb climate change.*[405]

*Environmental measures, therefore, are closely connected to social sustainability. Improvements taken in port operations can benefit not only the lives of people who work there but also those who live beyond the dock walls. There is limited value in making changes within the port if attention is not also paid to the polluting effects (including the hours of operation) of heavy transport which comes and goes. As well as breathing cleaner air, noise and bright lights that affect one's wellbeing can all be reduced.*[406]*And these are not the only social factors under consideration, with safety in ports and resilience to unexpected events high on the agenda too.*[407]

## Innovation hubs

As is often the way, radical change comes about not so often by direction, nor necessarily in tandem so that everything happens at the same time, but sequentially through the innovative approach of particular pathfinders. For various reasons, in improving port practices, Rotterdam demonstrates some of the best in current transformation.

The main reason for singling out Rotterdam is that the very scale of its operations increases the magnitude of the challenge. It is the largest seaport in Europe, and the largest outside East Asia – extending inland some 42 kilometres from the sea and offering a combined length of nearly 80 kilometres of quays. As well as its direct port activities, it contains the country's main petrochemical refineries and production units. Sailing into the port is an experience one can never forget, a seemingly never-ending complex of ships and containers, of tall cranes and floodlights that enable a 24-hour working day. Behind the initiative to make it sustainable is a single body, the Port of Rotterdam Authority, its core tasks being 'the sustainable development, management and operation of the port, the maintenance of the smooth and safe handling of shipping and supporting the future resilience of the port of Rotterdam'.[408] It is striving for net-zero emissions by 2050, and in pursuit of that it supplies LNG to tenants, incentivises use of shore power for ships, and includes renewable energy in its electricity mix.[409]

To work towards sustainability, the Authority groups its various activities within three clusters: a safe and healthy environment; climate and energy; and people and employment. A summary of headline projects is shown in the table below.

| Safe and Healthy Environment | |
| --- | --- |
| *Flood-Risk Management* | Protection measures are sound and regularly monitored. There is no increased risk of flooding in the port area. |
| *Truck Stops* | Dedicated spaces for visiting trucks to park when not in use, with good facilities for drivers. |
| *Discount for Cheap Shipping* | Both sea-going and land-based vehicles qualify for a discount on port dues when they meet designated environmental standards. |
| *Nature in the Port* | Nature reserves have been established in different locations. |
| *E-Noses* | Electronic sensors are used to detect noxious and hazardous emissions. |
| Climate and Energy | |
| *Wind and Solar Power* | Pilot study in progress for solar panels to fuel various installations; and space allocated for equipment to create wind energy. |
| *Heat Alliance* | Residual heat generated in the industrial sector of the port can be transferred by pipeline to other users within and beyond the port. |
| *Carbon Capture and Storage* | In place of releasing carbon emissions, these can be stored through a system of pipelines and under-sea storage. |

| Climate and Energy | |
|---|---|
| **LED for Public Lighting** | Replacement of all lighting with LED installations. |
| **Carbon Footprint** | As well as encouraging other users to reduce their carbon footprint, the Authority has taken steps to reduce its own too. |
| **People and Employment** | |
| **Social Agreement** | The Port Authority has joined with trade unions and container companies to produce an agreement on employment conditions. |
| **RDM Rotterdam** | A centre for research, design and manufacturing to identify new employment opportunities for the future. |
| **Port Welfare Committee** | Supports various projects for the benefit of seafarers in Rotterdam. |
| **Futureland and EIC Mainport** | Futureland is the main information centre for visitors. EIC Mainport shows young people a range of port-related jobs and training opportunities. |
| **Startbaan** | Gives young people without formal qualifications a chance to obtain a Diploma and possible jobs on completion. |

Even taken together, the above initiatives are nowhere near enough to lead to the port's sustainability. But they do show a commitment to work towards that ambitious goal. And it is encouraging to see that this is certainly not an isolated example. One of the innovations that can be seen in a number of progressive ports is the increased use of automation, particularly for operating cranes but also for other potentially dangerous equipment. This is not only highly efficient but it is safer to do this remotely from a control room rather than on site. As well as Rotterdam, automation in their operations is being extended in Singapore, Taiwan and Hong Kong. Other ports are promoting different initiatives.

Europe has a number of exemplary schemes, in addition to Rotterdam. The ports of Amsterdam, Antwerp and Gothenburg, for instance, all show a comparable commitment to sustainability. With justification, Hamburg claims not only to be the largest but also the most sustainable port in Germany. It has been using sulphur-free fuels for its own craft since 2009 and, to reduce emissions, all visiting ships when berthed are connected to land-based power connections. In southern Spain, the port of Algeciras is showing the way in the use of digitalisation. Through an innovative modular platform called Digital Port, it aims to optimise logistics processes in all its operations.

So, too, some North American ports are committing to sustainability. One sign of continent-wide interest is through a certification programme called Green Marine:

> Green Marine is an environmental certification program designed to promote environmental best practices across the North American marine industry. Green Marine sets benchmarks for performance across 14 indicators, including greenhouse gas emissions, community impacts, waste management, and underwater noise, and offers educational programs to help companies reduce their environmental footprint.[410]

The sustainability performance of North American ports is patchy but some have a deserved reputation for innovation. The Port of San Diego, for example, has been focusing on energy efficiency for the best part of a decade, when it first subscribed to climate action, leading to significant reductions in greenhouse gas emissions. To the north, also on the Pacific coast, with the dual advantage of tapping into the vast North American hinterland and routes across the Pacific to East Asia, Vancouver aspires to be the most sustainable port in the world. As well as generic initiatives, like reducing greenhouse emissions, it is interesting to see specific projects that are oriented to local conditions. One such project is the sensitivity of the port authority to how noise pollution can affect the survival of whales, and how the situation can be improved.[411]

In contrast, on a much smaller scale and in a different cultural setting, the Port of Krishnapatnam, on the east coast of India, is owned and operated by a private company, which from the outset has integrated sustainability objectives in its growth plans.[412] Under the banner of becoming a 'garden port', its environmental projects are seen as contributors to its commercial success. These various projects include the planting of 50 hectares of mangroves and 3.5 million trees on neighbouring coastal land, with a view to managing the impact of sea-level rise and reducing the local temperature. It is interesting that to encourage commitment by workers at the port, planting is carried out by its own employees in addition to their normal duties. Of its energy requirements, 60 per cent is provided naturally from the wind. Water management is also a priority and includes the use of atomisers for dust suppression, recycling water for its planting schemes, and conservation of reserves through rainwater harvesting ponds. Dust emissions are reduced by the use of electricity for cranes and internal transport. And the port authority has signed 'green MOUs' with other organisations to help in spreading good practice.

*Mangroves at Krihnapatnam Port: the port workers themselves engage in planting schemes around the site*

In spite of some undoubted achievements, the record, however, of ports becoming more sustainable remains something of a patchwork. As well as the obvious high-fliers, there will be numerous ports around the world which continue with outdated and unsustainable practices. The International Maritime Organization can introduce regulations but is unable to enforce them; some port operators have little interest in new ways of working; and, in any case, one must acknowledge that the size of the task, having to address so many activities, is monumental. So, inevitably, the change process is slower than many of us would like to see. However, I take heart from the fact that the situation is better than it was when I wrote my earlier book on the Blue Economy. In the intervening years, there has undoubtedly been progress in making practices more sustainable. And, with new practices, safer too. All of this counts for progress. This should be cherished. Further change is needed but at least the direction is now surely set. I would hope that by 2030 there will be more exemplary schemes and a general commitment to sustainable practices.

## Beside the Sea

An all-too-often ignored aspect of the Blue Economy is the impact of housing development close to the sea; unlike ports, it is not there because it has to be but because people choose to live by the ocean. In the words of an old British music-hall song (dating from 1907), popular with working-class audiences who were lucky if they made even an annual trip to their nearest seaside resort:

> *Oh! I do like to be beside the seaside!*
> *I do like to be beside the sea!*

Industrial societies in Europe and North America, and then in countries like Australia with cultural affinities, followed a similar pattern of enabling, first, people from industrial cities to make occasional visits to the seaside and, later, to buy homes for retirement. In the rush to meet an insatiable demand, developers paid little attention to how their buildings looked, the result being quickly-completed houses that would not be out of place in any suburban location. They were all much the same, although better-off occupants favoured large plate-glass windows, through which to gaze endlessly at the sea beyond. For everyone else, looking at rows of seaside development from the outside, the result was a scene of dull uniformity. One house was much the same as another. Surely the ocean deserved better neighbours than that.

Traditionally, long before mass housebuilding, the relationship with the sea was symbiotic. From one country to another, one can still find evidence of this. Take, for instance, the brightly painted buildings in far northern latitudes, as in Greenland and Iceland, where simple structures make their own statements in an otherwise bleak landscape, blanketed in darkness and semi-darkness for several months of the year. Or, in contrast, tropical villages where homes are on stilts, above the normal high-water mark, or carefully located marsh cabins on low mounds; there is nothing self-conscious about them, just the product of a natural harmony between living-space and nature. Often, too, harbours have attracted small rows of cottages, huddled around the waterfront where social as well as economic interaction was concentrated. I think of the example of Cornish fishing villages in south-west England, with grey, stone-built homes for fisherfolk. Or, performing the same function but in appearance very different, the dazzling white buildings that fringe island harbours in Greece, sometimes with a shrine on a higher slope where fishermen would look to give thanks for their safe return. I recall, too, the distinctive sight of homes tumbling down steep slopes in other parts of the Mediterranean, like the Amalfi coastline in Italy, seemingly unplanned but creating their own sense of harmony.

*Sometimes settlements seem to tumble down the hillside to be close to the sea*

In contrast, modern development is so often bland and dissociated from the sea itself. Yet, I know from other observations that it need not be like this. Coastlines have been desecrated by thoughtless development motivated solely for profit. I know that there are examples of exotic architecture on rocky outcrops overlooking the sea – the kinds of places built for celebrities and oligarchs – but these are exceptions to a dull norm. It is time, I believe, that under the banner of the Blue Economy a start be made to reverse this unsightly legacy. New designs can be introduced to explore the potential of such a unique location: within sight, sound and even the scent of the ocean. And, in a modest way, there is evidence that this reversal has already started. I am thinking here of the interesting projects derived from a movement called the New Urbanism.[413] Starting in America, the idea is to create places that restore a sense of community, with buildings that reflect local conditions and where people are encouraged to walk and shop locally. Critics (of which there many) say it is an attempt to turn back the clock, embracing everything that is traditional and rejecting modernity. Advocates, on the other hand, argue that there is no virtue in modernity if all it does is lead to its own uniformity, using artificial materials that bear no relationship to their surroundings and forcing people to use cars rather than making it possible to walk, say, to a local school or a community centre.

## Seaside, Florida

To illustrate this new approach in a coastal context, I turn to the example of Seaside, a novel experiment in Florida's Panhandle, on the northern shore of the Gulf of Mexico.[414]

As is so often the case with innovation, it features the commitment and ideas of a few leading individuals, in this case spearheaded by a wealthy but also benevolent developer named Robert Davis, and a progressive architect renowned for his espousal of the New Urbanism, Leon Krier. Davis, a Harvard graduate, recalled boyhood vacations spent on land by the sea which had been bought by his idealistic grandfather, who had a vision of turning it into a summer camp for his employees, with the name of Dreamland Heights. By the time Robert inherited the site, it was still largely undeveloped, although his personal experience of staying in traditional buildings was enough to inspire him to create something new. Former architecture, he believed, typified the old South – homes with generous porches shaded by deep roof overhangs and with gentle breezes blowing beneath the raised floors and through the well-ventilated rooms. With his wife, he travelled through the neighbouring states of Alabama and Georgia, making it his business to find out more about the intricate ways in which traditional buildings responded to local conditions.

In turn, Leon Krier brought to the project his European experience and warmed to the prospect of creating a small township where a car was not needed and people would soon get to know each other. Sustainability was high on his agenda. But there were two other architects, Andres Duany and Elizabeth Plater-Zyberk – not at that stage so well known – who were to deliver the masterstroke. Their genius was to recognise that Seaside (as the development was called) should be about more than taking commissions from prosperous clients. Instead, they produced a series of pattern books: 'A system of codes prescribing in considerable detail the placing of buildings, setbacks, lot lines, fences, road widths, style even, window design and so forth.'[415] Every house in Seaside had to have a porch, and all the picket fences were to be made of real wood and painted white.

It was not only the initial design that was prescribed: owners were given a limited choice of colours to paint their houses. At the same time, there was scope for individuals to introduce interesting features such as towers, pavilions, follies and gazebos.

*Towers and picket fences are iconic features of Seaside*

Nor was it just individual buildings which characterised Seaside. No less important was the attention paid to the public domain, a conscious attempt to revive the lost qualities of small-town America. Bucking a trend, rather than travel to a distant mall, provision was made for a post office and general stores, a church and school, all of which could be reached on foot. There is a market and an amphitheatre for open-air performances, and local artists are encouraged to exhibit their works along the sidewalks in the appropriately named Ruskin Square. A 1 per cent levy to support the arts is added to every purchase in the town.

And the sea is never far away, whether viewed with a drink in hand at sunset from the distinctive towers, or approached by the boardwalks which cross the line of sand dunes onto the sandy beach. Every morning, joggers and walkers make their way along the shoreline, exuding a sense of wellbeing. A striking feature are the beach pavilions, all with their own design and offering a natural point of gathering for the nearest residents, as well as focal points on the horizon.

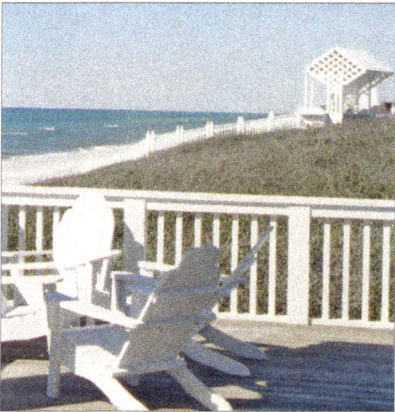

*The beach pavilions are a feature much loved by residents and tourists*

Seaside has evolved to become a successful township in its own right, inspiring the creation of other small settlements along the same stretch of coastline. It is a commercial success but, more than that, something of an architectural landmark, attracting a regular stream of visitors who want to see for themselves what is so different. For some visitors it is all too folksy, a make-believe world for the privileged, a ready-made film set that was used in 'The Truman Show'. And altogether too smug to be real. But that is surely not the point. It is not that everywhere should necessarily look exactly like Seaside, nor serve the same cultural preferences. Instead, the use of design codes enables endless variations from one place to another. It would be entirely inappropriate to try to emulate this Florida creation in a contrasting coastal location in, say, the Indian Ocean or the Baltic. The beauty of design codes is that they are adaptable and enable planners working in different cultural and landscape settings to produce much higher standards than present systems allow. Pattern books for coastal development, inspired by the principles of the New Urbanism, have the potential to transform what has become an unacceptable norm. They should not be seen as a blueprint but as a valuable tool, to be used to bring to life this hitherto neglected aspect of the transition to a sustainable Blue Economy.

# Chapter 12

# Reducing Risk
*Respecting the might of the ocean*

In the course of describing (in earlier chapters) the various ocean activities and showing how they can become more sustainable, the devil lurks in the shadows. Such are the attractions of the sea that it is all too easy to ignore this unwelcome presence. But it would be folly in the extreme to do so. For good reason, the maritime security expert, Christian Bueger, describes his specialism as the dark end of the spectrum.[417] Ocean sustainability cannot be achieved in its entirety without ensuring that there are no unnecessary dangers; that all activities are as safe as possible.

Particular risks have been addressed in the course of the earlier chapters, whether they be in relation to ship design or fishing far from shore, tourists who are unfamiliar with the might of the sea or planners who ignore the implications of rising tides. It is time now to bring together common themes for a safer future. The focus will be on ways to remove needless risk: coming to terms with the ocean rather than burying one's head in the sand. First, I will consider the element of risk itself and why we do not always see (or want to see) the threats before us. This leads, in turn, to measures of safety, and what interventions can be most productive.

In the final part of this chapter, I will turn to a number of examples to illustrate not only the threats but also how issues of maritime security might more effectively be tackled. In turning the spotlight on maritime security, the aim is to emphasise that, unless the sea can offer free and safe access, it will fall short in an important way of the goal of a sustainable Blue Economy.

## 'For Those in Peril on the Sea'

All coastal cultures will have experienced their share of tragedies, of fellow countrymen and women drowned close to shore or on long voyages. Prayers will be spoken and hymns sung, in a mixture of memory and invocation of a higher power:

> *Oh, hear us when we cry to Thee,*
> *For those in peril on the sea!* [418]

The sea can be unforgiving, capricious in the extreme, given to sudden changes of mood. And surely we would not want it any other way, for is not part of its appeal that inherent free spirit, although it can bring sadness as well as joy? The sea can never be tamed but we can, at least, come to terms with the challenges presented. It is within our own ability to reduce risk and improve safety, although even this is by no means straightforward.

For a start, not all risk is to be avoided. Business analysts worry about the uncertainty associated with it but they also appreciate that there is risk in doing nothing. Standing still while others forge ahead is hardly a sustainable strategy. Innovators, for instance, are inherent risk-takers and breakthroughs would not be possible without their moving beyond safe ground. We are indebted in many ways for their doing so. In another context, too, as fans of adventure movies will agree, it's the risk-takers who win the plaudits. Would Bruce Willis chasing a perpetrator, faced with the chasm of an open shaft, choose to wait patiently for the elevator? All of this is true enough but there is also a world of difference between good risks and bad, the one driven by careful calculation and the other by impossible odds. And, of course, it is one thing to choose to take a risk and quite another to have no choice but to live under a volcano.

In searching for an understanding of the issues, I am indebted to the work of Lloyd's Register and its Foundation. The original company was founded in the eighteenth century as the world's first marine classification society, with the aim of improving the safety of ships. For all the busy mercantile traffic at the time, there was remarkably little order and few rules to guide the process. The Register was an early attempt to redress this. Together, the two organisations now work together to offer not only a core of business activities but also a reliable source of information on international shipping and other marine activities. The reach is global, revealing a wide range of ideas and practical measures to make the ocean a safer place in which to operate.

> *Lloyd's Register is wholly owned by the Lloyd's Register Foundation, a politically and financially independent global charity that aims to engineer a safer world through promoting safety and education. The Foundation focuses on the most pressing global safety challenges, establishing the best evidence and insight to understand the complex factors that affect safety, and by building partnerships for change. For a thriving ocean economy, Lloyd's Register and Lloyd's Register Foundation work together to fund research, foster industry collaboration and develop action-oriented solutions.*[419]

As an example of their universal scope, in 2019 (and again in 2021) a global survey – the World Risk Poll – was organised to measure what people regard as the greatest risks in their lives.[420] Not surprisingly, the issues that most concerned the 126,000 respondents polled, reflected those concerns which were affecting individuals directly and on a daily basis: for instance, a fear of street crime and the possibility of road accidents were ubiquitously high on the agenda. Although it was a peak period in terms of the Covid pandemic, the virus was ranked well below other items. And, in spite of the high level of publicity given to climate change in general, concern was more marked amongst those who had personally experienced the effects of severe weather incidents. Again, it was not a surprise that low-income groups generally felt more at risk on all counts than those who could afford to mitigate threats. This was not universally true as low-income groups in Africa saw themselves as more at risk on most issues than their counterparts in Asia. Perhaps the most disappointing finding in the latest report is the low level of confidence people have in their governments to protect them from the issues that are of greatest concern.

The World Risk Poll, in general, is certainly of interest in providing a global context but, perhaps, it is the reasons why some issues are not seen as prime risks that offer the more intriguing insights into the subject. Risk is a product not only of knowledge but also of perception, and the things that people are most concerned about are not always predictable. Given the huge number of fatalities and damage to property, one might have thought that the 2004 Indian Ocean tsunami would have lasting effects on where to live.[421] In the event of another tsunami, living in low-lying coastal regions in the Indo-Pacific carries the greatest risks. But there is no evidence of large-scale evacuation; on the contrary, with population growth there will almost certainly be more people living in the vulnerable areas than before. Partly, this is because low-income families would find it difficult to move, but there is also the fact of perception. People weigh up the chances of another tsunami on this scale affecting a particular location, and they decide to stay. In other words, they know about the risk but choose to live with it. After all, they might consider there is more chance of getting run down by a car tomorrow or contracting a life-threatening disease.

*People assess risk in different ways. In spite of the widespread destruction caused by the 2004 tsunami in the Indian Ocean, there is no evidence of mass migration to other places*

As an important outcome of the poll, the Foundation (in association with Gallup) drilled into the responses to highlight the element of resilience, showing how people might react to critical events and how prepared governments are to take a lead. Especially relevant to this discussion is the report on resilience to a changing climate.[422] It showed that, at the level of individuals and households, only half of the people believed there would be anything they could do in the event of a natural disaster. Nearly one in three said they would be unable to support their families for more than a month (and in many cases for a shorter time) if they suddenly lost their income. Internet connections are far from universal but for those who have this access, the continuance of the service in a disaster was seen as a lifeline. And in only 14 of the 121 countries polled did a majority claim to have a plan for survival in the case of a natural disaster.

At the level of community and society, fewer than one in four respondents worldwide said they could count on their neighbours in a time of crisis; a proportion that generally increased in low-income countries and was lower in places with higher incomes. Essential infrastructure, to include healthcare, education and roads, was lacking in countries with longstanding political and economic issues, where people felt most at risk. Likewise, a recent history of discrimination undermined confidence in governments to provide support fairly and equally. Three quarters of those polled felt they could not rely on their governments to adequately provide for them in their hour of need, with Central and Western Africa, and Latin America and the Caribbean showing the most adverse results.

From these findings, a resilience index can be calculated, the purpose of which is to provide a valuable tool for policymakers. Where can international resources best be directed to improve rates of resilience? The areas most in need largely reflect differences in income although other factors intervene. For instance, South-Eastern Asia records low incomes but high resilience. Not surprisingly, the most vulnerable groups are women with low incomes in in Afghanistan and also in Central and Western Africa.

In parallel with the polling exercises, the Foundation commissioned a study to show ways in which it is possible to engineer a safer future.[423] The outcome is a formidable report which seeks to reconcile the enormous changes which lie ahead, with the joint aims of minimising harm to the ocean and offering restorative measures in the long term for overall global benefit. This present summary (in this chapter) hardly does justice to the detailed evidence and arguments in the report, but it is worth recounting what are considered priority action areas for ocean safety. Six such areas are identified: public awareness and policy; evidence insight and ocean data; decent work at sea; ocean engineering (infrastructure and systems); ocean infrastructure (education and skills); and ocean foresight.

Firstly, public awareness and policy calls for a new generation of 'ocean citizens' who can actively participate in campaigns and support for compatible projects. The Foundation itself can help to create partnerships, working with bodies like the UN Global Compact (with its orientation to businesses), to encourage the adoption of safety and sustainability principles in future ocean engineering. Reference is also made to the Foundation's maritime heritage collection and how that can be used to increase public awareness. Nor is that just historical, as future generations can be encouraged to see present changes as the start of a new model of heritage.

Secondly, the report stresses the fact that so little is still known about the ocean and how vital it is to build a credible evidence base to underpin policies. Where data does exist, it is often kept in 'silos'; a policy of sharing these sources needs to become second nature. The Foundation, it is asserted, can be a leader in building and sharing actionable insights on all aspects of ocean safety.

A third priority is the achievement of decent work at sea (a point that I have already highlighted in an earlier chapter). Working in partnerships, it is proposed that: 'The Foundation should support others to ensure that new jobs created in the ocean economy have high standards of welfare and safety, that actively protect workers and vulnerable groups, and support equity, diversity and inclusion.'

*Engineering a safer future embraces a wide variety of sensible practices, from checking equipment to keeping a clean ship*

Next is considered the hardware aspect of ocean engineering, in the form of infrastructure and systems. It is acknowledged that the sheer volume of investments needed for groundbreaking research and development will normally exceed the budget of any one organisation and, as a result, the Foundation can have a role in 'supporting knowledge transfer across sectoral and geographic boundaries and by catalysing cooperation and action in areas where new approaches and thought leadership is needed'. The Foundation can also 'build on its [own] investments in areas such as autonomy and robotics, data centric engineering, decarbonsation and complex systems; and accelerate new research and development in emerging areas such as multi-use infrastructures, nature-based engineering, marine spatial planning and full life-cycle assessments'.

As the fifth priority action area, the report turns to another aspect of ocean engineering, namely, education and skills. Given the transformational developments underway, it follows that present models of education and training must make a commensurate leap. Ideally, they should be leading the changes but, at the very least, they need to keep pace in providing workers with appropriate skills and understanding. Once again, the Foundation can play a key role, including to facilitate a global conversation about the skills needed for ocean safety in the new ocean economy.

Finally, attention is turned to ocean foresight. Global communication is vital so that evidence is shared and all parties have a chance to be part of ongoing progress. As a 'ringmaster' in the process, the Foundation can 'monitor and forecast new trends, support technological and skills road mapping, and highlight and promote the safety risks and opportunities in emerging sectors'.

## 'The Dark End of the Spectrum'

In the previous section, I concentrated on issues of risk and safety that can be influenced through domestic and non-military actions. But there is another dimension, which takes us into a military and quasi-military arena. This is usually referred to as maritime security and is an aspect of a sustainable Blue Economy in its own right. To match expectations, the ocean should offer a safe and reliable means of carrying goods from one port to another; a peaceful setting where tourists are unthreatened;

a place where different jurisdictions are respected; an absence of illegal activities on the High Seas; and, not least of all, freedom from national and international conflicts. Maritime security is an important and multi-faceted subject that defies easy definitions.[424] To illustrate its role, rather than adopt an encyclopaedic approach in which all aspects are individually addressed, I have, instead, selected just a few cameos; in doing it this way, there are, inevitably, different aspects of maritime security omitted but, even allowing for this, I hope to convey a sense of why this aspect of the Blue Economy matters.

The first of the cameos offers a topical example of why wars are incompatible with the idea of a sustainable ocean, one in which there is free movement of shipping. This is followed by a brief insight into the continuing practice of piracy, which is what I call, unequivocally, theft by another name. My third cameo looks to another type of criminal activity, namely the use of the sea to trade in drugs. Fourthly, I turn to some of the safety implications of greater volumes of maritime traffic and, particularly, how this is affecting shipping bottlenecks.

As far as possible, I have taken these examples from different parts of the world, if only to emphasise that maritime security is a global issue. Each is the result of human intervention and, in theory, it follows that each is capable of correction. As we will see, some solutions are more accessible than others. Or, as I liken it, there is some low-hanging fruit ready to be picked and some which remains elusively on the higher branches.

## *Bread deliveries*

Wheat is one of the world's essential commodities. It is a vital element in food security. Some countries are self-sufficient but many rely on imports to meet their needs. Transfers are normally made through the various mechanisms provided by globalisation. But globalisation itself is susceptible to events that interrupt complex flows of trade and finance. This happened during the Covid pandemic and, currently, in the face of the ongoing conflict between Russia and Ukraine.

Wars at sea have perennially constituted the ultimate threat to a free and open use of the ocean. Not only does the occurrence of conflict itself disrupt trade routes by making it unsafe for normal traffic to continue, but vital food supplies are sometimes themselves directly targeted. Grain is one such item where a blockage leading to shortages can affect morale and even physical survival. This is all too well illustrated at the present time.

Thus, Ukraine is a major wheat exporter and in normal times ships sail south from its main Black Sea ports, centred on Odessa, through the Bosphorus Strait to all parts of the world. But these are not normal times and, since February 2022, Ukraine has been unable to guarantee the regular movement of wheat exports (and other grains, such as maize and barley) to countries where they are needed. For the first six months of the conflict, it was not safe for ships to leave Odessa and other ports along the same coast, prior to an agreement brokered by the UN and Turkey with Russia. As a result of these negotiations, exports were then permitted to follow a 'grain corridor' across the Black Sea, subject to a review of the arrangement after 120 days. Russia is itself a major grain exporter but sanctions on financial transactions, imposed by the West, put limits on where and what it is free to export.[425]

Through the agreement to allow Ukraine to send grain overseas, at the time of writing some 800 ships to date have crossed the Black Sea with this valuable cargo. Because of the need to impose checks on whether the ships are acting in accordance with the agreement, movements have sometimes been delayed; sometimes as many as a hundred ships are forced to wait in line for clearance. Once these delays are overcome, however, ships laden with grain have offered a lifeline for countries facing severe food shortages and rising prices (although critics point out that most of the early supplies released in this way were sent to high-income destinations and not necessarily to those poorer nations most in need).[426] Even with shortcomings, however, one might assume that, in practical terms, there is now a state of near-normality. That, however, is far from the truth. For one thing, the volume of exports is well below what was commonplace before the conflict. There is also a critical question of safety: the war is ongoing and crews find themselves embroiled in a conflict where one can never be certain if the designated corridor will be respected and their safe passage assured. This is no way to manage the ocean, in the interests of all, and the situation will not be normalised until the war itself is brought to an end.

## *Theft by another name*

In spite of all that we now know about modern piracy, the very name still conjures up images of swashbuckling adventurers and commandeered chests brimming with unimaginable treasures. The romanticisation of piracy was misguided then – for the practice is as old as international trade – just as it is now. A more realistic view is that it is no more than another aspect of organised crime, which involves theft and violence.

*An anti-piracy exercise in the Gulf of Guinea*

Far from being consigned to history, modern piracy reared its head early in the present century with incidents in the Indian Ocean off the coast of Somalia. At the same time, the Malacca Strait also attracted its own criminal activities, directed in that case mostly towards the lure of valuable oil supplies. And a third focus of piracy emerged off the coastline of north-western Africa, in the expansive Gulf of Guinea, extending on both sides of the equator in an arc from Gabon in the south to Liberia in the north. In total, it includes over 6,000 kilometres of coastline and is bordered by 20 countries. Roughly at a mid-point, it contains the lucrative oilfields of the Niger Delta. The Gulf of Guinea soon acquired the unwanted reputation of being the world's 'hotspot' for maritime piracy, with container ships, fishing vessels and oil tankers all targets of armed attacks and kidnappings. Little wonder the shipping industry has been foremost in urging strong measures to prevent this:

*Pirate groups in the Gulf of Guinea are resilient and determined,*

*often attacking at more than 200 nautical miles from the shore.
Their main objective is to kidnap seafarers and demand ransoms
from shipping companies for their release. They are often violent, and
seafarers and navy personnel have been killed during attacks. Given
the severity of the crimes it is essential that voyages in the GOG
are fully threat and risk assessed and self-protection measures applied
by ships.*[427]

Towards the end of 2022, various reports suggested that the number of
incidents in the region was decreasing. The fall was by no means dramatic
and it was too early to be sure that it would continue. Causes for this
modest decline were by no means certain yet credit was given for measures
taken by countries in the region and international partners, coupled with
the first piracy convictions in 2020 in the courts of Nigeria and Togo. In
its own report, the International Maritime Organization recommended
additional actions that could be taken.[428] A more sceptical view is that the
underlying causes remain and all that is happening to reduce the number
of incidents is a switch by pirates to other maritime criminal activities. It is
a troubled region with far from a unified approach to tackle the problems.
Attempts to control the situation are piecemeal and, after ten years, a
proposal to establish a strong security framework has still to be adequately
implemented.[429]

## Drug smugglers at sea

It would be folly to claim that drug smugglers have total freedom to operate
at sea but their illicit activities are extremely difficult to trace. In a ship with
up to 20,000 containers piled high, who is to say whether drugs are hidden
in a false compartment or amongst cargo in just one of these? And that is
apart from the vast expanse of the ocean and the inability of surveillance
craft to patrol more than a small fraction of their assigned territory. To add
to the challenge, some smugglers now use underwater drones to transport
their contraband from a source country.[430] Even though there is the prospect
for smugglers, if they are caught, of very long prison sentences, the potential
monetary rewards for the perpetrators are high enough to make the risk
worthwhile. In any case, it is the carriers who are likely to be caught and
not the drug barons in the countries of origin.

There are few parts of the ocean where drug smuggling is absent – but the
two heaviest trafficked routes are those from South America which target

the lucrative markets to the north (the US is the world's largest consumer of illicit drugs, accounting for about a third of global consumption),[431] and from the ports of western Asia, where heroin from Afghanistan is conveyed mainly to Europe and Africa. Most of the cocaine available in European drug markets (which originates in South America) is smuggled in by sea, primarily in maritime container shipments entering major container ports such as Antwerp, Rotterdam, Hamburg and Valencia.[432]

To take a small but specific example of how drug smuggling operates, heroin is taken from the growing areas in Afghanistan to be loaded onto dhows in Iran and Pakistan, *en route* to meeting points in the western Indian Ocean. From Seychelles (which has the unwelcome reputation of being home to the highest *per capita* rate of heroin addiction), fast boats are sent to meet the dhows and transfer the valuable cargo for subsequent sale in the small island state. Occasionally, individuals are caught at the mid-ocean point of transfer and taken to Seychelles for prosecution. But that is not the end of it as long terms of captivity are expensive to sustain, while there is also evidence that the foreign prisoners use the experience of mixing in the prisons with other criminals to establish stronger domestic networks for future sales.[433]

Why does this matter? Quite apart from the ethics of drug cultures, the use of the ocean in this way matters because it enables various operators to flout the laws of legitimate jurisdictions. Moreover, it is a corrosive activity which increases the strength of criminal networks. The ocean becomes a venue for organised crime instead of a peaceful place for the benefit of all humanity. In short, it matters because it is wrong, and totally at odds with the principles of a sustainable Blue Economy.

## *Drive safely*

Such is the volume of shipping traffic and the potential for accidents that the exhortation to drive safely might now be applied at sea as well as on roads. In spite of increased efficiency and the use of larger vessels, the number of ships in the world fleet is increasing. With a present total of some 63,000 merchant ships, there is evidence from the order books of the world's shipyards, together with global trends in trade, to suggest a continuing annual growth rate of at least 3 per cent.[434] When projected across the open seas, this increase might not seem significant but on a number of the main shipping routes there are bottlenecks where greater traffic is giving rise to its own problems. Even with lower speeds mandated in these areas, there is an added risk of collisions. Apart from damage to the ships and harm inflicted on crews, the disruption to other ships in the area can be considerable.

In recent times, the most dramatic illustration of what can happen occurred in March 2021, when the mega-container ship, the Panamanian-registered *Ever Given*, was unceremoniously grounded in the Suez Canal.[435] This was not the result of volume of traffic but the sheer size of one of a new generation of container ships that everyday pose problems for the nineteenth-century canal. As they pass through the narrow channel, the leeway for error is minuscule and no one was surprised when an accident of this magnitude finally happened. In the event, no one was hurt but traffic was halted for six days and *Ever Given* was impounded for a further three months.

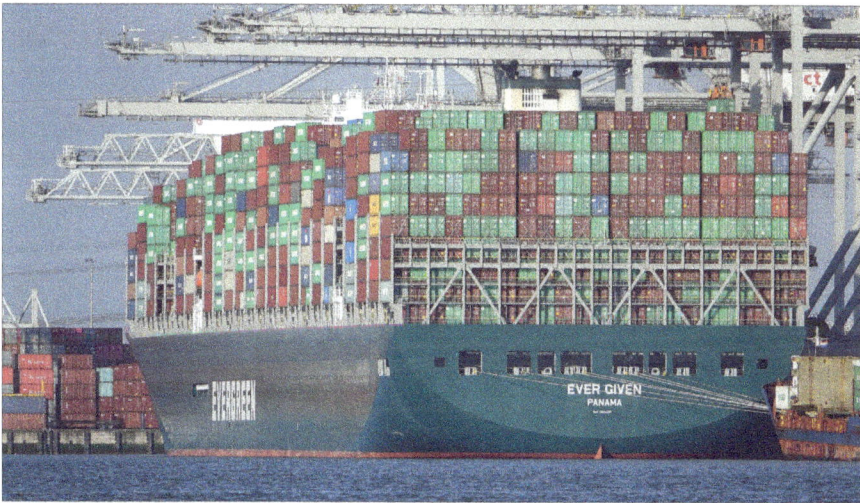

*This massive container ship was simply too large to be manoeuvred through the Suez Canal in sub-optimal conditions*

Such a high-profile event obviously attracted worldwide attention but the possibility of less dramatic incidents increases daily. Thus, a recent study of the Malacca Strait, where shipping is forced to reduce speeds and follow designated channels, shows that the growing volume of traffic has to be taken into account if accidents are to be avoided.[436] Systems have been put in place to provide up-to-date information for ship captains but these are not foolproof. Examples are given of incidents where a following ship in a convoy failed to detect a warning signal and, in another case, human error was to blame. To add to the effects of accidents, there have been repeated instances of oil spillages from tankers.

One should not exaggerate the number of mishaps at sea as, compared with the past when much was left to intuition, modern devices have undoubtedly assisted navigators. At the same time, the greater size and unwieldy nature of modern vessels, coupled with more traffic, pose challenges that cannot be ignored.

## The Old Adage of Low-Hanging Fruit

Defining and illustrating maritime security is one thing, but what can be done about transgressions? Each represents a threat to a sustainable ocean, yet there are no easy solutions.

Following the order of the above cameos, war is the most intractable issue of all. An unbroken history of conflict between nations and different ethnic groups confounds any foreseeable possibility of creating a world of peace. It is a sad observation but true. Optimists dared to wonder whether, after the Second World War and in the face of unprecedented material progress in peacetime, Europe would turn its back on 'old-fashioned' wars. Then, in February 2022, a new conflict arose and images were shown of devastated towns and inhabitants huddled amongst the ruins without food and warmth. It seemed that nothing had changed. At the same time, with a build-up of naval forces in other parts of the world, one can sense the threat of new battlegrounds. Unless the world's leaders finally come to their senses, the shared ocean, for so long acting as theatres of war, might yet be centres of conflict again.

The second cameo, which looks at piracy, offers more hope of resolution – provided the political will is there. What is needed is a more vigorous response from the countries which generate illegal activities and, at the same time, strong measures by the international community to prevent transgressions at sea. I was able to witness significant progress in the fight against piracy off the coast of Somalia earlier in the century, and it would not be impossible, in theory at least, to initiate a comparable strategy in the

Gulf of Guinea. Admittedly, the latter region is more complex, with some 20 countries directly affected, but ways could be found to alleviate the situation. To date, however, there seems to be more talk than action. The fruit is within reach but there is an absence of commitment.

In the case of the third cameo, that of drug smuggling, there is no easy solution. Given the size of the ocean and the sheer volume of seaborne traffic, criminals retain the upper hand. Some seizures will be made and these will be rightly publicised but, in the meantime, other consignments of contraband trade will continue undetected. Advanced technology might help in law enforcement, and improved intelligence can lead to arrests, but there will be little in the way of low-hanging fruit. Realistically, if noticeable inroads are to be made to reduce drug smuggling it will more likely depend on ways to achieve falls in drug consumption and changes in the pricing structure to make the whole process of smuggling less attractive. For now, though, the most prolific clusters of fruit dangle on the higher branches.

Only in the case of the final cameo is there a realistic prospect of improving the situation. The volume of traffic will almost certainly continue to rise (even if not as much as originally expected) and exceptionally large vessels have a role to play. None of this necessarily means that the security of the Blue Economy needs to be compromised. If we look again at the Suez Canal debacle, weather conditions on the day were difficult and communication between the ship's captain and pilots was problematic. But, with better training and use of technical systems, the grounding could have been avoided. Likewise, in spite of heavier traffic, there is no inherent need for collisions in the Strait of Malacca. In both cases, the spotlight should be focused on high-level training for all parties and effective use of advanced technologies to provide precise information of the whereabouts of nearby ships and other obstacles. If the right things are done, the fruit is all but ready to pick.

## Last Word

Reviewed together, some initiatives can be taken now to reclaim the ocean for peaceful and lawful purposes. But some of the potential solutions remain elusive. We speak of maritime security but in all cases the problems have to be addressed not at sea but on land – in international forums, in national parliaments, in user networks of shipowners and seafarers, and in community organisations. There is also the insurance sector, where more effective scrutiny can reduce claims in cases for vessels engaged in illegal fishing.[437]

Just because the issues are difficult to resolve does not mean that progress on some, or even all, fronts cannot be made. But there is no sense in trying to do everything at once, much as I would like to see this. As I have found when considering other aspects of the Blue Economy, I believe the way forward calls for a two-tier approach: keeping one's sights firmly on the vision of a sustainable ocean, while at the same time tackling problems incrementally. In that way, there is every chance of making progress. Above all, there must be no slipping back.

# Part 3

# The Reckoning

In this final section of the book, I offer two cameos to illustrate the present state of play. I look, first, at what is happening on a global scale through the UN and, at the other extreme, I show how goals at that level are supported through the contribution of individuals dedicated to the cause of ocean improvement. There is no shortage of effort around the world, at all levels, to win the day. But is it enough?

The fact is that undoubted progress in some areas is countered by a strong undertow holding things back. In the face of national self-interest, there is by no means unanimity about the Blue Economy. And, for all their good intentions, international organisations can only move as far and as fast as their member states allow. Fine words are spoken about renewable energy but when a major supply of oil and natural gas is threatened, old coal-fired power stations are reopened and new ones planned. Richer nations speak well about achieving sustainable goals but there is scant evidence of sufficient funds being transferred to enable poorer countries to make their own necessary changes. Good and bad signs abound in equal measure.

I can see plenty of grounds for hope but we are not where we want to be yet. There is still a long way to go. The UN is working towards sustainable development goals and, at a different level, ocean champions are doing their best to achieve specific improvements. But there is no easy assessment of success and failure. We need the Blue Economy but will it happen? The jury is still out and an existential decision is awaited.

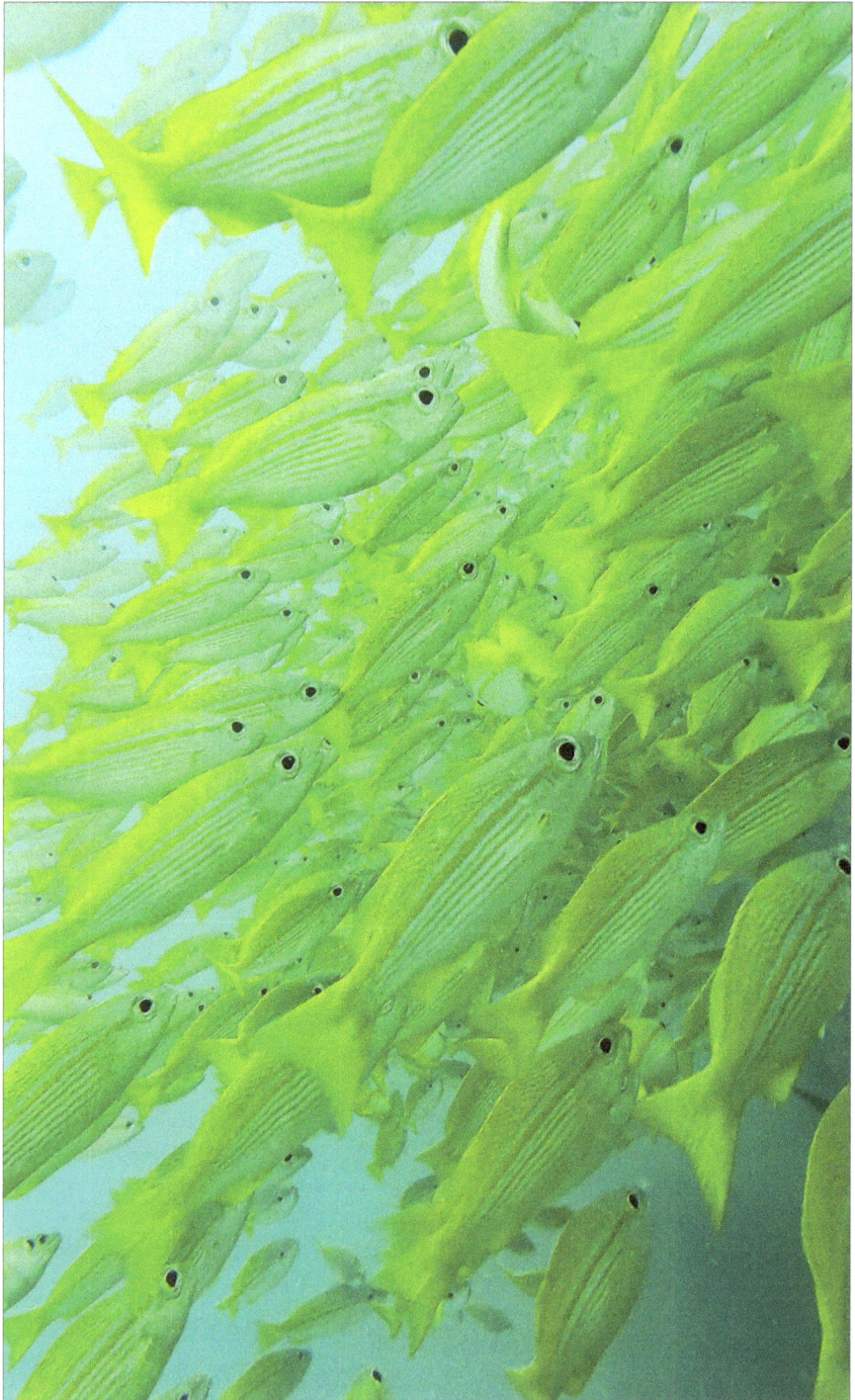

# Chapter 13

# Words, Words
*Follow the money*

In 2015, a year before the publication of my original book on the Blue Economy, the UN ostensibly made a landmark contribution to the cause of sustainable development. Commonly known as the 2030 Agenda, it identified 17 goals and associated targets where action was urgently needed to restore the health of the planet – the welfare of its people as well as the environment.[438] By 2030, it was anticipated that most of what was proposed could be achieved. Improving the state of the ocean was one such goal. Of course, at that stage, these were just words and, in themselves, hardly a guarantee of the kind of radical change called for. But, coming from the UN, the foremost international body, words count. For the many individuals and agencies around the world working for the same cause, this kind of endorsement was important. Collective action was called for; no longer would any one country have to act alone. Along with the other goals, the sustainable development of the ocean was, in this way, formally integrated as a global priority.

Beneath the well-formulated declaration, however, with its high-profile goals, one soon began to wonder whether there was any real substance and serious intent. Was it anything more than an attractive box of chocolates without fillings, appealing enough on the outside but hollow within? Initial hopes that the world could really come together to make things better soon began to fade. Eight years into the plan – just past the halfway mark – has anything happened to lift the spirits? Measures to reduce global warming are by now clearly understood and yet, even as I write this final chapter, I can read of further warnings that targets continue to be ignored.[439] In relation specifically to the ocean, there is scant evidence that serious progress has been made; on the contrary, over this period, on the basis of the main indicators, the situation has actually deteriorated. As in any big match, it is goals that count. At half-time, the score is not even 0-0. The home side is already trailing badly and showing few signs of turning things round.

In this chapter, I review what has been done to date and, in the face of currently-disappointing outcomes, I suggest harder-hitting targets and more demanding ways to reach them. Words alone are not enough. The present formula is clearly not working. But the world cannot afford to lose the match.

## Connecting the Parts

As already asserted, the process of setting goals, and targets to achieve them, has some value in itself. Together they highlight the importance of reversing present trends. So, who would gainsay the overall goal 'to conserve and sustainably use the oceans, sea and marine resources for sustainable development'?[440] We know what the main threats to a healthy ocean are and it follows from that knowledge that we also know what needs to be done. This is the essence of the UN agenda for the ocean, numbered Goal 14.

To be fair, a dream of overnight success is unrealistic. Working towards ocean improvements has so far been, at best, an evolutionary process, one step at a time. Sustainable development came onto the agenda in the last quarter of the past century, albeit in the early days with a strong environmental focus and not at that stage at the heart of a comprehensive movement that includes subjects as wide-ranging as gender equality and international justice. First came the green economy, then the blue. Over the past decade, the pace has quickened and, in different countries, governments, academics and NGOs have joined in calling for action to save the ocean. It was inevitable, to start with, that the various initiatives were piecemeal and largely unconnected. That is typical of how change emerges on this scale. To use a well-worn metaphor, it takes time and distance to turn an ocean tanker.

Ideas were, at first, drawn together incrementally, and not (until the UN declaration in 2015) in a single manifesto. The subject was intensively discussed, nationally and internationally, and protocols were signed; conferences were held and joint research provided evidence to support the cause; while demonstration projects inspired others to make the changes required. There is nothing more convincing than practical projects to show what is possible. In this way, sustainability has emerged to take its place on the world stage, a concept little understood at first by most people. Indeed, the idea of 'sustainable development' was seen by some as an oxymoron

– as two parts which were in themselves incompatible, the one forging ahead and the other portrayed as holding back. But, over time, its meaning and good sense took hold on the public imagination so that, by the time the UN announced its own goals, the ground was already prepared. The announcement was timely and there was fair reason to be optimistic.

International bodies are not always good at reaching their widely-dispersed audience but, in this case, the UN formulated and disseminated an effective message – clearly presented and comprehensive in coverage. Before long, everyone working for planetary change knew that there were 17 sustainable development goals. The scope was broad – far more than when Gro Harlem Brundtland explained the meaning of the term 'sustainability' in 1987. If only to indicate this breadth, the following table lists the different themes. The footnote makes the point that only one of the 17 goals is specifically about the ocean but all are related, some more than others. Thus, the link between ocean sustainability and climate change is an obvious one, just as sustainable policies on land are strongly connected to the sea. In the preceding chapters, I have also shown how other factors, like safe working conditions for seafarers, and the rule of law to limit illegal actions, are equally important to the ultimate success of the whole. Indeed, the message from the UN is that to achieve any one goal there has to be progress in the others too, a point that is well taken in this present book. The UN list helps to tease out the inter-related nature of the various parts, not only referring to problems but, equally, solutions.

| UN SUSTAINABLE DEVELOPMENT GOALS ||
|---|---|
| 1 | No Poverty |
| 2 | Zero Hunger |
| 3 | Good Health and Wellbeing |
| 4 | Quality Education |
| 5 | Gender Equality |
| 6 | Clean Water and Sanitation |
| 7 | Affordable and Clean Energy |
| 8 | Decent Work and Economic Growth |

| UN SUSTAINABLE DEVELOPMENT GOALS | |
|---|---|
| 9 | Industry, Innovation and Infrastructure |
| 10 | Reduced Inequalities |
| 11 | Sustainable Cities and Communities |
| 12 | Responsible Consumption and Production |
| 13 | Climate Action |
| 14 | Life Below Water * |
| 15 | Life on Land |
| 16 | Peace, Justice and Strong Institutions |
| 17 | Partnership for the Goals |

*\* Goal 14 is addressed exclusively to the ocean. All other goals are related, some more strongly than others*

It would be short-sighted to suggest that any one of these goals does not merit a place. They are all important in an interconnected model of sustainable development. But I am not sure if it is as inclusive as it could be. If there is one obvious omission, I would question the absence of anything directly on population targets. From the time that Thomas Malthus (at the end of the eighteenth century) ventured his view – that if the population of the world continued to grow at its then rate, widespread starvation would ensue – the issue has been treated with kid gloves. Even to suggest that population growth should be restrained offends different interests: religions, for instance, which see virtue in every living soul; businesses which rely on an ever-growing demand for their products; and nations which rely on new generations to join the workforce and which measure their importance in numbers of people. Malthus, of course, misjudged the impact of technological advances on agricultural productivity and refrigerated shipping, both of which brought a huge increase in food availability. But we are doing ourselves a disservice if we fail to acknowledge the inseparable link between numbers of people and sustainability.

The world's population has grown to a level that would not so long ago have been beyond most people's imagination. Just a hundred years ago, it stood at 2 billion; now it is fast approaching 8 billion, with the sharpest rise being over the past 50 years. Yet, still it is not seen by the UN as a sustainable development goal. Surely, there are critical questions to be asked? Can globalisation be relied upon to balance a shortage of food in one part of the world with potential supplies in another? How many people can the natural environment reasonably sustain, in the face of a sharp increase in visitor numbers? Each day, we generate mountains of waste at a faster rate than we can sustainably dispose it? The warning signs are there but, far from putting this at the top of the list, we see countries lamenting a fall in their population as an existential threat. This is not the stage in the book to explore the ethical issues surrounding population restraint, and my interest is, in any case, altogether more basic. I simply observe that most of the problems that stand in the way of a smooth transition to a sustainable Blue Economy would be less severe if there were fewer people, or at least not more. Because it is a potentially contentious subject is not a good reason to avoid it. On the contrary, I believe it matters to everyone that it is properly addressed.

## Ocean Targets

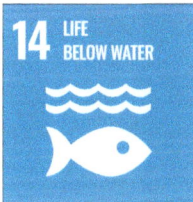

Goal 14, 'Life Below Water', is dedicated solely to the sustainable development of the ocean. Below, each of the ten targets to achieve this goal is listed. Some of the first-stage deadlines (those for 2020) have already passed, which in those cases enables measurable outcomes to date; the rest represent work in progress, with 2030 as the main milestone.

| TARGETS: LIFE BELOW WATER |
|---|
| 14.1 | By 2025, prevent and significantly reduce marine pollution of all kinds, in particular from land-based activities, including marine debris and nutrient pollution. |
| 14.2 | By 2020, sustainably manage and protect marine and coastal ecosystems to avoid significant adverse impacts, including by strengthening their resilience, and take action for their restoration in order to achieve healthy and productive oceans. |

| TARGETS: LIFE BELOW WATER | |
|---|---|
| 14.3 | Minimize and address the impacts of ocean acidification, including through enhanced scientific cooperation at all levels. |
| 14.4 | By 2020, effectively regulate harvesting and end overfishing, illegal, unreported and unregulated fishing and destructive fishing practices and implement science-based management plans, in order to restore fish stocks in the shortest time feasible, at least to levels that can produce maximum sustainable yield as determined by their biological characteristics. |
| 14.5 | By 2020, conserve at least 10 per cent of coastal and marine areas, consistent with national and international law and based on the best available scientific information. |
| 14.6 | By 2020, prohibit certain forms of fisheries subsidies which contribute to overcapacity and overfishing, eliminate subsidies that contribute to illegal, unreported and unregulated fishing and refrain from introducing new such subsidies, recognising that appropriate and effective special and differential treatment for developing and least developed countries should be an integral part of the World Trade Organization fisheries subsidies negotiation. |
| 14.7 | By 2030, increase the economic benefits to Small Island Developing States and least developed countries from the sustainable use of marine resources, including through sustainable management of fisheries, aquaculture and tourism. |
| 14.a | Increase scientific knowledge, develop research capacity and transfer marine technology, taking into account the Intergovernmental Oceanographic Commission Criteria and Guidelines on the Transfer of Marine Technology, in order to improve ocean health and to enhance the contribution of marine biodiversity to the development of developing countries, in particular Small Island Developing States and least developed countries. |
| 14.b | Provide access for small-scale artisanal fishers to marine resources and markets. |
| 14.c | Enhance the conservation and sustainable use of oceans and their resources by implementing international law as reflected in United Nations Convention on the Law of the Sea, which provides the legal framework for the conservation and sustainable use of oceans and their resources, as recalled in paragraph 158 of 'The future we want'. |

What can we say about these ten targets? On the face of it, they all make good sense and if they were to be achieved we would be able to celebrate an altogether different ocean than the one we have now. To take the first of these, reducing marine pollution is an obvious target and the world would be a better place without the sea being used as a dumping ground. But, who amongst the great and the good who presented it this way could honestly have expected that it could be achieved by 2025? This very first target alerts the reader to the fact that what follows might well be no more than a wish-list. The second target – in relation to the better management and protection of marine ecosystems – is no less laudable but even more unrealistic, with an earlier deadline of 2020. The third target, to tackle the problem of ocean acidification, is also to be welcomed but anyone who has studied this issue will know that, especially in the face of global warming and the continuing volume of carbon emissions, there are no easy or quick remedies.

And so it goes on. One of the biggest threats to the ocean is the widespread incidence of overfishing, whether a result of legitimate (but misguided) practices or through illegal activities. Solutions are simple enough in theory but they are invariably opposed because they would erode profits and challenge national interests. Even when it is apparent to all concerned that the stock of fish in the sea is being depleted, it has so far been impossible to achieve a consensus to manage things better. And the situation is complicated by the perennial issue that poorer nations can ill afford to lose income as well as essential proteins for their diets. There is another aspect of fishing, too, which is addressed in a related target, namely, the negative influence of subsidies.

Only in relation to one of the targets, that of achieving protection of 10 per cent of the ocean by 2020, was some progress made, and even that fell short of the mark. In a study in that year, it was suggested that, instead of the figure of 7.5 per cent claimed by countries with MPAs, a more accurate assessment might be closer to 3 per cent.[441] Areas with effective protection are clearly smaller than the designated areas, although, with the recent biodiversity treaty (brokered by the UN) there is real hope that more effective controls will now be possible. This is one of the few bright spots in an otherwise bleak review of the situation, and we should at least rejoice in that.

There are seven substantive targets in Goal 14 and then, without explanation, three more with a different numbering system. One of these – 'to provide access for small-scale artisanal fishers to marine resources and markets' – might well have been included in the main list. The other two are worthy enough in themselves but, in their cumbersome text, give an impression that they were added by a committee as an afterthought to please different parties. Of the two, one speaks of increasing scientific knowledge and capacity, and the other is about adhering to international law.

## Lagging Well Behind at Half Time

It is against my nature to be pessimistic and I would like nothing more than to offer a positive report on progress towards the UN goals since 2015. Sadly, the evidence tells me otherwise. For all the increase in public awareness of the plight of the ocean, and improved technological capacity to address the problems, conditions in the sea have actually deteriorated in the period to date. That is a terrible indictment, for which we must all bear some responsibility.

In the UN's own review in August 2022, on how the condition of the ocean has changed since the goals were set in 2015, the findings are consistently gloomy. We have confirmation that the situation has worsened on all of the key fronts:

> *Continuing ocean acidification and rising ocean temperatures are threatening marine species and negatively affecting marine ecosystem services. Between 2009 and 2018, for example, the world lost about 14 per cent of coral reefs, often called the 'rainforests of the sea' because of the extraordinary biodiversity they support. The oceans are also under increasing stress from multiple sources of pollution, which is harmful to marine life and eventually makes its way into the food chain. The rapidly growing consumption of fish (an increase of 122 per cent between 1990 and 2018), along with inadequate public policies for managing the sector, have led to depleting fish stocks.*[442]

Given, for instance, all the publicity on the harmful impact of plastic and other forms of waste, one might have thought there would by now be at least some signs of relief. But the contrary is true. Far from slowing the rate of depositing waste in the ocean, the pace has increased and the UN predicts a doubling or even tripling of the volume of plastic pollution by 2040.[443] Nor is it only plastic which is the problem. The use of artificial fertilisers in agriculture generates its own problems for coastal areas, where 'eutrophication caused by nutrient pollution shows an increasing trend from 2016 to the present'.[444] This is resulting in a growing number of 'dead zones' across the world. The fact is that any progress can only be measured through the evidence of the ocean, and what one sees there is almost universally dire. No matter that, as the UN reports, there are better observation and monitoring facilities than in 2015, it is the state of the sea and the life within it that counts. [445] Words alone, as I say repeatedly, are not enough – a point that is colourfully endorsed by another observer:

> *...mere talk can backfire by conferring legitimacy on unsustainable behaviour, letting corporate leaders wave colourful SDG flags while prizing profits above all else. Simply talking about SDGs can demobilise civil society by creating a false impression of action. Even as promised, transformations remain elusive. Idle talk acts as a smokescreen, hiding the reality of delay and stagnation.*[446]

So much, it would seem, for the good intentions of SDG 14, seemingly lost in a sea of words. But who is most responsible for the poor performance to date? In many ways, as I will show, it is a shared responsibility, although I believe the UN itself (and its various agencies) has to take a large share of the blame. Although the goals it has set are clear enough, the means of reaching them are not. In fact, there is a serious gulf between aspirations and the routes – often described as road maps – to be followed. Conditions vary round the world, and so, although it is not a question of being too prescriptive, clear guidance might have been provided to assist effective implementation. I see this shortcoming as a basic fault of management rather than subject expertise. Indeed, reading through the UN documents and other reports, I am impressed with the enthusiasm and professional understanding that lies behind them, not to mention the ability of the UN to call on the assistance of all manner of specialists. There can be no doubting the commitment or competence of individuals. Instead, I believe the barrier to non-achievement lies further up the line, in a poor understanding of modern management methods combined with the debilitating effects of an obstructive bureaucracy. If the UN does some good things – which I believe it does – it is in spite of, rather than because of, the cumbersome way it works.

The fact is that the UN is a giant organisation, spread widely across different countries and subdivided into numerous agencies. One might say this is true of all multinational bodies, but in the commercial sector they share the single goal of being profitable; in contrast, the aims of the UN are more diffuse. For one reason and another, I fear that the UN has become ungovernable. This is not just a question of size but, more divisive is the effect of factional fragmentation, in which different countries and interests prevent a clear process of decision-making at all levels. The problems of the UN have become legendary, well summarised in the single paragraph below:

> ...it has been dismissed as a shameful den of dictatorships. It has infuriated with its numbing bureaucracy, its institutional cover-ups of corruption and the undemocratic politics of its security council. It goes to war in the name of peace but has been a bystander through genocide. It has spent more than half a trillion dollars in 70 years.[447]

Given it has such a questionable record in managing its own affairs, it is little wonder that the UN is failing to deliver on its SDGs. And the cost of failure is too high a price to pay. If one takes the single example of SDG 14, the ocean is too precious to entrust to an organisation that is in so many ways not fit for purpose. Tragically, the same is true of the other 16 goals. What is even more telling is that, in the face of such obvious shortcomings (as its own review admits), there are no convincing signs that anything will be different in the years through to 2030. To say that 'combatting the decline in ocean health requires intensified protection efforts and the adoption of solutions for a sustainable blue economy' is a truism that takes one no further than when the goals were first announced in 2015. It was known then that the situation was dire and something needed to be done to reverse negative trends, and the SDGs were intended to do just that. Now that they are so obviously failing to make a difference, it is not enough simply to repeat the intentions. We have to move on – the time for action is long overdue. Instead, we need an alternative strategy.

Of course, it might be said that it is not all the fault of the UN. What about the constituent nations that comprise its membership? Surely, they have a responsibility too? And that is absolutely true. But what we find is that some nations are at least partially responsive, while others are not at all. One might expect, for instance that the European Union, with its generally wealthy membership, would be ahead of the field. But that is, seemingly, not the case. Thus, in a hard-hitting report, one of the largest international NGOs, the Worldwide Fund for Nature (WWF), directs much of its criticism for the failure to implement SDG 14 to the European nations:

> *WWF finds the EU Member States to be unequivocally missing the mark on provisions for biodiversity conservation, healthy marine ecosystems and sustainable and viable fisheries. The absence of effective protection of marine ecosystems with sustainable management plans, failure to align the EU's fleet capacity with fishing opportunities, the reintroduction of harmful fishing subsidies and sustained overfishing indicate critical gaps in compliance with existing EU legislation...*[448]

It is not a lack of resources which is holding it back but a lack of commitment. WWF (early in 2020) predicted that three of the four targets for 2020 would not be achieved, and one (on MPAs) only partially so. It is cold comfort to learn in another critical study that a failure to achieve this first tranche of targets is not confined to the EU. In fact, the claim is made that 70 per cent of all countries had not by then met a single one. Belgium and Germany had the best record to date but most nations around the world were trailing well behind.[449] One of the problems, according to another commentary, is that ways to record indicators like the amount of plastic waste in the sea, are neither effective in themselves nor universally consistent.[450] This means that some trends might be wrongly measured so that it becomes hard to compare figures from one year to the next, nor between countries. More worrying, though, is the conclusion that, for many countries the ocean is simply not a priority. It is no coincidence that of all the 17 goals, SDG 14 attracts the least funding; the shortfall to enable targets to be met is estimated to be close to $150 billion.[451]

In other words, performance varies greatly between nations, and not always on the basis of contrasting incomes, rich and poor. But income, although not the only factor, is critical and, not surprisingly, the UN goals expose the different abilities of countries to achieve the desired outcomes. Small island states are a case in point, all of which are totally dependent on the surrounding ocean but which are invariably without sufficient funding to invest in improvements. The unifying factor, though, is not geography but economic performance, which can be evident in large as well as small countries. As early as 2018, this was recognised when the UN convened a meeting of all member states, opening with the obvious point that some countries were struggling more than others to achieve sustainable development:

> *Hampered by such obstacles as trade barriers, debt distress, food insecurity, climate change and meagre resources, the world's poorest countries lagged furthest behind in reaching the Sustainable Development Goals.*[452]

The basic contradiction, of course, is that getting to a state of sustainable development costs money – but if that is in short supply, how can everyone get there? It follows from this that it is in the world's interest to transfer funds from richer to poorer nations to make the changes that will benefit the world. Alas, the outcome of this lengthy discussion has so far failed to offer any practical suggestions to achieve this. Words again, without action.

In the next section, I will suggest that one has to go down the scale, to the level of individuals, communities and NGOs to find more promising ways to rescue the situation. The UN can be retained to add gravitas (given its record, an irony in itself) but the real energy for change will come from those who care most and are not shackled by endless rules and factional interests.

## Making a Sea Change

In looking for a new approach, let me start with a visit to the Kenyan coastline. Once it would have been fringed with a thick belt of mangrove forest. Decline set in during the colonial era and has continued since then, leaving a scarred landscape with isolated patches of mangrove in place of the former green strip. With the loss of trees went natural flood protection, a profusion of fish and crabs, and an effective source of carbon capture. But, thanks to a number of innovative community schemes, this is now changing.

Women are playing a key role in the revival – people like Mwatime Hamadi, who is engaged with other women in her village in a programme of mangrove restoration that is already bringing benefits.[453] One of her tasks is to work as an ecotourism guide, responding to the interest the project is attracting. Profits from carbon capture income are used to pay salaries and invest in village infrastructure. The important thing is that it is a community-based approach, supported, in turn, by the national government and international NGOs. And it is far from being an isolated project, with other restoration schemes along the Kenyan coastline as well as comparable ones in Madagascar and Mozambique.[454]

The purpose of this excursion to East Africa is to demonstrate the energy and innovative ideas that can be found at the community level. I have earlier in this book pointed to other examples where local action is directed to preventing species extinction, whether of particular seabirds and marine mammals or vulnerable seabed ecosystems. I am certainly not claiming that community projects are enough on their own, and they undoubtedly benefit from specialist advice, funding, and publicity from higher-level support. The Nature Conservancy, for instance, is active in assisting some of the mangrove restoration in Kenya.[455] And the UN, no less, has an important role in providing grants and news coverage.[456] In the end, it is about teamwork, calling for different types of intervention.

Thus, at a higher level, one looks for more involvement from national governments. Of course, there will always be individual countries that are serious about the fulfilment of SDG 14 but the record is very patchy. As noted above, the EU is heavily criticized by WWF for not doing more. In turn, WWF urged that various steps be taken to remedy the situation:

⟡ *EU Member States ensure that the main priority of Marine Protected Areas is the conservation of biodiversity and marine ecosystem services, not short-term economic opportunity. MPAs must effectively conserve and restore ecosystems, and include zones that are fully protected from destructive activities.*

⟡ *EU decision makers commit to double the EU's current level of removing $CO_2$ from the atmosphere by 2030, achieved by supporting the activity and expansion of European carbon sinks, in particular through ecosystem restoration.*

⟡ *EU Member States follow advice based on the best-available scientific evidence to set fishing opportunities aligned with sustainable levels and apply the precautionary approach when data on the status of marine populations is lacking.*

⟡ *EU decision makers maintain the ban on harmful subsidies that increase fishing capacity and eliminate all subsidies to operational effort-enhancing costs, including engine replacement.*

> ✧ *The EU fully implements the Illegal, Unregulated and Unreported (IUU) Regulation and applies sanctions for non-compliant vessels to deter IUU activities and help compensate for the damage done to marine ecosystems, as well as to the communities impacted by reduced marine stocks and diminished seafood production economies.*[457]

These recommendations would certainly help to make a difference but I do wonder whether even these would be enough. To go further, I believe there needs to be an upfront commitment to transfer funding to poorer countries, coupled with effective penalties when the marine environment is degraded. Thus, if we are really serious about improving the health of the ocean, I am suggesting three ways forward that would make an immediate (or at least short-term) difference.

> ✧ Firstly, tackle the problem of illegal and over-fishing, showing that we really mean to stop it. The technology exists to make this possible, and for nearly a decade Global Fishing Watch has been spreading good practice. Why not, within a year, fit every fishing boat with a compulsory tracker and map the movements on a regional basis? Whether boats are apprehended at sea or when they arrive in port, the penalties will have to be punitive, including the option of confiscation of a vessel and its catch. There are still technical challenges but the main obstacle is the lack of governmental commitment. This has to change.
>
> ✧ Secondly, transfer funds from rich to poor nations to enable environmentally-friendly waste-disposal facilities in every country. These facilities should be in place within two years. When that is done, no longer will it be permitted to dump truck-loads of trash directly into the sea or to allow untreated sewage to pollute surrounding waters, as is the case now. Once again, it is a lack of political will which holds things back.
>
> ✧ Thirdly, capture agricultural run-off containing a high proportion of chemicals through effective filter systems, monitored and (in the case of poorer countries) funded through an international source. A start should be made in those areas where there are already dead zones. Prioritising action in this way will make best use of available funds.

There are other solutions that can be offered for other problems, but the principle is the same. Funding is crucial and there will have to be an international commitment to transfer monies to poorer nations. The ocean is an international resource and solutions need an international response. A second principle is that actions taken for contravention need to be punitive – sufficiently so to deter future offenders. The time for sweet-talking is over.

All of these measures can be implemented in time to make a real difference by the target date of 2030. Time has been lost in the first seven years but it is not too late to catch up. But only if there is a strong commitment by all parties to do so.

## Turning to the UAE

As a last word, I turn to an unexpected source for inspiration. In any discussion of ocean sustainability, who would necessarily associate the idea with the barren deserts of the Middle East? It is not simply that desert and ocean will at first seem poles apart, but add the presence of oil and any prospect of synergy will seem like a case of mission impossible. The juxtaposition of hope amongst these elements is unlikely but true. I have myself been greatly stimulated by what I see taking place in the United Arab Emirates and it is this which I wish to share. I am not greatly impressed by the intent of most nations to make a difference; too often political leaders are distracted by short-term interests. But with the UAE there is not only a long-term plan but also the financial means to make it work.

Sustainable goals are now central to all aspects of the nation's economy and it is fortuitous that COP28 will be held in the UAE. Hopes are running high that, after years of disappointment at previous gatherings, this one could make a difference. That is certainly the intention of the country's leader, His Highness Sheikh Mohamed bin Zayed Al Nahyan, President of the UAE and Ruler of Abu Dhabi, who is urging nations to move 'beyond setting goals to achieving them'.[458] The desert kingdom has an unparalleled record in getting things done and 'it could be the perfect stage for the UAE to showcase its sustainability efforts to the world'.[459]

Oil may now be everyone's *bête noire* but it has been the massive reserves within its boundaries which have fuelled the remarkable rise of a previously poor desert kingdom. Rather like Singapore, there is also a history of visionary leadership which has led in this case to the creation of two world-class cities, Abu Dhabi and Dubai, as well as modern industrial infrastructure. The supply of oil and natural gas, though, is not inexhaustible, and it is expected that it will not be many years before output will start to decline. Rather than simply wait for this to happen, plans have been put in place to switch to renewable energy.[460] This will be matched by a wholesale conversion to a sustainable economy. Indeed, one can already witness a wide range of exemplary projects.

With an average of ten hours of sunshine a day, and only a few days when its rays are obscured by cloud cover or dust storms, the sun is a natural successor to oil. Solar farms can be seen across the seven emirates, with the largest ones close to the main cities. With research an important part of the strategy, production costs are constantly being driven down. Together with other sources, like wind, the nation is working towards 50 per cent renewable energy by 2050. There are parallel developments, too, in nuclear power, where the UAE is the first country in the region to achieve zero carbon emissions; and in the production of hydrogen as another clean fuel.

An integrated goal of the energy strategy is carbon capture and a drastic reduction in harmful emissions. To achieve this, as well as changes to the various fuel-production processes, it is encouraging to see attention paid to natural solutions. I have mentioned elsewhere the value of mangrove forests as areas of carbon capture, and the planting of 100 million new trees along the UAE shoreline by 2030 is to be warmly welcomed. In the words of the Minister of Climate Change and Environment, Mariam bint Mohammed Saeed Hareb Almheiri: 'We focus on nature-based solutions to achieve two very important benefits; contributing more effectively to achieving net zero, and strengthening efforts to protect ecosystems and biodiversity.'[461]

Nor is the UAE approach just inward-looking, and its international reach includes generous financial support for less fortunate nations, as well as contributing to an important international dialogue. In relation to the latter, Sheikha Shamma bint Sultan bin Khalifa Al Nahyan shares her experience of leading her country's bid to achieve net zero by 2050. She already has her sights on what can be done beyond the mid-century target date: 'It's the synergies we create today that will allow us to live a more sustainable future, far beyond 2050.'[462]

*I was honoured to meet Sheikha Shamma bint Sultan bin Khalifa Al Nahyan at the Abu Dhabi Sustainability Week earlier in 2023*

Also of international importance, one name that has become synonymous with sustainable development in the UAE is Masdar. Formed by the government some 15 years ago to spearhead developments in renewable energy, it has engaged not only in some major developments within the UAE and overseas but also in different aspects of energy research. In turn, Masdar City (in Abu Dhabi) is an ambitious plan to attract other companies to join in creating a hub to further the cause of sustainable development. The UAE is an experienced proponent of creating 'cities' to bring together cognate businesses and activities (for instance, education, media or medicine) with the aim of encouraging synergies. It is an interesting strategy and I often think of the value of following this example with something comparable for the Blue Economy – a hub where researchers, startups, established companies and investors could work closely together. Perhaps the UAE itself would be a suitable location for, say, Ocean City?

صاحب السمو الشيخ محمد بن زايد آل نهيان
رئيس دولة الإمارات العربية المتحدة
HIS HIGHNESS SHEIKH MOHAMED BIN ZAYED AL NAHYAN
PRESIDENT OF THE UNITED ARAB EMIRATES

*An ocean champion in his own right is His Highness Sheikh Mohamed bin Zayed Al Nahyan who has introduced a progressive environmental policy for the UAE*

# Chapter 14

## Ocean Champions
### *People who are making a difference*

One thing I have become more aware of in writing this book is just how much difference individuals can make. We are dealing with issues on a global scale and yet some of the most effective interventions come down to a personal contribution. People with tenacity and skills, combined with vision, play an immeasurable part in moving us closer to the goal of a sustainable ocean.

Some of these exceptional individuals are already well-known internationally, but in the course of writing this book I came into contact with the work of others who are not so much in the limelight but who also play important roles. In this final chapter, I would like to offer a sense of what is being done by some of these remarkable individuals. Those I have selected are all 'ocean champions', and together they are making the transition to a Blue Economy a realisable objective. I salute them all.

Doubtless, there are others who might have been included and I hope they will understand that this is no more than a sample rather than an exhaustive list. Further, it would be invidious to attempt to rank these champions in terms of importance, and so below I simply present their profiles in alphabetical order. For each, I offer a short biographical description followed by their personal visions for a future ocean.

## Dona Bertarelli

*Dona Bertarelli is a Swiss businesswoman of Italian ancestry. She is Co-President of the Bertarelli Foundation, a philanthropic organisation dedicated to implement real change in marine science and conservation, life science research and support for local communities. Stemming from this, she joined forces with the Pew Charitable Trusts to form the Pew Bertarelli Ocean Legacy Project, which is a leading advocate for marine protected areas. Her commitment is total and, not stopping there, she urges the added value of connecting them to create even larger, continuous ecosystems. She also acts as Special Adviser for the Blue Economy for the UN Conference on Trade and Development. Before spending most of her time campaigning for a healthier ocean, she achieved international renown for her sailing achievements, including breaking the record for the fastest solo voyage around the world by a woman. Dona is also a founding patron of Womanity Foundation, which works to accelerate gender equality through innovative investments.*

Spending days and weeks alone on the ocean inspired her to ask why the wondrous sea has been treated so badly, and what can be done about it? Her link to the ocean and commitment to its cause is inexorable. In her own words: 'The science is clear, marine protected areas are an effective tool to help protect and restore biodiversity, enable the ocean to be more resilient to climate change and recover from the impact of extractive activities such as overfishing, improve carbon sequestration, and secure the food and livelihoods of billions of people who rely on a healthy ocean.' As one of the Pew Bertarelli Ocean Ambassadors, I know just how much she cares about this.

Since the project was launched, notable successes include the designation of the Rapa Nui Rāhui MPA and Motu Motiro Hiva Marine Park, the Revillagigedo Archipelago National Park, protection of the New Caledonia Remote Reef, and the Hermandad Marine Reserve around the Galapagos Islands . Together – working with philanthropic partners, indigenous groups, community leaders, government officials and scientists – Pew Bertarelli is responsible for helping to safeguard over 8 million square kilometres of ocean. That alone is quite a legacy but these are still early days in a continuing campaign. Asked what she would do if she had a free hand to change the world, Dona is unequivocal: 'My first step would be to immediately enforce fully or strongly protection for 30 per cent of the planet, and ensure the remaining 70 per cent is sustainably managed. Given that the ocean covers two thirds of our planet, I hope we could protect more than half of the ocean, in strict no-take zones.'

## Vincent Doumeizel

*Vincent started working in Africa for the French government, supporting international aid. There he realised the impact of poverty and global hunger and decided to devote his life to mitigate them. With 20 years' experience in the food sector, he is now Senior Adviser for the Ocean at United Nations Global Compact, as well as Director for the Food Programme at Lloyd's Register Foundation. Partnering with institutions and large brands, Vincent led in the making of the 'Seaweed Manifesto', a call to scale up the seaweed industry to address a number of critical challenges (hunger, climate change, pollution, poverty). He is now leading the first global platform for seaweed stakeholders, the Global Seaweed Coalition, and argues the cause in all media and at high-level events around the world. The English version of his book, The Seaweed Revolution, was launched in early 2023.*

Our food systems, he says, have reached maximum capacity on land and have now become the biggest contributor to global warming, soils depletion, biodiversity loss and water scarcity. Yet we still have almost one billion people starving – with 215,000 extra mouths to feed every day – whilst our land productivity keeps decreasing. In the face of these figures, in spite of covering 72 per cent of our planet, the ocean contributes less than 3 per cent of our food calories. Vincent urges that we should start by treating it more responsibly and stop acting like hunter-gatherers in the stone age. We must, instead, cultivate and protect the largest part of our blue planet!

Algae, at the lowest trophic level in the ocean and the origin of life on our planet, offers our greatest hope in turning things round. Seaweed cultivation could be the way to provide sustainable food for people and livestock, and to replace fertilisers and plastics as well as innovations in medicine. It could also restore biodiversity in the ocean by providing food and habitat for marine life; it can decarbonise our economy and sequester more carbon than any land forest. Eventually, it can bring a new source of revenue, notably to women, in coastal communities where fishing resources will keep declining. With 12,000 very different types of seaweed still unexplored, offering a wide range of applications, these organisms may well be the greatest untapped resource on our planet and a great source of hope for future generations. But to do this we will have to bridge the science gap, increase public and private investment, share knowledge globally, and educate people so they understand that using seaweed is good for our body and our planet. To achieve all of this, we will need a revolution. A seaweed revolution!

## Sylvia Earle

*Surely, few would dispute recognition of Sylvia Earle as the doyen of ocean science and discovery. For seven decades she has studied, lived and spread the message about the wonders of the ocean and how vital it is to the future of humanity. Sylvia has excelled in everything she does, whether in the most advanced laboratories or on the sea floor, whether speaking to governments or enthusiasts, whether in the written word or broadcasts. Little wonder she was appointed in 1999 as a National Geographic Explorer in Residence and then Explorer at Large. One of the many projects in her long and varied career was to form an organisation, Mission Blue, which identifies what are known as 'hope spots' – special places that are seen as critical to the health of the ocean. Her numerous accomplishments would merit a book in itself and one can do no better than to turn to her own volume – Ocean: A Global Odyssey.*

Sylvia is a respected scientist but also an advocate; when she speaks of 'hope spots', she urges the role of champions in communities around the world who are willing to stand up and take action to protect the ocean. That, she says, is what these special places are about. In her unassuming way, she has also enhanced the contribution of women in what was, in the early stages of her career, largely a man's world. Her love of the ocean stems from her firsthand experience of it – like walking untethered on the seabed and notching up 7,000 hours spent beneath the waves. She has seen the best of the ocean in its hidden splendours, and also the worst, where people have treated it with disrespect. Sometimes that is due to ignorance but, as she says, we can remedy that. More problematic is the lasting damage where continuing bad practices pose a threat to the very existence of human settlement on earth: 'No water, no life; no blue, no green.'

Whenever I am with her, I warm to her positive approach: 'It is easy to find despair, but don't let it own you. Don't let the bad guys win; be a force for good. You can be that connection to turn things from despair to recovery, from letting earth decline and society rip it apart, or you can become a healer. You can become the beginning of something. It starts with somebody doing something. Just go back to that recognition that being alive is a miracle, and as long as you're alive, you've got a chance to really make a difference for yourself and for the world.'

## Ameer Ebrahim

*Ameer was nominated in 2015 as one of 28 young people making a difference in Seychelles. He wasted no time in registering with the University of Queensland, where he became one of the youngest Seychellois to receive a PhD. He has already held several high-level portfolios, including Head of Fisheries Management and Technical Coordination at the Seychelles Fishing Authority, Chief Scientific Advisor to the James Michel Foundation, and Director of Conservation and Science at the Island Conservation Society. Ameer has led some ground-breaking scientific research on home soil, most recently exploring Blue Carbon opportunities with a team of experts from Deakin University. He is a published scientific author, and has been classified (on oceanexpert.org) as an Ocean Expert internationally. He has also been nominated as a FishPath member, adding his expertise to the international network of fisheries scientists and practitioners guiding fisheries towards sustainability.*

Ameer's philosophy is that everyone has a responsibility to keep the oceans healthy. It is our duty to protect our finite resources. This includes making a conscientious choice to abstain from littering and to encourage others to do the same, and to collect plastics or marine debris from the beach whenever the opportunity arises. It also includes making the effort to lessen one's carbon footprint.

The eyes of the world, he says, are now on decision-makers; there is no time to lose. Decision-makers cannot remain disconnected from the natural world. Solutions to any challenges being faced by governments need to be guided by science. A collaborative approach should be employed in order to effect any lasting change, which engages local communities, different ministries, the private sector, relevant non-profit organisations, and other stakeholders. It is evident that our actions are directly affecting the world's seas. The vastness of the ocean seems to lull people into a false sense of security, and prompt a mistaken belief that fish stocks exist in abundance. However, the reality is that rampant over-fishing, illegal fishing, coral reef and seagrass meadow destruction, dredging, and unchecked pollution are already draining the ocean's lifeforce, depleting fish stocks to near extinction of certain species, and it is only a matter of time before we end life as we know it through sheer greed and narrow-mindedness. We all have the potential and the capacity to effect change, and even the smallest step in the right direction can make a positive difference. How we treat our oceans reflects directly on us. Protecting our oceans means protecting our futures, and the futures of generations to come.

## James Ellsmoor

*James Ellsmoor is an award-winning serial entrepreneur, writer and advocate for islands, known for his work in renewable energy and sustainable development. He has written extensively for many publications, including as the first contributor at Forbes, focused on sustainability, with a regular column educating readers about sustainable practices and global development policy. James takes a systems approach, with expertise including climate, oceans, energy, tourism and conservation particularly in Small Island Developing States and sub-national island jurisdictions. Through his advocacy, he spearheads initiatives such as the Virtual Island Summit, which convenes island representatives from all corners of the globe to highlight islands as models for global sustainability and leaders on pressing global issues such as climate action. He co-founded Solar Head of State, with the goal of raising awareness of solar power by installing free solar systems on government buildings and the homes of world leaders. James' expertise, combined with his ability to effectively communicate complex concepts, has made him a sought-after speaker and consultant in the field of sustainable islands, with his dedication to driving positive change continuing to shape the future of sustainable development worldwide.*

The global community, James believes, is taking great strides in improving the governance of the ocean. The vast distances, limitations of EEZs and the ability to enforce them, as well as the sheer complexity of the biosphere and processes that happen below the waves can make the ocean the subject of both wonder and discomfort. A realisation that often goes unnoticed is the fact that our planet relies on the ocean to keep its natural balance. We, as a global collective, rely on the ocean.

When developing policies for better governance and use of ocean resources, there must be a space for the communities that have long been the custodians of these marine environments. James reminds us that islanders have an intrinsic link to the ocean, and have built their culture, heritage and history on their relationship with the environment that surrounds them. Island nations and coastal communities see firsthand the importance of the ocean in a way that is lost on many others, and it is islanders who are at the forefront of a changing climate. These communities must have their voices heard and be featured more prominently in discussions on managing the world's marine ecosystems. We all rely on the ocean and we should listen to the island and coastal communities who are the traditional custodians. As such, the vision he has for the ocean is one of stronger collaboration and inclusivity towards achieving our shared goals, and pursuing the just transition that is critical to sustainable development and climate action around the world.

## Ginger Garte

*Ginger is America's Environmental and Sustainability Director for Lloyd's Register, and is part of the Lloyd's Register Foundation's Maritime Decarbonisation Hub. Having obtained a Geological Science degree, she was selected to serve as a U.S. Commissioned Officer with the National Oceanic and Atmospheric Administration. Upon completion of officer training, she served for five years onboard NOAA's research vessels and land-based laboratories. Her geological research led to several publications on South Florida ecosystems. She has also held roles in the Environmental Health and Safety Department, and in the Environmental Stewardship Department within the Royal Caribbean Group. Ginger takes an active role in the community where she is a board member of UpGyre's.org, a non-profit that develops technologies that transform ocean pollution into useful products; and she is on the steering committee of Vancouver Maritime Centre for Climate. She also serves as council member and judge for The Fairchild Challenge, and the Women's International Shipping and Trading Association.*

Ginger is a passionate guardian of the ocean, devoting herself to all aspects of marine life and the various organisations that serve it. Her vision says it all: 'I'm an optimist, I find purpose and inspiration in being a global ocean steward! To me this means being mindful in all that you do, and with the intention of leaving your heart mark. I've always listened to my heart and recognise that being a good steward gives me great purpose, joy and peace of mind. To be impactful, we form alliances, follow science and commit to a 'net positive' life! As a leader, to get to net-zero (carbon, water, waste), we must have the courage to strive for sustainability solutions and answers that are not within reach. This must be accomplished in a just, equitable way and leave no one behind. The United Nations developed 17 Sustainable Development

Goals and they show you how to be a Zero Hero! The apps are fun ways for us all to give back and tap into our SDG (#) talent! As a family, we have been net positive for the past five years – not perfect, yet! We are energy independent, and our net-zero carbon targets have been exceeded! This was a long process and we do not claim to have all the answers, but the solar array on our home produces more energy than we consume, so any extra energy is sent back to the electricity grid and provided to our neighbors. Our electric car is charged in our home charging station or at the electric charging infrastructure stations -- connecting us throughout the US. I plan to leave behind what I call my 'heart mark'. Once you find your purpose and listen to your inner voice – the one driving you to change behaviours, habits and ways of doing things to be better stewards, it sparks the magic and then you align with like-minded people finding their net positive place in this amazing planet ... continuing this circle=hope for a better more regenerative future!'

## Ellen MacArthur

*Ellen MacArthur is a renowned English sailor, who in 2005 circumnavigated the world faster than anyone else (man or woman) before then. A few years later, she retired from competitive sailing in order to set up the Ellen MacArthur Foundation. Although this might have seemed a change of career, in many ways it was a natural progression. Days alone on the ocean, dependent on her boat and the supplies she brought with her, led Ellen to reflect on the fragility of finite resources in the world as a whole. As she explained: 'No experience in my life could have given me a better understanding of the word finite.' This realisation is at the heart of the foundation she established. Ellen believes that if humanity is to have a future, the time has come to go back to basics, to recognise that we cannot continue to live in a 'throw away' society. Thus, the Ellen MacArthur Foundation is synonymous with the development of a circular economy.*

Survival, MacArthur contends, is dependent on our ability to transform an extractive, throwaway economic model to one that is based on the principles of a circular economy – an economy designed to keep materials in use, eliminate waste and regenerate natural systems. 'The economy', she observes, 'is entirely dependent on finite materials. Burning fossil fuels for energy suddenly seemed illogical. Designing things in ways that meant materials would ultimately end up in a landfill, is equally troubling. And then there was the damage that was being done to the environment through extraction, undermining its ability to regenerate and provide us with the things we need for life. There had to be a better way.'

To sail alone around the world (as Dona Bertarelli, another ocean champion would later demonstrate too) calls for a special person – someone of enormous strength of will who would never give up. So, when Dame Ellen (the honorific was bestowed in recognition of her sailing feats) decided to set up her own foundation, it was always going to be a success. And it was too important to ignore: 'When I circumnavigated the globe, it didn't really matter, but sustainability is part of all our lives.' The idea of the circular economy is profound but simple enough to be widely understood, so, combined with her personal charisma, it was soon adopted not only by environmentalists but across the corporate and governmental sectors. Numerous case studies are available as models of its application and universities are amongst those institutions which now offer courses on the circular economy. From plastics to the design of cities, from food to fashions, the circular economy questions current practices. Not surprisingly, the attraction of the concept is international and Ellen travels extensively to make the connections. Everywhere she goes, the basic message is well received: 'If we could build an economy that would use things rather than use them up, we could build a future.'

## Angelique Pouponneau

*Angelique qualified as a lawyer in Seychelles. She holds an LLM in Environmental Law, specialising in the law of the sea and legislation surrounding natural resources. Building on these qualifications, she is currently pursuing a PhD on the subject of an enabling legal environment for a sustainable ocean economy in Small Island Developing States. At the same time, she is currently serving as an advisor to the Chair of the Alliance of Small Island States on climate change and ocean negotiations. Angelique has worked in different countries on a wide range of projects relating to sustainable fisheries and management of marine biodiversity within and beyond national jurisdiction. She serves on the advisory board of the UN Ocean Decade for Sustainable Development and previously held the post of Chief Executive Officer of the Seychelles' Conservation and Climate Adaptation Trust. Angelique was recently recognised by The New African Magazine as one of the 100 most influential Africans.*

As a young ocean champion, Angelique has already worked at multiple governance levels, from grassroots to national and international. She co-founded the Seychelles chapter of the SIDS Youth AIMS Hub, equipping young people with the knowledge and tools to become ocean and climate advocates. At a national level, she led the Seychelles' Conservation and Climate Adaptation Trust, a trust fund dedicated to supporting a healthy ocean through empowering local communities, private sector and government to take appropriate action. All of our efforts, she says, were directed towards the cause of sustainability of marine protected areas, fisheries and coastal and marine ecosystems. Inclusion was always placed at the heart of her work and most of the projects were led by local communities – showing the agency of individuals to take their futures in their own hands. Her latest role is at the international level, as an advisor to the Chair of Alliance of Small Island States. Climate change is one of the biggest threats to the ocean and she is adamant that we must address this issue to give the ocean a chance to support its ecosystems and humanity, while also reducing and, in some cases, eliminating other anthropogenic pressures.

Angelique's vision for a healthy ocean begins with the reversal of harm that we have for so long inflicted on the ocean. Above and below the surface, she envisages an ocean that is at a temperature and acidity that supports life, healthy habitats and biodiversity. It must be an ocean that is not degraded by plastic pollution – teeming with thriving marine ecosystems. She envisages a future where we have found a way of living together – with nature and not against it. She celebrates the positive news of the BBNJ (High Seas) treaty. It is evidence that the world can still come together to address pressing challenges and it has provided us with an opportunity to do better for the ocean. Her only concern is that treaties are treaties, laws are laws – it is political will, resources and capacity that will ensure that implementation is effective.

## Enric Sala

*Enric obtained a bachelor's degree in Biology from the University of Barcelona and a Ph.D. in ecology from Aix-Marseille University, France. He is a former university professor who saw himself writing the obituary of ocean life and quit academia to become a full-time conservationist as a National Geographic Explorer in Residence. He founded and leads Pristine Seas, a project that combines exploration, research, and media to inspire country leaders to protect the last wild places in the ocean. To date, Pristine Seas has helped to create 25 of the largest marine reserves on the planet, covering an area of more than 6.5 million square kilometres. He has earned numerous honours for his work, including 2008 World Economic Forum's Young Global Leader, 2013 Explorers Club Lowell Thomas Award, 2013 Environmental Media Association Hero Award, 2016 Russian Geographical Society Award, 2018 Heinz Award in Public Policy, 2021 Prince Albert I Grand Medal, and 2021 National Geographic Society's Hubbard Medal. He is a Fellow of the Royal Geographical Society.*

Enric is one of those rare individuals who is able not only to explore the ocean's frontiers but who is equally talented in communicating his thoughts and findings. To understand his vision, his widely acclaimed book – *The Nature of Nature: Why We Need The Wild* – is a treasure trove of ideas and inspiration. He wants nothing less than to change the world and his book tells how this can be done. Once we know how nature works, he asserts, we will understand why conservation is economically wise and essential to our survival. He recounts the story of his own journey from academic to activist, using science to question long-held assumptions about the ocean. He draws on his experience and those of other scientists to show the economic wisdom of making room for nature, even (or especially) as the world becomes more urbanised. Saving nature, he affirms, can save us all – by reversing conditions that led to the coronavirus pandemic and preventing other global catastrophes. For a sense of his vision of a healthy and sustainable future, one can do no better than select a few quotes from his challenging text:

⟡ *A healthy mature ecosystem is not like a picture of a single color, but a multicolor quilt that evolves and responds... It takes a long time – centuries or millennia – for old ecosystems to assemble.*

⟡ *Humans want quantity over quality, growth over development, production over protection... The truth is, we need forests more than we need cathedrals.*

⟡ *A degraded environment is a hotbed of all the problems affecting humanity... We have turned wild habitats into cities, farmland, and shopping malls, crowding in on the species with whom we share this planet. We have created the perfect conditions for a modern plague.*

⟡ *We are in the midst of an existential crisis, not only affecting the survival of our very society, but also about our place in the world.*

⟡ *We need to build for stability and resilience instead of unfettered growth.*

# Epilogue

Much has happened in the seven years since I wrote my first book on the Blue Economy. Not all of it good. Illegal fishing remains a critical problem; the ocean continues to be a dumping ground for all kinds of waste materials; coastal communities face the reality of rising sea levels; advocates for seabed mining ignore the fact that we know too little about the damage that will be caused. And so on. It is too early to claim we are 'living the Blue Economy'. That is hardly surprising. It will take longer than seven years to reverse forces which are embedded in the very structure of modern industrial society. But, even now, I can take heart from many promising signs of progress.

Above all, there is a level of awareness that was absent before. People across the world speak knowledgeably about climate change and what can be done to achieve not just a healthy ocean but a sustainable planet. Children in schools play their part in cleaning beaches and they have a key role in bringing to fruition a better future; dedicated groups work night and day to ensure the survival of endagered sea mammals; and there are few governments that would openly counter this mounting tide of popular aspirations. After years of effort, international agreement has finally been reached to work towards the protection of large swathes of the ocean that remain unregulated. In the still-faltering journey towards net zero, great strides have been made in capturing energy from the wind and sun. The shipping industry is taking seriously the need to ensure decarbonisation of its vessels, with a variety of new fuels already in use. Some of the major corporations are fulfilling their own responsibilities to counter climate change. Groundbreaking ideas like the circular economy are challenging old practices where waste has for so long been endemic. And, everywhere, one can see examples of business start-ups and NGOs in common pursuit of the goal of a sustainable ocean.

In spite of important steps forward, however, it would be folly to underestimate the magnitude of the task that lies ahead. The obstacles remain formidable. At root, human nature and self-interest too often stand in the way of change; if this resistance is to be eroded, the separate dimensions of 'self' and 'society' need to be more closely aligned. Those corporations which remain focused on the bottom line, to the exclusion of everything else, have to be convinced that externalities must be factored into their business models. And, to fund the changes needed, nations which have become rich in the past must be prepared to make sacrifices to assist those less fortunate. There is a long history of inequality but, within a new global framework, a healthy and productive ocean offers opportunities to create a better balance of wealth and welfare for all.

We are daily assaulted with facts and figures, arguments for and against. This is the information age and we can hardly complain that we are unaware of what is going on. But my belief is that the future will be shaped, not so much by science as by a shared vision of what we want to achieve. Of course, science is absolutely essential to ways in which the world can change but, above all, it is our common belief in the future that will keep us on track. In my own experience, there have been moments when the idea of the Blue Economy has shone brightly, and other times when critics have dimmed the lights. In bad times as well as good, I have been sustained by my conviction of how much better things can be. In the previous pages, I have repeatedly asserted aspects of this theme but it is time now that I assemble these various fragments in the shape of a single vision:

*The Blue Economy is synonymous with the safe and sustainable use of the ocean. It replaces years of neglect and wilful harm with a respect for beauty combined with utility; a resource to be shared fairly by all of humanity; an enduring habitat for marine life in its entirety; a source of enjoyment and fulfilment; the assertion of spiritual values in harmony with material needs. It will be a credit to all who inhabit this planet, the ultimate triumph of the benign and creative side of human nature. The ocean holds the key to our very survival; the ocean is our future.*

Is this really too much to ask for?
Let us now work together to make it happen.

# Notes and References

## Prologue

1    James Alix Michel (2016). *Rethinking the Oceans: Towards the Blue Economy*. St Paul, MN: Paragon House.

## Chapter 1

2    Helen Czerski (2023). *Blue Machine: How the ocean shapes our world*. UK: Torva.
3    Bas Verschuuren (2006). An overview of spiritual and cultural values in ecosystem management and conservation strategies. The Netherlands: Foundation for Sustainable Development, paper presented at a conference 'Endogenous Development and Bio-Cultural Diversity', Geneva, 3-5 October. https://www.researchgate.net/profile/Bas-Verschuuren/publication/241673426
4    *Ibid.*
5    Rita Joubert Lawen (2022). 'Adamantine Energy seeks to start oil exploration in Seychelles, agreement expected in May. *Seychelles News Agency*, 12 May. http://www.seychellesnewsagency.com/articles/16740 Adamantine+Energy+seeks+to+start+oil+expected+in+May
6    Lloyd's Register Foundation (2021). *Foresight Review of Ocean Safety: Engineering a safe and sustainable ocean economy*. London. https://www.lrfoundation.org.uk/en/publications/download-foresight-review-on-ocean-safety/
7    For instance, Health and Safety Executive UK (2011). *A quick guide to health and safety in ports*. https://www.hse.gov.uk/pubns/indg446.pdf
8    Gro Harlem Bruntland (1987). *Report of the World Commission on Environment and Development: Our Common Future*. New York: United Nations. http://www.un-documents.net/our-common-future.pdf
9    *Ibid.*, Section I.3, 'Sustainable Development'.
10   *Ibid.*, op.cit., Section III. 16. 'Managing the Commons'.
11   UN Environment Programme (2021). *7 conservation projects win grants for underwater innovation*, 3 December. https://www.unep.org/news-and-stories/story/7-conservation-projects-win-grants-underwater-innovation
12   *Ibid.*

13    *Ibid.*

14    Camilla Novaglio *et al.* (2021). 'Deep aspirations: towards a sustainable offshore Blue Economy'. *Springer,* 21 January. https://link.springer com/article/10.1007/s11160-020-09628-6

15    Leah V. Gibbons (2020). 'Regenerative – the new sustainable?'. *Sustainability,* Vol.12, Issue 13, 7 July. https://www.mdpi.com/2071-1050/12/13/5483

16    *Ibid.*

17    *Ibid.*

18    *Ibid.*

19    Stuchtey, M., Vincent, A., Merkl, A., Bucher, M. *et al.* (2020). *Ocean solutions that benefit people, nature and the economy.* Washington, DC: World Resources Institute. www.oceanpanel.org/ocean-solutions

20    J.J. Freijo (2021). 'Regeneration: The next step in sustainable supply chains'. *LinkedIn.* https://www.linkedin.com/pulse/regeneration-next step-sustainable-supply-chains-juan-jos%C3%A9-freijo

21    Wavepiston website (n.d.). https://www.wavepiston.dk/#top

22    *Ibid.*

23    Blueinvest Africa (2022). https://blueinvest-africa-2022.b2match.io/

24    OECD (2016). *The Ocean Economy in 2030.* Paris: OECD Publishing. http://dx.doi.org/10.1787/9789264251724-en

25    EU (2021). *The EU Blue Economy Report 2021.* Luxembourg: Publications Office of the European Union. https://oceans-and-fisheries ec.europa.eu/system/files/2021-05/the-eu-blue-economy-report-2021_ en.pdf

26    *Ibid.*

27    Heidi Schroderus-Fox (2022). *The business case for building a Blue Economy in small island nations.* UN 'Our Ocean Conference', 13 April, organised by the UN Office of the High Representative for the Least Developed Countries, Landlocked Developing Countries and Small Island Developing States. https://www.un.org/ohrlls/news business-case-building-blue-economy-small-island-nations

28    I would include Goals 1 (No Poverty), 2 (Zero Hunger), 3 (Good Health and Wellbeing), 5 (Gender Equality), and 10 (Reduced Inequalities).

29    Dona Bertarelli (2021). 'The blue economy is an ocean of opportunity to advance gender equality'. *UNCTAD,* 22 March. https://unctad.org news/blue-economy-ocean-opportunity-advance-gender-equality

30    Roland Duval (2021). 'Getting a broader youth perspective on the Blue Economy'. *The Nation,* 4 December. https://nation.sc/articles/11636/ getting-a-broader-youth-perspective-on-the-blue-economy

31 Sharon Ernesta (2020). 'Now 5 years old, SeyCCAT celebrates Blue Economy project successes'. *Seychelles News Agency,* 12 November. http://www.seychellesnewsagency.com/articles/13847/Now++ years+old%2C+SeyCCAT+ celebrates+Blue+Economy+project+successes

32 NLA International (2021). *The Blue Economy in Practice: Raising lives and livelihoods.* https://nlai.blue/wp-content/uploads/2021/06/NLAI Blue_Economy_In_Practice.pdf

33 *Ibid.*

34 'How to drive investment into the blue economy'. *The Economist*, 8 July 2021. https://ocean.economist.com/blue-finance/articles/how-to-drive investment-into-the-blue-economy

35 https://www.bertarelli.com/family/dona-bertarelli/

36 https://www.pewtrusts.org/en/projects/pew-bertarelli-ocean-legacy

37 'Ocean exploration and awareness' (n.d.). *Dalio Philanthropies.* https:/ www.daliophilanthropies.org/initiatives/ocean-exploration-and- awareness/

38 http://leonardodicaprio.com/

39 'Case study: Innovative financing – debt for conservation swap, Seychelles' Conservation and Climate Adaptation Trust and the Blue Bonds Plan'. *The Commonwealth*, 28 November 2020.

40 Nicholas Owen (2022). 'Swapping debt for nature'. *IMF News*, 4 May. https://www.imf.org/en/News/Articles/2022/05/03/CF-Belize swapping-debt-for-nature

41 Belinda Bramley (2022). 'BE Pulse #12: Accelerating the Blue Economy – the role of Multilateral Development Banks'. *Blue Economy Pulse*, 6 December. https://www.linkedin.com/pulse/pulse-12-accelerating blue-economy-role-multilateral-?trk=article-ssr-frontend-pulse_more articles_related-content-card

## Chapter 2

42 OECD (2016). *The Ocean Economy* in 2030, Paris: OECD Publishing. http://dx.doi.org/10.1787/9789264251724-en

43 See, for instance, (i) *The Potential of the Blue Economy: Increasing long-term benefits of the sustainable use of marine resources for small island developing states and coastal least developed countries.* World Bank: United Nations Department of Economic and Social Affairs, Washington, DC, 2017. https://openknowledge.worldbank.org/handle/10986/26843 (ii) *Blue Economy Reports: Reports, White Papers and other analyses on the* Blue *Economy.* https://theliquidgrid.com/blue-economy-reports/

(iii) Additionally, although with its 18 authors the result is something of a scattergun approach, some useful examples can be found in Lu Wenhai *et al.*, 'Successful Blue Economy examples with an emphasis on international perspectives'. *Frontiers in Marine Science*, 7 June 2019. https://doi.org/10.3389/fmars.2019.00261

[44] United Nations (2022). *Oceans as the next great economic frontier.* 14 March. https://unric.org/en/blue-economy-oceans-as-the-next-great economic-frontier/

[45] IUCN (2022). *Reflections on the closing of the UN Ocean Conference, Lisbon, Portugal.* 4 July. https://www.iucn.org/blog/202207/reflections closing-2022-un-ocean-conference-lisbon-portugal

[46] It was still the case when I was drafting this section that the proposal from Lisbon was meeting further resistance from a host of nations which continued to place self-interest before common gain.

[47] UN Secretary-General (2023). 'UN delegates reach historic agreement on protecting marine biodiversity in international waters'. *UN News*, 5 March. https://news.un.org/en/story/2023/03/1134157

[48] IUCN, *op.cit.*

[49] *Ibid.*

[50] Pew Charitable Trusts (n.d.). *Ocean Conservation.* https://www. pewtrusts.org/en/topics/oceans

[51] https://www.stimson.org/2018/70-countries-100s-ngos-pledge-new action-protect-oceans-billions-commitments-show- continued/

[52] National Geographic award ceremony, June 2019. Personal record.

[53] *Ibid.*

[54] Ocean Panel (n.d.). *High level panel for a sustainable ocean economy.* https://oceanpanel.org/

[55] *Ibid.*

[56] UN (2014). *The Samoa Pathway.* https://www.un.org/ohrlls/content/ samoa-pathway

[57] Heidi Schroderus-Fox (2022). *The business case for building a Blue Economy in small island nations.* UN 'Our Ocean Conference', 13 April 2022, organised by the UN Office of the High Representative for the Least Developed Countries, Landlocked Developing Countries and Small Island Developing States. https://www.un.org/ohrlls/news business-case-building-blue-economy-small-island-nations

[58] *Ibid.*

[59] *Ibid.*

[60] Blue Recovery Hubs are a joint initiative introduced by the Organisation for Economic Cooperation and Development (OECD), Friends of

Ocean Action and the Sustainable Development Impact Partnership at the World Economic Forum.

[61] World Economic Forum (2022). *A sustainable path to lasting recovery for Small Island Developing States lies in the ocean and the building of a robust blue economy*, 28 June.

[62] IUCN (2021). *Global launch of the Great Blue Wall*, 10 November. https://www.iucn.org/news/secretariat/202111/global-launch-great-blue-wall

[63] *Ibid.*

[64] European Commission (2022). *The EU Blue Economy Report 2022*. Luxembourg: Publications Office of the European Union. https://op.europa.eu/en/publication-detail/-/publication/156eecbd-d7eb-11ec-a95f-01aa75ed71a1

[65] European Union (2021). *EU Strategy for the Baltic Sea Region*. Rostock: Intereg Baltic Sea Region. https://interreg-baltic.eu/about/eusbsr/

[66] The United Nations Convention on the Law of the Sea was signed in December 1982 but it did not come into force until 1994, after it had been ratified by the requisite 60 countries. By the early 21st century, the signatories totalled more than 150 countries.

[67] Felipe Paredes Vargas (2021). *Why protect the ocean: moving towards a blue economy*. State Alumni Chile, 16 June. https://statealumni.cl/en/why-protect-the-ocean-moving-towards-a-blue-economy/

[68] *Australia: National Waters*. Marine Protection Atlas. https://mpatlas.org/countries/AUS

[69] Norwegian Ministry of Trade, Industry and Fisheries (2017). *Blue Opportunities: The Norwegian Government's updated ocean strategy*. https://www.regjeringen.no/globalassets/departementene/nfd/dokumenter/strategier/w-0026-e-blue-opportunities_uu.pdf

[70] Reuters and Laura Paddison (2023). 'Norway discovers huge trove of metals, minerals and rare earths on its seabed'. CNN Business, 30 January. https://edition.cnn.com/2023/01/30/business/norway-minerals-seabed-deep-sea-mining-climate-intl/index.html See also https://news.mongabay.com/2023/04/norway-proposes-opening-germany-sized-area-of-its-continental-shelf-to-deep-sea-mining/

[71] Government of India (2020). *India's Blue Economy: A Draft Policy Framework. Economic Advisory Council to the Prime Minister, New Delhi, September.* https://incois.gov.in/documents/Blue_Economy_policy.pdf

[72] Michael Fabinyi *et al.* (2021). 'China's Blue Economy: A state project of modernisation'. *The Journal of Environment and Development*, 30 (2),

April. https://journals.sagepub.com/doi/10.1177/1070496521995872

73   *Ibid.*

74   Daria Solovieva (2021). 'What's holding back America's Blue Economy?'. *Fortune*, 27 September. https://fortune.com/2021/09/27/whats-holding-back-americas-blue-economy/

75   Belinda Bramley, in personal correspondence with the author, May 2023.

76   WWF (2020). *Coastal community-led conservation: Ocean Witness.* https://wwf.panda.org/discover/our_focus/oceans_practice/coastal_community_led_conservation/

77   Nature Seychelles website (n.d.). http://www.natureseychelles.org/home

78   Sarifa Karapetyan (2022). 'Coral reef restoration: 3 sites in Seychelles chosen for REEFFISH restoration'. *Seychelles News Agency*, 28 July. http://www.seychellesnewsagency.com/articles/17145/Coralreef+restoration++sites+in+Seychelles+chosen+forREFFISH+ project

79   GIF website (n.d.). https://greenislandsfoundation.blogspot.com/

80   GVI website (n.d.). https://www.gviusa.com/blog/what-you-need-to-know-about-shark-conservation-in-seychelles/

81   UNESCO (n.d.). *Aldabra Atoll.* https://whc.unesco.org/en/list/185/

82   Hajira Amia and Sharon Uranie (2016). '5 fascinating facts about Aldabra, a remote Seychelles atoll'. *Seychelles News Agency,* 4 August. http://www.seychellesnewsagency.com/articles/5680/+fascinating+facts+about+Aldabra%2C+a+remote+Seychellois+atoll

## Chapter 3

83   Some sources cite a higher figure. The OECD, for instance, maintains that shipping accounts for 90 per cent of world trade by volume. See OECD report, *Ocean shipping and shipbuilding.* https://www.oecd.org/ocean/topics/ocean-shipping/
In order not to overstate the case, I have preferred to adopt the more conservative estimate favoured in other publications, including Lloyd's Register Foundation, *Foresight Review of Ocean Safety: Engineering a safe and sustainable ocean economy,* Report Series No. 2021/2, November 2021. https://www.lrfoundation.org.uk/en/news/foresight-review-of-ocean-safety/

84   As with the estimated proportion of goods, actual figures vary. Before the pandemic, it was widely expected that growth would be significant. See, for instance, OECD (2016). *The Ocean Economy in 2030.* Paris: OECD Publishing. http://dx.doi.org/10.1787/9789264251724-en
More recently, a new consensus is forming, in which a slower rate of

growth is predicted. Belinda Bramley, in personal correspondence with the author, May 2023. See also:
https://lloydslist.maritimeintelligence.informa.com/LL1145339/Longterm-demand-for-shipping-to-fall-says-Nobel-Prizewinning-economist

[85] International Maritime Organization (2020). *Fourth Greenhouse Gas Study 2020.*
https://www.imo.org/en/OurWork/Environment/Pages/Fourth-IMO-Greenhouse-Gas-Study-2020.aspx

[86] Ships that are associated with specific functions, like fishing and seabed exploration, are dealt with separately in later chapters. Likewise, ports, too, represent an essential part of the shipping network and are also addressed separately, in the context of coastal development and infrastructure.

[87] International Maritime Organization (2021). *IMO's work to cut GHG emissions from ships.* https://www.imo.org/en/MediaCentre/HotTopics/Pages/Cutting-GHG-emissions.aspx

[88] Hanna Bach and Teis Hansen (2023). 'IMO off course for decarbonisation of shipping: three challenges for stricter policy'. *Marine Policy*, Vol.147, January.

[89] Lloyd's Register (2021). 'Decarbonising shipping – the global challenge'. *Maritime Decarbonisation Hub*, www.maritimedecarbonisationhub.org

[90] Ginger Garte, in personal correspondence with the author.

[91] Lloyd's Register (2021). 'First movers in shipping's decarbonisation. A framework for getting started'. *Maritime Decarbonisation Hub*. www.maritimedecarbonisationhub.org

[92] The table is derived from information in different sources: Sean T. Pribyl (2022). 'Decarbonization of shipping – emerging alternative fuels from a US perspective', *Gard*, November.
https://www.gard.no/web/updates/content/33127327/decarbonization-of-shipping-emerging-alternative-fuels-from-a-us-perspective
Global Maritime Forum (2021). *A strategy for the transition to zero-emission shipping.*
www.globalmaritimeforum.org/getting-to-zero-coalition
Environmental Defense Fund (2022). *Alternative fuels for shipping*, November. https://www.edfeurope.org/alternative-fuels-shipping

[93] Raucci, C., Karan, A. and Balani, S. (2022). 'Experience and initial lessons from a green shipping corridor cluster'. *Lloyds Register*, November. https://www.lr.org/en/marine-shipping/maritime-decarbonisation-

hub/decarbonising-shipping-the-global-challenge/

94  'Paris summit on climate and finance ends without deal on global shipping tax'. *France 24*, 23 June 2023. https://www.france24.com/en/environment/20230623

95  Paul Polman and Andrew Winston (2021). 'The net positive manifesto: Is the world better off because your company is in it?'. *Harvard Business Review*, September/October 2021. https://hbr.org/2021/09/the-net-positive-manifesto

96  Paul Polman and Andrew Winston (2022). *Net Positive: How courageous companies thrive by giving more than they take*. Boston: Harvard Business Review Press.

97  Harry Dempsey and Dave Lee (2021). 'Amazon, Ikea and Unilever commit to zero-emission shipping by 2040'. *Financial Times*, 19 October. https://www.ft.com/content/850eee4b-2c2d-4186-99d7-fdbe8131ddd0

98  Shell plc (2020). *Decarbonising shipping: All hands on deck*. In collaboration with Deloitte.
https://www.shell.com/business-customers/marine/decarbonising/_jcr_content/root/mainsection/promo_copy_copy/links/item0.stream/1651646057912/b4878c899602611f78d36655ebff06307e49d0f8/decarbonising-shipping-report.pdf

99  Maersk, Press Release (2020). *New research center will lead the way for decarbonizing shipping*, 25 June. https://www%20Maersk%20Press%20Release%20about%20the%20%20Mc-Kinney%20Moller%20Center%20for%20Zero%20Carbon%20Shipping%20-%20(1).pdf

100  IRENA (2021). 'A pathway to decarbonise the shipping sector by 2050'. International Renewable Energy Agency, Abu Dhabi. https://www.irena.org/-/media/Files/IRENA/Agency/Publication/2021/Oct/IRENA_Decarbonising_Shipping_2021.pdf

101  Lloyd's Register (2020). *About the Maritime Decarbonisation Hub*. https://www.lr.org/en/marine-shipping/maritime-decarbonisation-hub/about/#accordion-thegettingtozerocoalition

102  *Ibid.*

103  Raucci *et al., op.cit.*

104  Lloyd's Register Foundation (2021), *op.cit.*

105  Maritime and Port Authority of Singapore (2022). *Maritime Singapore Decarbonisation Blueprint: Working Towards 2050*. https://www.cdn.imo.org/localresources/en/OurWork/Environment/Documents/Air%20pollution/Maritime%20Singapore%20Decarbonisation%20blueprint.pdf

[106] An essential source for the rest of this chapter is Lloyd's Register Foundation (2021), *op.cit.*

[107] I have reflected on this whole sequence of events involving pirates in the western Indian Ocean, in my book (2021), *Legacy: New Millennium, New Seychelles.* Blue Gecko Books.

[108] I am grateful to Beth Elliot of LRF for her own perception of the balance of causes.

[109] Shishir Upadhyaya (2022). 'Harmonizing maritime governance in the Indo-Pacific region'. *Journal of the Indian Ocean Region*, Vol.18, No.2.

[110] Christian Bueger (2015). 'What is maritime security?'. *Marine Policy*, Vol. 53, March. https://www.sciencedirect.com/science/article/pii/S0308597X14003327

[111] ILO (2006). *The Maritime Labour Covention 2006.* Geneva. http://https://www.ilo.org/global/standards/maritime-labour/convention/lang--en/index.htm

[112] Lloyd's Register Foundation (2021), *op.cit.*

[113] Criselle David (2021). 'The able-skilled seafarer: re-envisioning the seafarer of the future'. *Global Maritime Forum.* https://www.globalmaritimeforum.org/news/the-able-skilled-seafarer-re-envisioning-the-seafarer-of-the-future/

[114] See, for instance, the work of the European Maritime Safety Agency. https://www.emsa.europa.eu/

[115] Nautilus General Secretary, Mark Dickinson, speaking at 'Safety onboard: a meeting of minds at Maritime Safety Week', September 2022. Nautilus is a global trade union for seafarers. https://www.nautilusint.org/en/news-insight/telegraph/safety-onboard-a-meeting-of-minds-at-maritime-safety-week/

[116] 'The future of maritime safety' (2021). *Inmarsat Maritime*, August 2021. https://www.inmarsat.com/content/dam/inmarsat/corporate/documents/maritime/insights/Inmarsat%20-%20The%20future%20of%20maritime%20safety%20report%20-%20August%202021.pdf.gc.pdf

[117] Notably, Daryl Attwood (2018). *Insight report on safety in the passenger ferry industry: a global safety challenge.* Lloyd's Register Foundation. https://www.lrfoundation.org.uk/en/publications See also, Neil Baird (2018). *Fatal ferry accidents, their causes, and how to prevent them.* Doctoral Thesis, Australian National Centre for Ocean Resources and Security, University of Wollongong. https://ro.uow.edu.au/theses1/498

[118] Baird, *op.cit.*

[119] *Ibid.*

120 '1994 Baltic ferry disaster: new dive finds no evidence to back alternative theories'. *The Guardian*, 16 November 2021. https://www.theguardian.com/world/2021/nov/16/1994-baltic-ferry-disaster-examination-prompts-new-theory-about-sinking

121 Nick Kampouris (2022). 'Samina ferry disaster haunts Greece more than 20 years later'. *GreekReporter.com*, 26 September 2022. https://greekreporter.com/2022/09/26/deadly-samina-sinking-haunts-greece-18-years-later/

122 Baird, *op.cit.*

123 *Ibid.*

124 For instance, Nishan Degnarain (2020). 'Is the UN shipping agency, the IMO, still fit for purpose?'. *Forbes*, 28 October. https://www.forbes.com/sites/nishandegnarain/2020/10/28/is-the-un-shipping-agency-the-imo-still-fit-for-purpose/?sh=4cc77e22458f. Also, Psaraftis, H.N. and Kontovas, C.A. (2022). 'Influence and transparency at the IMO: the name of the game'. *Maritime Economics and Logistics*, 22. https://doi.org/10.1057/s41278-020-00149-4

125 Baird, *op.cit.*

## Chapter 4

126 Christopher Costello *et al.* (2020). 'The future of food from the sea'. *Nature*, 19 August. https://www.nature.com/articles/s41586-020-2616-y

127 University of Tasmania (2019). 'More fishing vessels chasing fewer fish, new study finds'. ScienceDaily, 28 May. https://www.sciencedaily.com/releases/2019/05/190527152737.htm

128 Ilaria Perissi and Ugo Bardi (2020). *The Empty Sea: The future of the Blue Economy*. Switzerland: Springer Nature.

129 *Ibid.*

130 Ian Urbina (2020). 'How China's expanding fishing fleet is depleting the world's oceans'. Yale Environment 360, 17 August. https://e360.yale.edu/features/how-chinas-expanding-fishing-fleet-is-depleting-worlds-oceans

131 Sjarief Widjaja (2020). 'Illegal, unreported and unregulated fishing and associated drivers'. *High Level Panel for a Sustainable Ocean Economy*, 8 February 2020. https://oceanpanel.org/publication/illegal-unreported-and -unregulated-fishing-and-associated-drivers/

132 Emma Witbooi et al (2020) 'Organised crime in the fisheries sector', *High Level Panel for a Sustainable Ocean Economy*, 18 August. https://oceanpanel.org/publication/organised-crime-in-the-fisheries-sector/

133 Elizabeth Fitt (2022). 'Delegates come close but fail again to clinch

high seas protection treaty'. *Mongabay*, 29 August. https://news.mongabay.com/2022/08/delegates-come-close-but-fail-again-to-clinch-high-seas-protection-treaty/ Since then, a defining decision was taken in March 2023 to provide protection in the High Seas. This is dealt with more fully in a later chapter.

134 Maddie Molloy (2022). 'Vast marine area "boosts tuna stocks"'. *BBC News Climate and Science.* https://www.bbc.com/news/science-environment-63291104

135 *Ibid.*

136 Pew Charitable Trusts (2018). *The case for marine protected areas.* 31 October 2018. https://www.pewtrusts.org/en/research-and-analysis/fact-sheets/2018/10/the-case-for-marine-protected-areas

137 Basten Gokkon (2022). 'As Indonesia protects more marine areas, the top priority is management'. *Mongabay*, 14 October. https://news.mongabay.com/2022/10/as-indonesia-protects-more-marine-areas-top-priority-is-management-experts/

138 National Geographic (n.d.). *Marine Protected Area.* https://education.nationalgeographic.org/resource/marine-protected-area

139 Ameer Ebrahim, in a personal submission received for the present book.

140 National Geographic (n.d.). *North America's Marine Protected Areas.* https://education.nationalgeographic.org/resource/north-america-marine-protected-areas-gallery

141 Nature Conservancy (2022). *Marine Spatial Planning.* https://marineplanning.org/

142 Sedrick Nicette (2023). 'Ocean conservation: Seychelles' marine spatial plan in final stages of completion'. *Seychelles News Agency*, 13 January.

143 Pew Charitable Trusts (n.d.). *Conserving life in Canada's oceans.* https://www.pewtrusts.org/en/projects/conserving-life-in-canadas-oceans/northern-solutions

144 *Ibid.*

145 'The Ocean Foundation', website (n.d.). https://oceanfdn.org/

146 Bianca Haas *et al.* (2021). 'The future of ocean governance'. *Springer Link*, 12 January. https://link.springer.com/article/10.1007/s11160-020-09631-x

147 Pew Charitable Trusts (2022a). *Improving management of international fisheries.* https://www.pewtrusts.org/en/projects/improving-management-of-international-fisheries

148 Pew Charitable Trusts (2022b). *Ecosystem-based fisheries management needed to help marine life thrive in Northeast Atlantic Ocean.* 10 October. https://www.pewtrusts.org/en/research-and-analysis/issue-

briefs/2022/10/ecosystem-based-fisheries-management-needed-to-help-marine-life-thrive-in-northeast-atlantic-ocean

[149] Information provided by Dr Ameer Ebrahim, based on his experience of working with the Seychelles Fishing Authority.

[150] Haas, *op.cit.*

[151] *Regulating fisheries subsidies* (n.d.). United Nations Conference on Trade and Development.
https://unctad.org/project/regulating-fisheries-subsidies#

[152] World Trade Organization (2022). *Introduction: Agreement on fisheries subsidies.* Briefing Note, 17 June. https://www.wto.org/english/thewto_e/minist_e/mc12_e/briefing_notes_e/bffish_e.htm

[153] OECD (2017). *Sustaining Iceland's fisheries through tradeable quotas.* Environment Policy Paper No. 9. https://www.oecd.org/environment/resources/Policy-Paper-Sustaining-Iceland-fisheries-through-tradeable-quotas.pdf

[154] European Union, Oceans and Fisheries (2020). *Fishing fleet.* https://oceans-and-fisheries.ec.europa.eu/facts-and-figures/facts-and-figures-common-fisheries-policy/fishing-fleet

[155] Widjaja, *op.cit.*

[156] World Economic Forum (2022). *How date and tech can combat illegal fishing.* Davos 2022. https://www.weforum.org/agenda/2022/05/how-can-data-and-tech-help-the-seafood-industry-to-combat-illegal-fishing/

[157] Margot Stiles (2022). 'A data revolution in the ocean: an interview with Global Fishing Watch'. *Our Shared Seas*, 12 January. https://oursharedseas.com/data-revolution-in-ocean/

[158] *Illegal, Unreported and Unregulated Fishing Action Alliance Pledge.* Department for Environment, Food and Rural Affairs UK, 23 March 2023. https://www.gov.uk/government/publications/illegal-unreported-and-unregulated-fishing-action-alliance-pledge/illegal-unreported-and-unregulated-fishing-action-alliance-pledge

[159] 'Illegal, Unreported and Unregulated Fishing' (n.d). *United States Coast Guard.* https://www.uscg.mil/iuufishing/

[160] FAO (2022). *The State of World Fisheries and Aquaculture.* https://www.fao.org/publications/sofia/2022/en/

[161] Christopher Costello, Ling Cao and Stefan Gelcich (2022). 'The future of food from the sea'. *Ocean Panel.* https://oceanpanel.org/wp-content/uploads/2022/05/The-Future-of-Food-from-the-Sea.pdf

[162] European Institute of Innovation and Technology (2021). 'Seven aquaculture start-ups that are set for success'. *The Fish Site*, 8 June. https://thefishsite.com/articles/seven-aquaculture-startups-that-are-set-

for-success
163 *Ibid.*
164 *Ibid.*
165 Dr. Gero Nootz, assistant professor of ocean engineering at USM, speaking to Van Arnold, 'USM ocean engineering program produces first graduates, meeting needs of blue economy'. *USM*, 28 May 2021. https://www.usm.edu/news/2021/release/ocean-engineering-graduates.php
166 *Sustainable online aquaculture courses.* https://thefishsite.com/learn/standrews
167 Ioannis Nengas (2020). In '7 top digital farming innovations impacting aquaculture'. *Pearse Lyons Cultivator*, 27 October. https://www.pearselyonscultivator.com/2020/10/27/7-top-digital-farming-innovations-impacting-aquaculture/
168 *Ibid.*
169 See, for instance, 'The road ahead to a sustainable aquaculture industry in Norway'. *Innovations News Network*. 22 August 2022. https://www.innovationnewsnetwork.com/the-road-ahead-to-a-sustainable-aquaculture-industry-in-norway/24698
Also, 'Norwegian Sea ecoregion: Aquaculture overview', *International Committee for the Exploration of the Sea*, ICES Advice 2022. https://doi.org/10.17895/ices.advice.21252237
170 Innovation News Network, *op.cit.*
171 Perissi and Bardi, *op.cit.*
172 Business Norway (n.d.). *Moving fish farms out to sea.* https://prep.theexplorer.no/solutions/ocean-farm-1

## Chapter 5

173 Eliza Northrop (coordinating lead author) *et al.* (2022). *Opportunities for transforming coastal and marine tourism: Towards sustainability, regeneration and resilience.* High Level Panel for a Sustainable Ocean Economy. https://oceanpanel.org/wp-content/uploads/2022/06/Sustainable-Tourism-Full-Report.pdf
174 UNWTO World Barometer and Statistical Annex, January 2020. https://www.e-unwto.org/doi/abs/10.18111/wtobarometereng.2020.18.1.1
175 The estimate of 50 per cent is included in 'Sustainable coastal and marine tourism'. *Ocean Panel.* https://oceanpanel.org/opportunity/sustainable-coastal-marine-tourism/
176 Green Fins (n.d.). *Protecting coral reefs through sustainable tourism.* https://greenfins.net/

177 Caribbean Natural Resources Institute (n.d.). *Experience Nariva: creating a community-driven, sustainable cluster and brand to transform ecotourism in Nariva Swamp, Trinidad and Tobago.* https://canari.org/experience-nariva-creating-a-community-driven-sustainable-cluster-and-brand-to-transform-ecotourism/

178 Jeremie Fosse, Salvador Klarwein and Ioanna Kosmas (2021). 'Towards a Sustainable Blue Tourism in the Mediterranean: Ecosystem approach for a better environmental management of coastal and maritime tourism'. *eco-union.* https//www.ecounion.eu/wp-content/uploads/2021/06/EcAp_mediterranean_bluetourism02.pdf

179 Anowar Hossain Bhuiyan, Abud Darda, Wahidul Habib, and Belal Hossain (2020). 'Marine tourism for sustainable development in Cox's Bazaar, Bangladesh'. *ADBI Institute*, June. https://www.adb.org/sites/default/files/publication/616761/adbi-wp1151.pdf

180 Dan and Mikel Woodruff (n.d.). 'Cruise sustainability: who leads the way to a better future in travel?'. *Sometimes Sailing.* https://sometimessailing.com/about/

181 '5 key sustainability practices at Royal Caribbean'. *Sea Views*, 28 December 2021. https://www.royalcaribbean.com/blog/sustainability-at-sea/

182 Nicholas Kyriakides (2022). 'Sustainable cruises: are they worth it and what are the options?'. *Hospitality Technology*, 24 February. https://hospitalitytech.com/sustainable-cruises-are-they-worth-it-and-what-are-options

183 'Insights on the yacht global market to 2026: rising demand for luxury tourism is driving growth'. *Research and Markets*, 22 June 2022. https://finance.yahoo.com/news/insights-yacht-global-market-2026-113300357.html

184 *Green yachts: sustainable yachting evolution.* https://www.greenyachts.net/zero-34/?gclid=EAIaIQobChMIh8v3tN_D-gIVn5BoCR2UlAbiEAMYASAAEgKSdvD_BwE

185 'Sustainable yachting: is it achievable?'. *Ocean Web*, 19 April 2022. https://www.oceanweb.com/sustainable-yachting-is-it-achievable/

186 WI (Windward Islands) (n.d.). *Sustainable yachting: how is the boat industry becoming more eco-friendly?'.* https://www.worldwideluxuryyacht.com/blog/sustainable-yachting-the-industry-is-becoming-more-eco-friendly/

187 *Ibid.*

188 *The Monaco Yacht Show's new exhibition area dedicated to sustainable yachting solutions.* Press Release, 13 June 2022

https://www.monacoyachtshow.com/en/the-monaco-yacht-shows-new-exhibition-area-dedicated-to-sustainable-yachting-solutions

[189] 'Meet the creative eco-warriors crew taking action for sustainability in yachting'. *High Point Yachting.* https://www.highpointyachting.com/sustainability-in-yachting/

[190] Michael Donoghue (2018). *Development of marine species-based eco tourism in the Pacific Ocean.* https://www.forumsec.org/wp-content/uploads/2018/05/Regional-Initiative-ecotourism.pdf

[191] Nature Seychelles website. http://www.natureseychelles.org/about-us/who-we-are

[192] Lavanya Sunkara (2019). '10 coastal resorts conserving our oceans'. *Forbes*, 9 June.
https://www.forbes.com/sites/lavanyasunkara/2019/06/09/10-coastal-resorts-conserving-our-oceans/?sh=55e1741674bb

[193] *Ibid.*

[194] 'Japanese tourist boat sinks with at least ten dead, authorities confirm'. *Euronews with AP,* 25 April 2022. https://www.euronews.com/travel/2022/04/24/at-least-10-dead-in-japan-after-tour-boat-sinks-in-rough-waters-authorities-confirm

[195] 'Four people die in bus crash after Machu Picchu visit'. *France 24*, 22 August 2022. https://www.france24.com/en/live-news/20220822-four-tourists-die-in-bus-crash-after-machu-picchu-visit

[196] From my personal experience, Seychelles is generally a safe place to visit although a few tourists each year underestimate the strength of the currents around our islands.

[197] Merli, R., Preziosi, M., Acampora, A., Lucchetti, M.C. and Ali, F. (2019). 'The impact of green practices in coastal tourism: an empirical investigation on an eco-labelled beach club'. *International Journal of Hospitality Management*, Vol.77, January. https://www.sciencedirect.com/science/article/abs/pii/S0278431918303086

[198] Caroline Tippett (2022). 'Vision setting: a sustainable coastal and marine tourism sector: Part One'. *WWF* (World Wildlife Fund), 13 July. https://www.worldwildlife.org/blogs/sustainability-works/posts/vision-setting-a-sustainable-coastal-and-marine-tourism-sector-part-one

[199] *Ibid.*

[200] Tom P. Moorhouse *et al.* (2015). 'The customer isn't always right: conservation and animal welfare implications of the increasing demand for wildlife tourism'. *PLOS One*, 21 October. https://journals.plos.org/plosone/article?id=10.1371/journal.pone.0138939

[201] Of the numerous reports of this event, I have used an account by Rodrigo

[Duterte:] 'Philippines to shut down tourist island Boracay for six months'. *AlJazeera*, 5 April 2018. https://www.aljazeera.com/economy/2018/4/5/philippines-to-shut-down-tourist-island-boracay-for-six-months

202 Karta Cripps (2022). 'Tourism killed Thailand's most famous bay. Here's how it was brought back to life'. *CNN*, 1 August. https://edition.cnn.com/travel/article/maya-bay-thailand-recovery-c2e-spc-intl/index.html

203 See for instance, Northrop *op.cit.* for a review of different financial sources and the recognition that 'to finance a positive transformation of tourism, new revenue sources will be needed.'

## Chapter 6

204 Vincent Doumeizel, trans. Charlotte Coombe (2023). *The Seaweed Revolution: How seaweed has shaped our past and can save our future.* UK: Hero Press.

205 *Profile of Vincent Doumeizel, Senior Advisor on Oceans to the UN Global Compact.* Ocean Stewardship Coalition, United Nations Global Compact. https://www.unglobalcompact.org/take-action/ocean/doumeizel

206 'Seaweed'. *Encyclopaedia Britannica* (updated version 10 October 2022). https://www.britannica.com/science/seaweed

207 'Sargasso Sea'. The seaweed site: information on marine algae. https://www.seaweed.ie/sargassum/sargasso.php

208 Lucy Knight (2022). 'Sea forest would be a better name than seaweed, says UN food adviser'. *The Guardian*, I June. https://www.theguardian.com/environment/2022/jun/01/sea-forest-better-name-seaweed-un-food-adviser

209 *Ibid.*

210 Doumeizel, V. and Aass, K. (eds.) (2020). *Seaweed Revolution: A manifesto for a sustainable future.* UN Global Compact, Sustainable Ocean Business Action Platform. https://ungc-communications-assets.s3.amazonaws.com/docs/publications/The-Seaweed-Manifesto.pdf

211 *Ibid.*

212 FAO (2018). *The state of the world's fisheries and aquaculture.* Food and Agriculture Organization of the United Nations, Rome. https://agupubs.onlinelibrary.wiley.com/doi/full/10.1029/2019GH000204

213 GreenWave website (n.d.). *GreenWave replicates and scales regenerative ocean farms to create jobs and protect the planet.* https://www.greenwave.org/

214 Betty Gold (2022). 'Step aside, kale: in 2022, your favourite form of leafy green won't grow on land'. *Well+Good.* https://www.wellandgood.

com/fitness-wellness-trends/food/sea-greens/

215 IBM Institute for Business Value (n.d.). *Sustainability at a turning point: consumers are pushing companies to pivot.* https://www.ibm.com/downloads/cas/WLJ7LVP4

216 Global Market Insights (2020). *Commercial Seaweed Market to hit $85 billion by 2026.* 15 July.

217 NOAA Fisheries (n.d.). *Seaweed aquaculture.* https://www.fisheries.noaa.gov/national/aquaculture/seaweed-aquaculture

218 Global Market Insights, *op.cit.*

219 Seaweed Seychelles website (n.d.). https://www.seaweedseychelles.com/organic-soil-conditioner

220 Personal interview with Yohan Gallet in September 2022, at an EU-funded conference held in Seychelles under the banner of BlueInvest Africa. https://blueinvest-africa-2022.b2match.io/

221 RASSA (2022). *Irish seaweed: from famine food to foraged delicacy.* 25 July. RASSA is an organisation that provides educational events in creative activities, including food preparation. https://www.joinrassa.com/articles/irish-seaweed

222 'China plans to feed 80 million people with seawater rice'. *Bloomberg News*, 19 February 2022. https://www.bloomberg.com/news/articles/2022-02-19

223 'China to use seawater rice to ensure food security'. *Rice Today*, 21 February 2022. https://ricetoday.irri.org/china-to-use-seawater-rice-to-ensure-food-security/

224 *Ibid.*

225 Qian Qian, Fan Zhang and Yeyun Xin (2021). 'Yuan Longping and hybrid rice research'. *Rice*, 14 December. https://doi.org/10.1186/s12284-021-00542-4

226 Giullia Botaro (2022). 'Growing vegetables in seawater could be the answer to feeding billions'. *Euronews.green*, 25 May 2022. https://www.euronews.com/green/2022/05/24/growing-vegetables-in-seawater-could-be-the-answer-to-feeding-billions#

227 *Ibid.*

228 Etta di Leo (2021). *Creating a new vision for sustainable agriculture.* University of Waterloo, 26 October. https://uwaterloo.ca/news/global-impact/creating-new-vision-sustainable-agriculture

229 'Building the world's first floating farm in the Netherlands'. *Agritecture*, 2021. https://www.agritecture.com/blog/2021/8/24/building-the-worlds-first-floating-farm-in-the-netherlands

230 *Ibid.*

[231] Jonker, G.H. with Singla, P., Jainand, S. and Woldring, A.R. (2020). *Feeding our growing population and diminish land-usage by building on the idea of Floating Farms.* Faculty of Science and Engineering, University of Groningen, 18 August 2020.

[232] *Ibid.*

[233] Samuel Taylor Coleridge (1834). *The Rime of the Ancient Mariner.*

[234] Nina Lakhani and Oliver Milman (2023). 'First global conference in 50 years yields hundreds of pledges, zero checks'. *The Guardian,* 25 March. https://www.theguardian.com/world/2023/mar/24/united-nations-water-conference-new-york-pledges

[235] Information provided in private correspondence by NLA International.

[236] Michael Birnbaum (2021). 'Desalination can make saltwater drinkable – but it won't solve the US water crisis'. *Washington Post,* 28 September 2021.
https://www.washingtonpost.com/climate-solutions/2021/09/28/desalination-saltwater-drought-water-crisis/

[237] NLA International, *op.cit.*

## Chapter 7

[238] Haugan, P.M., Levin, L.A., Amon, D., Hemer, M., Lily, H. and Nielsen, F.G. (2020). What Role for Ocean-Based Renewable Energy and Deep Seabed Minerals in a Sustainable Future? Washington DC: World Resources Institute. www.oceanpanel.org/blue-papers/ocean-energy-and-mineral-sources

[239] Lyrics of a traditional English folk song, made famous through an early recording by Kathleen Ferrier.

[240] 'Why Britain is a world leader in offshore wind'. *The Economist,* 24 November 2022.
https://www.economist.com/britain/2022/11/24/why-britain-is-a-world-leader-in-offshore-wind

[241] 'Nine new countries sign up for global offshore wind alliance at COP27 in Sharm el-Sheikh'. *IRENA,* 8 November 2022.
https://www.irena.org/News/pressreleases/2022/Nov/Nine-new-countries-sign-up-for-Global-Offshore-Wind-Alliance-at-COP27

[242] Daniel Timblin (2022). 'The pros and cons of onshore vs offshore wind farms'. *True Expertise Delivered,* 16 August.
https://www.expertisedelivered.com/insights/blog/the-pros-and-cons-of-onshore-vs-offshore-wind-farms-29/

[243] Examples can be seen, for instance, in America and Ireland. Information

provided in correspondence with Beverley Bramley.

[244] Center for Environmental Science, University of Maryland (n.d.). *Wind energy and environmental impacts*. https://www.umces.edu/wind-energy

[245] 'Offshore wind power gains ground but faces environmental challenges'. *Insight*, 26 April 2019.
https://www.whitecase.com/insight-our-thinking/offshore-wind-power-gains-ground-faces-environmental-challenges

[246] 'Hornsea 2'. *Orsted*. https://hornseaprojects.co.uk/hornsea-project-two

[247] Jonah Fisher (2022). 'Hornsea wind farm claims title of world's largest'. *BBC News*, 31 August. https://www.bbc.com/news/science-environment-62731923

[248] 'How many more wind turbines will the UK build?'. *BBC News*, 28 November 2022. https://www.bbc.com/news/explainers-60945298

[249] Adnan Durakovic (2022). 'Largest wind farm in China fully grid connected'. *offshoreWIND.biz*, 27 December. https://www.offshorewind.biz/2021/12/27/largest-offshore-wind-farm-in-china-fully-grid-connected/

[250] Adrijana Buljan (2022). 'China's largest zero-subsidy offshore wind farm now up and running'. *offshoreWIND.biz*, 29 December.
https://www.offshorewind.biz/2022/12/29/chinas-largest-zero-subsidy-offshore-wind-farm-now-up-and-running/

[251] Norman Waite (2022). 'China's offshore wind energy giant stimulates global growth'. *Institute for Energy Economics and Financial Analysis*, 5 September. https://ieefa.org/articles/chinas-offshore-wind-industry-giant-stimulates-global-growth

[252] Mamoru Tsuge (2022). *China breezes to the lead of offshore wind power race*. 15 June. https://asia.nikkei.com/Business/Energy/China-breezes-to-the-lead-of-offshore-wind-power-race

[253] Maria Gallucci (2022). 'US offshore wind industry to hit major milestones in 2023'. *Canary News*, 26 December.
https://www.canarymedia.com/articles/wind/us-offshore-wind-industry-to-hit-major-milestones-in-2023

[254] '5 offshore wind projects and skills needed for the US Green New Deal'. *Airswift*, 19 August 2022. https://www.airswift.com/blog/offshore-wind-energy-projects-usa

[255] IRENA, *op.cit.*

[256] John Masefield (1902). *Sea Fever*.

[257] NLA International: commissioned project briefing on ocean energy.

[258] Haugan, *op.cit.*

[259] *Ibid.*

260  Amir Garanovic (2022). 'International wave energy project sets course for demonstration offshore Scotland'. *Offshore-energy.biz*, 17 October. https://www.offshore-energy.biz/international-wave-energy-project-sets-course-for-demonstration-offshore-scotland/

261  Admir Cavlaic (2022). 'Ocean current energy is the third source'. *Offshore-Energy.biz*, 18 November. https://www.offshore-energy.biz ocean-current-energy-is-the-third-source/

262  Kristin Houser (2022). 'Massive turbine turns deep ocean current into electricity'. *Freethink*, 6 June. https://www.freethink.com/energy/deep-ocean-currents

263  'Tidal power: the renewable energy source making a splash'. *Brunel. net*, 3 March 2022. https://www.brunel.net/en-au/blog/renewable-energy/tidal-power

264  Richard Youle (2023). 'Tidal lagoon, floating solar farm and battery manufacturing plant will be delivered in Swansea'. *Wales Online*, 12 January. https://www.walesonline.co.uk/news/wales-news/swansea-council-blue-eden-lagoon-25956956

265  NLA International, *op.cit.*

266  Wei-Shan Hsu *et al.* (2021). 'Miniaturized gradient density devices'. *Molecules*, September. https://www.ncbi.nlm.nih.gov/pmc/articles/PMC8466105/

267  NLA International, *op.cit.*

268  B. David Zarley (2022). 'This startup wants to build a radically new kind of wind turbine'. *Freethink*, 18 September. https://www.freethink.com/energy/vawt-offshore

269  Francesca Romana Piccioli (2022). '10 European wind startup projects that will blow you away'. *EU-Startups*, 23 December. https://www.eu-startups.com/2022/12/10-european-wind-energy-startups-that-will-blow-you-away/

270  *Ibid.*

271  Ørested (n.d.). *Our green business transformation: what we did and lessons learned.* https://orstedcdn.azureedge.net/-/media/www/docs/corp/com/about-us/whitepaper/our-green-business-transformation

272  The then CEO, Anders Eldrup, in Ørested, *op.cit.*

273  Ørested, *op.cit.*

274  Richard Gardham (2021). 'Is the wind still in Hull's sails?'. *Investment Monitor*, 11 March. https://www.investmentmonitor.ai/features/is-the-wind-still-in-hulls-sails/

# Chapter 8

[275] Lloyd's Register Foundation (2021). *Foresight review of ocean safety: Engineering a safe and sustainable ocean economy.* London. https://www.lrfoundation.org.uk/496707/siteassets/pdfs/lrf_foresight_review_of_ocean_safety_v3.pdf

[276] An invaluable source on the subject of the last frontier is Kathryn A. Miller *et al.* (2018). 'An overview of seabed mining including the current state of development, environmental impacts and knowledge gaps'. *Frontiers in Marine Science*, 18 January. https://www.frontiersin.org/articles/10.3389/fmars.2017.00418/full

[277] Throughout the book I have tried to use everyday terms rather than legalistic language. Strictly speaking, *'the high seas refers to the ocean water column that lies beyond the boundaries of any one country, also known as areas beyond national jurisdiction (ABNJ). The seafloor beyond the limits of the coastal continental shelf is what is termed the Area by the 1982 United Nations Convention on the Law of the Sea (UNCLOS).'*
https://oceanexplorer.noaa.gov/facts/high-seas-governance.html#:~:text=The%20high%20seas%20refers%20to,of%20the%20Sea%20(UNCLOS)

[278] Ben Westcott (2020). 'China breaks national record for Mariana Trench manned-dive amid race for deep sea resources'. *CNN*, 11 November 2020. https://web.archive.org/web/20201111184811/https://edition.cnn.com/2020/11/11/asia/china-record-dive-mariana-trench-intl-hnk/

[279] Pew Charitable Trusts (2017). *Deep sea mining: the basics.* 3 February (updated version, 5 July 2018). https://www.pewtrusts.org/en/research-and-analysis/fact-sheets/2017/02/deep-sea-mining-the-basics

[280] Rachel Mills (2017). 'Why are countries laying claim to the deep-sea floor?'. *BBC News*, 21 June.
https://www.bbc.com/news/world-40248866

[281] The company was renamed The Metal Company following a merger in 2021.

[282] *Ibid.*

[283] *Ibid.*

[284] In my own text, I prefer to use the English spelling (sulphides) although in some of the quotes the American version (sulfides) is used.

[285] Pew Charitable Trusts, *op.cit.*

[286] DeepSea Conservation Coalition. *'About deep-sea mining'.* https://savethehighseas.org/deep-sea-mining/

287  Haugan, P.M. *et al.* (2020). *What Role for Ocean-Based Renewable Energy and Deep Seabed Minerals in a Sustainable Future?* Washington, DC: World Resources Institute. www.oceanpanel.org/blue-papers/ocean-energy-and-mineral-sources.

288  *Ibid.*

289  DeepSea Conservation Coalition (n.d.). *Challenging deep-sea mining.* https://savethehighseas.org/deep-sea-mining/making-a-change

290  *Ibid.*

291  *Ibid.*

292  Kate Lyons (2021). 'Deep-sea mining could start in two years after Pacific nation of Nauru gives UN ultimatum'. *The Guardian*, 30 June. https://www.the guardian.com/Deep-sea mining could start in two years after Pacific nation of Nauru gives UN ultimatum

293  At one point, the company suffered a $10 million loss through the misdirection of a cheque; whether the result of mismanagement or fraud was never made clear but it hardly added to the security of the venture.

294  'The world is set to debate seabed mining regulations, but the U.S. will be on the outside looking in'. *Politico.* https://www.politico.com/news/2022/03/22/seabed-mining-regulations-00019005

295  Felicity Bradstock (2022). 'The pros and cons of deep-sea mining. *Oil Price.com*, 27 August. https://oilprice.com/Energy/Energy-General/The-Pros-And-Cons-Of-Deep-Sea-Mining.html

296  *Ibid.*

297  'Exploring the deep'. *National Science Foundation.* https://nsf.gov/news/factsheets/Factsheet_Submersibles_v1_D.pdf

298  Bradstock, *op.cit.*

299  Pryanka Shankar (2022). 'Deep-sea mining efforts gear up to meet clean energy demands amid concerns'. *Mongabay*, 26 October. https://india.mongabay.com/2022/10/deep-sea-mining-efforts-gear-up-to-meet-clean-energy-demands-amid-concerns/

300  Stuart Heaver (2022). 'Earth's final frontier: China and the deep-sea gold rush set to cause environmental catastrophe'. *Hong Kong Free Press*, 2 January. https://hongkongfp.com/2022/01/02/earths-final-frontier-china-and-the-deep-sea-gold-rush-set-to-cause-environmental-catastrophe/

301  *Ibid.*

302  Ahmed Khan (2022). 'Mauritius: Indian Ocean – why is Mauritius looking to deep-sea mining?'. *L'Express.* https://allafrica.com/stories/202201310691.html

303  Haugan *et al., op.cit.*

304  *Ibid.*

305  *Ibid.*

306  Julian Jackson (2022). 'Momentum builds to halt the commencement of seabed mining in international waters'. *Pew*, 8 December. https://www.pewtrusts.org/en/research-and-analysis/articles/2022/12/08/momentum-builds-to-halt-the-commencement-of-seabed-mining-in-international-waters

307  Louisa Casson (2019). 'Four reasons why the International Seabed Authority probably won't protect our oceans'. *Greenpeace*, 24 July. https://www.greenpeace.org/international/story/23397/four-reasons-why-the-international-seabed-authority-probably-wont-protect-our-oceans/

308  Todd Woody and Evan Halper (2022). 'A gold rush in the deep sea raises questions about the authority charged with protecting it'. *LA Times*, 19 April. https://www.latimes.com/politics/story/2022-04-19/gold-rush-in-the-deep-sea-raises-questions-about-international-seabed-authority

309  *Ibid.*

310  Karen McVeigh (2023). 'More than 5,000 new species discovered in Pacific deep-sea mining hotspot'. *The Guardian*, 25 May. https://www.theguardian.com/environment/2023/may/25

311  Danielle Hall (2021). 'The deep sea'. *Smithsonian Institution*, 22 September. https://ocean.si.edu/ecosystems/deep-sea/deep-sea

312  Rachel Carson (1951). *The Sea Around Us*. New York: Oxford University Press.

313  The original quote is by Sylvia Earle but it has since been adapted in various presentations e.g. 'The ocean is neither too big to fail nor too big to fix, but it is too big and too central to our future to ignore'. Jane Lubchenco (2020). Co-Chair of the Ocean Panel Expert Group, 2 December. https://oceanpanel.org/14-world-leaders-commit-100-percent-sustainable-ocean-management-solve-global-challenges/

314  Karen McVeigh (2020). 'David Attenborough calls for ban on *devastating* deep sea mining'. *The Guardian*, 12 March. https://www.theguardian.com/environment/2020/mar/12/david-attenborough-calls-for-ban-on-devastating-deep-sea-mining

315  Enric Sala, in his website, https://www.enricsala.com/

316  Kongsak Thathong. 'A spiritual dimension and environmental education: Buddhism and environmental crisis'. *Procedia - Social andBehavioral*

*Sciences, Elsevier*, Vol.46, 2012.
https://www.sciencedirect.com/science/article/pii/S18770428
12021222?ref=pdf_download&fr=RR-2&rr=78283a65fdb64f99

## Chapter 9

[317] Dame Ellen MacArthur (2015). 'The surprising thing I learned sailing solo around the world'. *Ted Talk*, June. https://www.ted.com/speakers/ellen_macarthur

[318] Ellen MacArthur (n.d.). *What is a circular economy?*. Ellen MacArthur Foundation. https://ellenmacarthurfoundation.org/topics/circular-economy-introduction/overview

[319] *Ibid.*

[320] Sarah Knapton (2017). 'Prince of Wales: Plastic in the world's oceans is a growing human disaster'. *Daily Telegraph*, 18 May. https://www.telegraph.co.uk/science/2017/05/18/prince-wales-plastic-worlds-oceans-growing-human-disaster/

[321] Simon Reddy and Winnie Lau (n.d.). 'Preventing ocean plastics'. *Pew*. https://www.pewtrusts.org/en/projects/preventing-ocean-plastics

[322] Pew Expert Panel (2020). 'Breaking the Plastic Wave: A comprehensive assessment of pathways towards stopping ocean plastic pollution'. *Pew Charitable Trusts*. https://www.pewtrusts.org/-/media/assets/2020/10/breakingtheplasticwave_mainreport.pdf

[323] Pew Expert Panel, *op.cit.*

[324] Pew Expert Panel, *op.cit.*

[325] United Nations Basel Convention (1992). *Text of the Convention*. http://www.basel.int/TheConvention/Overview/TextoftheConvention/tabid/1275/Default.aspx

[326] Madeleine Cobbing (2018). *A Crisis of Convenience: The corporations behind the plastic pollution pandemic*. Amsterdam: Greenpeace International. https://issuu.com/greenpeaceinternational/docs/crisis_of_convenience_final

[327] Robert Blasiak, *et al.* (2021). 'Corporations and plastic pollution: trends in reporting'. *Elsevier: Sustainable Futures*, Vol.3. https://www.sciencedirect.com/science/article/pii/S2666188821000204

[328] Cody Bay (2021). 'Companies that have committed to reducing waste and how they plan to do it'. *Go Banking Rates*, 22 April. https://www.gobankingrates.com/money/business/companies-have-committed-to-reducing-waste-how-they-plan-to-do-it/

[329] Shell plc website (2022). *Circular Economy and Waste*. https://www.

shell.com/sustainability/environment/circular-economy-and-waste.html

330 *Ibid.*

331 'Plastic pollution by country 2022'. *World Population Review.* https:// worldpopulationreview.com/country-rankings/plastic-pollution-by-country

332 The Oceanic Society, for instance, has a list of things which can be done to support the cause: reduce your use of single-use plastics, support legislation to curb plastic production and waste, recycle properly, participate in (or organise) a beach or river cleanup, avoid products containing microbeads, spread the word and support organisations addressing plastic pollution. https://www.oceanicsociety.org/resources/7-ways-to-reduce-ocean-plastic-pollution-today/

333 '10 different types of ocean pollution (and the laws that fight them!)'. *eLawtalk.* https://elawtalk.com/types-of-ocean-pollution/

334 Leila Mead (2021). 'The ocean is not a dumping ground: fifty years of regulating ocean dumping'. *International Institute for Sustainable Development,* 7 December. https://www.iisd.org/system/files/2021-11/still-one-earth-ocean-dumping.pdf

335 *Ibid.*

336 Greenpeace (n.d.). *Sewage pollution in the Pacific and how to prevent it.* http://www.pacificwater.org/_resources/article/files/Sewage%20 Pollution%20in%20the%20Pacific%20and%20how%20to%20 prevent%20it.pdf

337 World Economic Forum, quoted in 'Recycling and circular economy: what's the difference?', Ellen MacArthur Foundation. https://ellenmacarthurfoundation.org/articles/recycling-and-the-circular-economy-whats-the-difference#:~:text=a%20product's%20 lifecycle.-,The%20circular%20economy,created%20in%20the%20 first%20place.

338 Xianlai Zeng *et al.* (2022). 'Comparing the costs and benefits of virgin and urban mining'. *Journal of Management Science and Engineering,* Vol. 7, Issue 1, March. https://www.sciencedirect.com/science/article/pii/S2096232021000287#!

339 Rubi Medina-Mjangos *et al.* (2021). 'The economic assessment of the environmental and social impacts generated by a light packaging and bulky waste sorting and treatment facility in Spain: a circular economy example'. *Environmental Sciences Europe,* Vol. 33. https://enveurope. springeropen.com/articles/10.1186/s12302-021-00519-6

340 Waterhaul website (n.d.). https://waterhaul.co/

341  *Ibid.*
342  The three founding partners are Francesca Adrienne, Rosetta Alcindor and Kyle de Bouter.
343  EcoAct Tanzania exhibited at the BlueInvest Africa event held in Seychelles in September 2022. https://blueinvest-africa-2022.b2match.io/
344  Popular lyric originally identified with Nat King Cole in the 1950s.
345  The Ocean Cleanup website (n.d.). https://theoceancleanup.com/
346  Ryan Stuart (2021). 'Scooping plastic out of the ocean is a losing game'. *Hakai Magazine*, 21 September. https://hakaimagazine.com/features/scooping-plastic-out-of-the-ocean-is-a-losing-game/
347  Susan Gourvenec *et al.* (2022). 'Global assessment of historical, current and forecast ocean energy infrastructure: Implications for marine space planning, sustainable design and end-of-engineered-life management'. *Renewable and Sustainable Energy Reviews (Elsevier)*, Vol.154, February.
348  Sasha Marivel and Betymie Bonnelame (2019). '10 tonnes of waste – mostly from other countries – collected in massive beach clean-up in Seychelles'. Seychelles News Agency, May 13. http://www.seychellesnewsagency.com/articles/10953/+tonnes+of+waste+--+mostly+from+other+countries+--+collected+in+massive+beach+clean-up+in+Seychelles

## Chapter 10

349  Madeleine Cuff (2023). 'What is the UN High Seas treaty and will it save the world's oceans?'. *New Scientist*, 6 March. https://www.newscientist.com/article/2362921-what-is-the-un-high-seas-treaty-and-will-it-save-the-worlds-oceans/
350  Karen McVeigh (2023). 'Crucial high seas treaty stuck over sharing of genetic resources'. *The Guardian*, 3 March. https://www.theguardian.com/environment/2023/mar/03/crucial-un-high-seas-treaty-stuck-over-sharing-of-genetic-resources
351  Esme Stallard (2023). 'What is the UN High Seas Treaty and why is it needed?'. *BBC News*, 5 March. https://www.bbc.com/news/science-environment-64839763
352  UN Secretary-General (2023). 'UN delegates reach historic agreement on protecting marine biodiversity in international waters'. *UN News*, 5 March. https://news.un.org/en/story/2023/03/1134157
353  Gemma Parkes (2023). 'Why the High Seas treaty is a breakthrough for the ocean and the planet'. *World Economic Forum*, 10 March. https://climatechampions.unfccc.int/why-the-high-seas-treaty-is-a-

breakthrough-for-the-ocean-and-the-planet/

354 Julia Kim and Rachel Treisman (2023). 'What to know about the new high seas treaty – and the next steps for the accord'. *NPR*, 7 March. https://www.npr.org/2023/03/07/1161196476/un-high-seas-treaty-international-waters#:~:text=The%20Oceans,led%20commitment%20known%20as%2030x30.

355 Lisa Speer, Director of the Natural Resources Defense Council's International Oceans program, in an interview with NPR (National Public Radio, US), in Julia Kim and Rachel Treisman, *op.cit*. https://www.npr.org/2023/03/07/1161196476/un-high-seas-treaty international-waters#:~:text=The%20Oceans,led%20commitment%20known%20as%2030x30.

356 'High Seas Treaty: should we be celebrating?'. *Marine Biological Association (n.d.)*. https://www.mba.ac.uk/high-seas-treaty-should-we-be-celebrating/

357 *Ibid*.

358 Dona Bertarelli (n.d.). *Pew Bertarelli Ocean Legacy*. https://donabertarelli.com/projects/oceanlegacy/

359 'Enric Sala'. *Re:wild*, 2021. https://www.rewild.org/team/enric-sala Enric Sala is National Geographic's Explorer in Residence. He is the author of two books: *Pristine Seas: Journeys to the ocean's last wild places (2015)* and *The Nature of Nature: Why we need the wild (2020)*.

360 Carlos M. Duarte *et al*. (2020). 'Rebuilding marine life'. *Nature*. https://hal.science/hal-02502619/document

361 *Ibid*.

362 *Ibid*.

363 At the time of writing, the dispute has still not been settled although negotiations are currently underway to do so. See, for instance, Dennis Hardy, 'Chagos and the British Indian Ocean Territory: A colonial anachronism in the post-colonial era'. *Seychelles Research Journal*, Vo.5, No.2, August 2023. www.seychellesresearchjournal.com

364 Johnny Briggs (2020). 'How much of the ocean is really protected in 2020?'. *Pew Bertarelli Ocean Legacy*, 7 July. https://www.pewtrusts.org en/research-and-analysis/articles/2020/07/07/how-much-of-the-ocean-is-really-protected. It is worth noting that a lower figure of 2.9 per cent is cited in another source: https://mpatlas.org/

365 National Ocean and Atmospheric Administration (US). *Where are Marine Protected Areas located?*. 20 January 2023. https://oceanservice.noaa.gov/facts/mpaloc.html

366 Information provided by NLA International, together with accounts of

many other MPAs.

367 The idea of 30-30 was adopted in December 2022 by the UN Convention on Biological Diversity, denoting a target to protect 30 per cent of the earth's land and coastal and marine areas by 2030.

368 *Ibid.*

369 Sophie Kevany (2023). 'Here's proof fishing bans leave plenty to eat, says study of Mexico marine park'. *The Guardian*, 1 June. https://www.theguardian.com/environment/2023/jun/01/

370 Sebastian Stelios (2010). 'Save the Whales: 35th anniversary'. *Greenpeace*, 27 April.
https://www.greenpeace.org/usa/save-the-whales-35th-anniversary

371 Duarte, *op.cit.*

372 *Ibid.*

373 Anna M. Magera *et al.* (2013). 'Recovery trends in marine mammal populations'. *Researchgate.*
https://www.researchgate.net/publication/258350989_Recovery_Trends_in_Marine_Mammal_Populations

374 Chrissy Sexton (2020). 'Endangered Species Act helped recover marine animal populations'. *earth.com*, 28 January. https://www.earth.com/news/endangered-species-act-recover/

375 Joshua Rapp (2022). 'Sea turtle numbers explode after decades of protection'. *Discover*, 1 April. https://www.discovermagazine.com/planet-earth/sea-turtle-numbers-explode-after-decades-of-protection

376 'Study shows value of mangrove for coastal defence'. *National Oceanography Centre*, 9 February 2023. https://thefishsite.com/articles/study-shows-value-of-mangroves-for-coastal-defence

377 Morgan Erickson-Davis (2018). 'New study finds mangroves store way more carbon than we thought'. *Mongabay*, 2 May. https://news.mongabay.com/2018/05/new-study-finds-mangroves-may-store-way-more-carbon-than-we-thought/

378 Maricé Leal and Mark D. Spalding (eds.) (2022). 'The State of the World's Mangroves 2022'. *Global Mangrove Alliance*. https://www.mangrovealliance.org/wp-content/uploads/2022/09/The-State-of-the-Worlds-Mangroves-Report_2022.pdf

379 *Mangroves for the Future* (n.d.). http://www.mangrovesforthefuture.org/countries/members/seychelles/

380 See, for example, 'Community-based ecological wetland rehabilitation, Pasquiere, Praslin' (n.d.). *SeyCCAT*. https://seyccat.org/community-based-ecological-wetland-rehabilitation-pasquiere-praslin/

381 Ameer Ebrahim (2022). 'Developing Seychelles' Blue Carbon Roadmap

to reach net zero'. *Blue Carbon Lab*, 23 June. https://www.bluecarbonlab.org/developing-seychelles-blue-carbon-roadmap-to-reach-net-zero/

382  *Ibid.*

383  Seagrass-Watch (n.d). *What is seagrass?*. https://www.seagrasswatch.org/seagrass/

384  F. Short *et al.* (2007). 'Global seagrass distribution and diversity: a bioregional model'. *Journal of Experimental Marine Biology and Ecology*, Vol. 350, 9 November. https://www.sciencedirect.com/science/article/abs/pii/S002209810700305X#:~:text=Seagrass%20species%20in%20temperate%20areas,temperate%20parts%20of%20the%20world

385  Seagrass-Watch, *op.cit.*

386  *Ibid.*

387  'Save the dugong! A global effort to save dugongs and their seagrass habitats'. *Dugong and Seagrass Conservation Project*, 2023. https://www.dugongconservation.org/

388  'Corals'. *National Geographic*, n.d. https://www.nationalgeographic.com/animals/invertebrates/facts/corals-1

389  National Oceanic and Atmospheric Administration, US (2022). *Coral recovery after bleaching event in the Central Pacific*. 8 June. https://www.fisheries.noaa.gov/feature-story/coral-recovery-after-bleaching-event-central-pacific

390  The Nature Conservancy (n.d.). New hope for coral reefs. https://www.nature.org/en-us/about-us/where-we-work/caribbean/stories-in-caribbean/caribbean-a-revolution-in-coral-conservation/

391  Nature Seychelles (n.d.). *Coral reef restoration: The reef rescuers project.* http://natureseychelles.org/what-we-do/coral-reef-restoration

## Chapter 11

392  The facts in this introductory section are now common knowledge, and can be accessed from numerous news items and reports on the effects of climate change.

393  Hans Guenther Brauch, in Kiyala, J.C.K. and Harris, G.T. (eds.) (2022). *Civil Society and Peacebuilding in Sub-Saharan Africa in the Anthropocene.* Cham, Switzerland: Springer Nature.

394  Lord Raglan (1960). 'Canute and the waves'. *Royal Anthropological Institute of Great Britain and Ireland*, Vol.60, January.

395  The quote is by Rachel Gittman, East Carolina University, in Joseph Bennington-Castro, 'Walls won't save our cities from rising seas. Here's

what will'. *NBC News*, 27 July 2017. https://www.nbcnews.com/mach/science/walls-won-t-save-our-cities-rising-seas-here-s-ncna786811

[396] *Ibid.*

[397] *Ibid.* Evidence provided by the US National Oceanic and Atmospheric Administration.

[398] 'Adaptation strategies for sea-level rise'. *Environmental Resilience Institute*, Indiana University (n.d.). https://eri.iu.edu/erit/strategies/sea-level-rise.html

[399] Senay Boztas (2022). 'Sinking Maldives plans to reclaim land from the ocean'. *The Guardian*, 23 May. https://www.theguardian.com/environment/2022/may/23/maldives-plan-to-reclaim-land-for-tourism-could-choke-the-ecosystem

[400] Natalie Marchant (2021). 'Threatened by rising sea levels, Maldives is building a floating city'. *World Economic Forum*, 19 May. https://www.weforum.org/agenda/2021/05/maldives-floating-city-climate-change/

[401] *Ibid.*

[402] Regina Asariotis (2021). 'Climate change impact on seaports: a growing threat to sustainable trade and development'. *UNCTAD*, 4 June. https://unctad.org/news/climate-change-impacts-seaports-growing-threat-sustainable-trade-and-development

[403] In 2020, the IMO introduced a new regulation, promoting cleaner air, human health, high-quality fuels, industry guidance and compliance control: 'IMO Regulation 2020'.
https://www.imo.org/en/MediaCentre/PressBriefings/pages/34-IMO-2020-sulphur-limit-.aspx

[404] The Maritime Just Transition Task Force was set up at COP26 to develop a concerted approach to training. unglobalcompact.org/take-action/think-labs/just-transition/about

[405] Rebeca Grynspan (2022), in 'Why ports are at the heart of sustainable development'. *UNCTAD*, 13 May.
https://unctad.org/news/why-ports-are-heart-sustainable-development

[406] Anas S. Alamoush, Fabio Ballini and Aykut I. Ölçer (2021). 'Revisiting port sustainability as a foundation for the implementation of the United Nations Sustainable Development Goals'. *Journal of Shipping and Trade, Springer Open*, 8 November. https://jshippingandtrade.springeropen.com/articles/10.1186/s41072-021-00101-6

[407] Resilience4 Ports refers to 'the ability to prepare for and adapt to changing conditions and withstand and/or recover rapidly from disruptions, with the aim of ensuring continuity of services and movement of goods to, from and through ports'. www.resilienceshift.org/why-ports-matter-

for-resilience/
408 Port of Rotterdam Authority (n.d.). *Facts and figures: the port of Rotterdam in numbers*.
https://www.portofrotterdam.com/sites/default/files/2022-11/facts-and-figures-port-of-rotterdam_0.pdf
409 Tony Walker and Michelle Adams (2021). 'How shipping ports can become more sustainable'. *The Conversation*, 25 March. https://theconversation.com/how-shipping-ports-can-become-more-sustainable-156483
410 'Advancing environmental excellence'. *Green Marine*, 2022. https://green-marine.org/
411 Vancouver Fraser Port Authority (n.d.). *Responsible practices*. https://portvancouver.metrio.net/indicators/ healthy environment/responsible practices/improve sustainability
412 'Sustainable development at ports'. *Maritime Gateway*, 6 August 2018. https://www.maritimegateway.com/sustainable-development-ports/
413 See, for instance, Leccese, M. and McCormick, K. (2000). Charter of the New Urbanism. New York: McGraw-Hill. Also, Dennis Hardy (2006). *Poundbury: The town that Charles built*. London: Town and Country Planning Association.
414 See, for instance, Mohney, D. and Easterling, K. (eds.) (1991). *Seaside: Making a town in America*. New York: Princeton Architectural Press. Also, Hardy, *op.cit*.
415 Christopher Alexander (n.d.). *The vital work of Andres Duany: a commentary*. http://www.patternlanguage.com/townplanning/duany.htm
416 *The Truman Show*, filmed in Seaside, was first shown in 1998.

## Chapter 12

417 Christian Bueger (2017). 'We are all islanders now: Michel's blue economy kaleidoscope and the missing link to maritime security'. *Journal of the Indian Ocean Region*. Online 23 August. http://dx.doi.org.10.1080/19480881.2017.1317500
418 Well-known British hymn sung first in Anglican services and later adopted by the UK and US navies.
419 Lloyd's Register website (2021). https://www.lr.org/en/
420 Lloyd's Register Foundation (2022). *World Risk Poll 2021: A changed world? Perceptions and experiences of risks in the Covid age*'. https://wrp.lrfoundation.org.uk/LRF_2021_report_risk-in-the-covid-age_online_version.pdf

421 'Am I in danger? Tsunami risk zones'. *International Tsunami Information Center* (n.d.)
http://itic.ioc-unesco.org/index.php?option=com_content&view=article&id=1310&Itemid=1166

422 Lloyd's Register Foundation (2022). '*World risk poll 2021: a resilient world? Understanding vulnerability in a changing climate*'. https://wrp.lrfoundation.org.uk/LRF_2021_report2-resilience_online_version.pdf

423 Lloyd's Register Foundation (2021). '*Foresight review of ocean safety: engineering a safe and sustainable ocean economy*'. https://lloyds-register-foundation-static-assets.s3.amazonaws.com/LRF_Foresight_review_of_ocean_safety_V3.pdf

424 Christian Bueger (2015). 'What is maritime security?'. *Marine Policy*, Vol.53.

425 'Ukraine Black Sea grain deal extended, UN and Turkey say'. *AlJazeera*, 18 March 2023. https://www.aljazeera.com/news/2023/3/18/russia-ukraine-black-sea-grain-deal-extended-un-turkey

426 'What is the Ukraine grain deal and what good has it done?'. *BBC News*, March 2023. https://www.bbc.com/news/world-61759692

427 'Piracy in the Gulf of Guinea'. *International Chamber of Shipping* (n.d.). https://www.ics-shipping.org/current-issue/piracy-in-west-africa/

428 'IMO calls for further action to address Gulf of Guinea piracy', *IMO Maritime Safety Committee*, 19 May 2021. https://www.imo.org/en/MediaCentre/PressBriefings/pages/GulfOfGuineaMay2021

429 'Piracy, armed robbery declining in Gulf of Guinea, but enhanced national, regional efforts needed for stable maritime security, top official tells Security Council'. *UN 9198th meeting*, 22 November 2022. https://press.un.org/en/2022/sc15113.doc.htm

430 Leo Sands (2022). 'Drug smuggling: underwater drones seized by Spanish police'. *BBC News*, 4 July. https://www.bbc.com/news/world-europe-62040790

431 'War on drugs: a detailed look at maritime drug trafficking'. *Maritime Fairtrade*, 14 November 2022. https://maritimefairtrade.org/war-on-drugs-a-detailed-look-into-maritime-drug-trafficking/

432 Derived from UNODC 2020 World Drug Report, in: Are Solum, Beatriz Åsgård and Kristin Urdahl (2021). 'Ship operators at increased risk of drug smuggling'. Gard.
https://www.gard.no/web/updates/content/31640962/ship-operators-at-increased-risk-of-drug-smuggling

433 Personal conversation with a senior law enforcement officer in Seychelles.

434 Information from various sources in 2022, including 'Shipping fleet

statistics 2021'. *Gov.UK*, 6 April 2022.
https://www.gov.ukgovernment/statistics/shipping-fleet-statistics-2021/

[435] See, for instance, Vivian Yee and James Glanz (2021). 'How one of the world's biggest ships blocked the Suez Canal'. *New York Times*, 19 July. https://www.nytimes.com/2021/07/17/world/middleeast/suez-canal-stuck-ship-ever-given.html

[436] F. Nofandi, *et al.* (2022). 'Case study of ship traffic crowds in the Malacca Strait-Singapore by using vessel traffic system'. *IOP Conference Series: Earth and Environmental Science*. https://iopscience.iop.org/article/10.1088/1755-1315/1081/1/012009/pdf

[437] For instance, Sarah Bladen (2021). 'New technology to help tackle illegal fishing by alerting insurers to risk'. *Global Fishing Watch*. 5 November. https://globalfishingwatch.org/press-release/new-technology-insurers-to-risk/

## Chapter 13

[438] UN (n.d.). *Make the SDGs a reality* (originally announced in 2015). https://sdgs.un.org/

[439] Laura Paddison (2023). 'The climate time-bomb is ticking: the word is running out of time to avoid catastrophe, new UN report warns'. *CNN*, 20 March. https://edition.cnn.com/2023/03/20/world/ipcc-synthesis-report-climate-intl

[440] UN. *Make the SDGs a reality*, op.cit.

[441] Johnny Briggs (2020). 'How much of the ocean is really protected in 2020?'. *Pew Charitable Trusts*, 7 July. https://www.pewtrusts.org/en/research-and-analysis/articles/2020/07/07/how-much-of-the-ocean-is-really-protected
The lower figure is recorded in the MPAtlas, which reports that only 2.9 per cent of the ocean is fully or highly protected from fishing: https://mpatlas.org/

[442] UN. *The Sustainable Development Goals Report 2022*.
https://unstats.un.org/sdgs/report/2022/The-Sustainable-Development-Goals-Report-2022.pdf

[443] *Ibid.*

[444] *Ibid.*

[445] *Ibid.*

[446] Frank Biermann (2022). 'UN sustainable development goals failing to have meaningful impact, our research warns. *The Conversation*, 20 June. https://theconversation.com/un-sustainable-development-goals-

failing-to-have-meaningful-impact-our-research-warns-185269

447  Chris McGreal (2015). '70 years and half a trillion dollars later: what has the UN achieved?'. *The Guardian*, 15 September. https://www.theguardian.com/world/2015/sep/07/what-has-the-un-achieved-united-nations

448  WWF (2020). *Failing SDG 14: EU on a cliff edge for ensuring a sustainable ocean*. 3 March. https://www.wwf.eu/?360550/Failing-SDG14-EU-on-a-cliff-edge-for-ensuring-a-sustainable-ocean

449  Sea Around Us (2022). *Heading for failure: UN sustainable development goals for world oceans*. 2 August. https://www.seaaroundus.org/heading-for-failure-un-sustainable-development-goal-for-world-oceans/

450  Ellen Hayward (2021). 'The importance of SDG 14: implementation failure'. *World Wide Generation*, 21 January. https://www.worldwidegeneration.co/news/importance-sdg14-implementation-failure

451  UN (2020). *Keeping the momentum for ocean action: investing SDG 14*. Based on a webinar held under the auspices of the UN in November 2020.https://sdgs.un.org/news/keeping-momentum-ocean-action-investing-sdg-14-25034

452  UN (2018). 'World's Poorest Nations Left Behind in Reaching Sustainable Development Goals, Delegates Stress as Second Committee Begins General Debate'. *Seventy-Third Session*, 8 October. https://press.un.org/en/2018/gaef3495.doc.htm

453  Geoffrey Kamadi (2022). 'How Kenyans help themselves and the planet by saving mangrove trees'. *Science News*, 14 September. https://www.sciencenews.org/article/kenya-mangrove-trees-forest-carbon-storage-climate

454  *Ibid.*

455  The Nature Conservancy (2021). *Mother Mangrove: the women behind Kenya's mangrove restoration'*. 18 November. https://www.nature.org/en-us/about-us/where-we-work/africa/stories-in-africa/women-kenya-mangrove-forest/

456  Mikoka Pimoja, the Kenyan mangrove restoration scheme that was extended to other East African countries, was awarded the UN's Equator prize in 2017.

457  WWF, *op.cit.*

458  'Cop28 will "move beyond setting goals to achieving them," President Sheikh Mohamed says'. *COP28*, 22 April 2023. https://

www.thenationalnews.com/climate/cop28/2023/04/20/cop28-will-move-beyond-setting-goals-to-achieving-them-president-sheikh-mohamed-says/

459 Justin Harper (2022). 'UAE moves toward sustainability'. *Accounting and Business*, December. https://abmagazine.accaglobal.com/global/articles/2022/dec/business/uae-moves-towards-sustainability.html

460 'UAE energy diversification' (n.d.). *Embassy of the United Arab Emirates*, Washington DC. https://www.uae-embassy.org/discover-uae/climate-and-energy/uae-energy-diversification

461 'UAE to plant 100 million mangroves by 2030 through National Carbon Sequestration Project'. *Gulf News*, 17 December 2022. https://gulfnews.com/uae/environment/uae-to-plant-100-million-mangroves-by-2030-through-national-carbon-sequestration-project-1.92753516

462 'UAE set to launch the region's first independent climate change accelerators, led by Shikha Shamma bint Sultan bin Khalifa Al Nahyan' (2022). *Abu Dhabi Media Office*, 20 September.

# Index

www.ingramcontent.com/pod-product-compliance
Lightning Source LLC
Chambersburg PA
CBHW041016280326
41926CB00094B/4655